Notes on How to Live in the World . . . and Still Be Happy

Notes on How to Live in the World . . . and Still Be Happy

HUGH PRATHER

Doubleday

NEW YORK   LONDON   TORONTO   SYDNEY   AUCKLAND

Published by Doubleday, a division of
Bantam Doubleday Dell Publishing Group, Inc.,
666 Fifth Avenue, New York, New York 10103.

Doubleday and the portrayal of an anchor with a
dolphin are trademarks of Doubleday, a division of
Bantam Doubleday Dell Publishing Group, Inc.

Library of Congress Cataloging-in-Publication Data

Prather, Hugh.
  Notes on how to live in the world . . . and still be happy.

  1. Conduct of life. 2. Happiness. I. Title.
BJ1581.2.P74   1986   158'.1   85-16167
ISBN 0-385-18261-9

4   6   8   10   9   7   5

BG

Fortunately, this book has been equally Gayle's in the making and, together, we wish to dedicate it to our family at The Dispensable Church.

CONTENTS

CHAPTER IV

BEGINNING THE DAY   *51*

CHAPTER V

GOING THROUGH THE DAY   *71*

CHAPTER XII

MAY I WRAP THAT FOR YOU?   253

PREFACE

About the Exercises

As you will see, this is a workbook on happiness as well as a text. I modeled it somewhat after the workbooks I had in grade school in which theory and practice were mixed and each lesson was done within the pages of the workbook itself. The departure, of course, is that here you must provide your own writing materials.

Some of the exercises entail practices that should be carried on for several days before the next step is taken. To break up reading with demonstration is a very efficient means of learning, and yet this may interrupt the flow of the book for some readers. If this turns out to be true for you, you might first read it through, including the exercises, and then go back and do them, using perhaps a spiral notebook that will fit into purse or pocket.

These exercises, or some version of them, have been used often by my wife, Gayle, and me and by those we have counseled over the years. They are like old and trusted friends who time and again have proven their reliability. And they are essential to the value of this book. Frequently they are arranged in a progression that leads into the next concept presented. However, it is not required that you agree with them or even understand their individual purpose at the time you do them. If you will merely take them in order and carry out the instructions as conscientiously as possible, you will receive the full benefits of the book.

CHAPTER I

Just a Little Chapter on Unhappiness

Happiness is easy. It is letting go of unhappiness that is hard. We are willing to give up everything but our misery.

Of course we are quite crazy. Yet our stand against happiness appears sane at first glance. The good thing about a book is that it offers a second glance. So I hope you will permit me to begin by drawing attention to unhappiness or, more specifically, to one of our most pervasive rationales for its continuance. This rationale must be laid aside, at least until the effects of consistent happiness can be *felt,* or else the very aim of this book will seem shallow and silly in light of the weightiness of the reasons for being unhappy.

Is it realistic to think that you can live in the world and be happy?—because the inescapable fact is that this is not an easy place. Perhaps your life has been such that you have not yet had to confront this fact, but you do see clearly the effects of the world on others.

It is in the general course of things that, whatever it may be, if you desire it, it is not good for you, and if you pursue it, it will hurt you. But who can help desiring and pursuing? And just look at the unhappy results. It does not matter whether the idol is large or small, whether wealth, eminence, influence, or merely the spiciest gossip, the tastiest foods, the most erotic pleasures: The outcome is some degree of misery.

Yet what of simple hard work? What of the plodder who wishes little and seeks slowly? It is in the general course of things that the fruits of your labor, whatever slice of the world they represent and however patiently earned, must be taken from you in the end. For thousands of years, for lifetime after lifetime, the story is retold of eventual loss, loneliness, and a painful death. How many truly escape this end? And do you actually expect to yourself?

And what of the many years leading to death—those times that should have made the way it ends all worthwhile? No matter what our age, nothing we see here is wholly reliable. Even the preschool playground is a place where someone is your best friend today but tomorrow will play only with another. Is there in fact any spot in the world where you cannot wear out your welcome? Parents turn away from children in a thousand ways, and when the children grow up they in turn abandon their parents. In all walks of life, in every form of life, the strong prey upon the weak until they, too, are weak and are preyed upon. The world contains much physical beauty and yet everything lives off the death of everything else. This is certainly not all there is to reality, but despite the few scattered exceptions one can list, this is indeed the basic nature of the world we live in. And so the question naturally arises, *is the nature of the world a sufficient reason for you not to be happy?* It would certainly seem so, wouldn't it? And if there really is another course, would it be *right* for you to walk that way?

Is it moral to be happy when a quarter or more of the people of this earth are starving? When a third or more of the nations are in armed conflict? When the numbers who can cause nuclear accidents or global devastation are inexorably growing? And what of pollution, discrimination, endangered species, detention and torture, plagues and degenerative illnesses, the growth of terrorism, signs of pending geological catastrophes, and the increase in crimes of violence? How could anyone dare think of being happy? What our mood *should* be is. . . .

Angry? Shocked? Sad? Outraged?

And instead of applying ourselves to becoming happier, what we *should* be spending our time doing is . . .

Identifying and bringing to light the people who are causing all of this? Working to defeat candidates who disagree with us? Taking steps to protect our personal supplies of food, money, and shelter? Giving away what we have to the needy? Marching? Writing letters? Forming organizations? Giving speeches? Holding prayer vigils?

These are indeed bitter questions. And who have agreed upon an answer? Obviously there is no widespread agreement, and it is equally as obvious there never has been. Nor is it the purpose of this book to make another futile attempt to rally universal support for still one more solution. However, at least it should be clear that there is entrenched guilt over lightheartedness and great fear that when we take time to be happy we are not guarding our own interests, and certainly not doing all we could for the world.

Although it is perhaps unconscious for many, we carry with us the sabotaging belief that we do not deserve to be happy. To have any aspect of our lives run more smoothly than is "natural" is somehow proof of our guilt. Whenever things are going "too" well (in every life a little sunshine must fall), we fear some vague, undefined retribution, as if the world has a consciousness that keeps track of these things, and since we are not getting our quota of hardship, the balance soon will be set right.

At this time our various news and even our entertainment media contribute to this attitude.[1] It is very difficult to sit before a television set night after night and not come to believe, at least unconsciously, that tragedy is to be expected in every life, and that some form of natural law is being violated if this is not presently true for us.

From radio, newspapers, TV, from cause-oriented movies, books, and magazines, from scare letters on behalf of every conceivable cause, from a constant stream of out-of-town speakers, and from the sprinkling of grapevine news and warnings tucked in little conversations throughout the day, we get a steady picture of a world ever fretting and wringing its hands. The ordinary and the prominent do it alike, and so we have assumed there must be some value in this time-honored form of fear. But is there?

The underlying supposition is that we must keep our guard up, and that if we are happy we have let it down. Somehow keeping our guard up has come to mean keeping our mind focused on the dark corners. We must never allow ourselves to forget a single painful experience. We must persistently catalog every upcoming event that could turn against us. But have you noticed how much of what you think will happen simply never does? And just consider for a moment the countless hours we all spend fantasizing reactions to things that will never be. It is indeed sad to realize how we could use our mind instead. If

---

[1] A few years ago Gayle and I realized that the overall effect of newspapers, radio, magazines, movies, and TV was so disturbing to the state of mind we needed to be consistently good and gentle parents and to do our chosen work in life that, with a few carefully selected exceptions, we simply eliminated them altogether. Should you choose to take this step, which you should definitely not take if it would entail any sense of sacrifice, I would suggest that you not talk a great deal about it because most people will interpret it as your turning your back on reality, even though your motive would be the reverse. The "lust to know" is deeply held and cherished, and those who do not honor it cannot realistically expect to be understood.

some simple protective step can be taken in the present that will make us or those around us feel safer, then let us by all means take it, but that of course is not what we are speaking of here.

The world is indeed a dangerous place and obviously there are times when the worst we fear does happen, but of the little that does, what did being sick with dread ever do to protect us? *Fear neither causes the thing feared to happen nor prevents it.* It is mere static. It is an absence of music. It is not power. There is calmness at the center of us, a very deep well of happiness that cannot be exhausted, but it is not experienced while our perceptions are twisted by doubt.

A thousand times a day our love of happiness is cut short by our even greater fear of it. Even a little cheerfulness is checked if it goes on too long. If we find ourselves laughing with complete freedom, singing in the shower, or maybe just whistling loud enough to be overheard, the old anxiety begins seeping in. Our "frivolous" mood is being called into question. For some nagging reason we must resume a "serious" state of mind, although just why this is helpful or proper we are not quite sure.

Happiness is serious. It is very serious, not only as it affects our health, job, children, and all other aspects of our life, but in my opinion how it also influences, perhaps even changes, the world. I am obviously not in a position to know the effect each individual's state of mind has on the whole. All I can do is give you my opinion of the role it plays, and I will do so in the hope that if there are readers who are conflicted about studying a book on happiness, if maybe they think it would be selfish, or unfair to those who are in no position to study, then perhaps what I personally feel will encourage them to look in their own hearts, for that is the only place where the answer will be found. One thing is certain: to be conflicted about studying how not to be conflicted will do very little good.

It seems to me that we clearly have a mental influence that extends beyond our mere words and physical gestures. This is most commonly given credit in a negative way. People talk of the "vibes" being bad in a certain home or place of business. But of course it should go both ways, and I believe it does. We are either throwing our emotional weight into the balance of fear and anger or we are adding to the world's measure of hope and kindness. This cannot be seen of course, but it is most certainly felt. So if some readers need a justification for feeling happy, they might ask themselves what is their alternative, and what do they believe this other feeling will do to relieve the world's misery.

My belief is that we will not lessen anguish by maintaining the very state of mind we wish to see the other members of our worldly family released from. No matter what our words or actions, to be bitter and outraged is to teach our faith in the value of those emotions.

It is curious how often peace is spoken for unpeacefully, and how often in the name of a broader kindness we feel justified in being unkind to a few people. Okay to snipe and lash out, or to be insensitive and selfish, provided the cause is grand. We even think it is logical to attack our children in order to teach them not to attack, to scold them into being more respectful. But a temporary change in the outward appearance is all we get, for doesn't our *mood* teach what we really believe the most effective approach to life is?

I believe that to be consistently harmless is to bolster this urge within the mental atmosphere of the world—even if in small measure only. And I believe that a little gain is better than none.

Who really knows the effect of one happy thought? Is it possible that it circles the globe, finding entry into any open heart, encouraging and giving hope in some unseen way? I am convinced it does. For whenever I am truly loving I feel the warmth and presence of the like-minded, a growing family whose strength lies in their gentleness and whose message is in their treatment of others. I believe it is good and right to be happy, and I know from experience that it is the only way I personally can be kind.

CHAPTER II

What Is a Happy Person?

Is There Consistent Happiness?

The belief that there is no permanent happiness is so widespread and deeply rooted that it is simply one of the hard facts of life for most people. Should some holy foreign visitor claim, or even appear, otherwise, he or she is either not believed or is thought to be a fake and swindler. And why not? Who has experienced even one day of "perfect peace"? A whole life of it seems ridiculous.

I have even heard it said that no one in his right mind would *want* consistent happiness. Which raises an interesting question. Is it possible to not want what by definition one wants? In order to start this book with the proper tone of scholarship and authority, I had better first define happiness.[1]

---

[1] I want you to know that having written that sentence I had to leave my awesomely upholstered recliner, go to the next room, lift the baby's water bed—complete with sheepskin hammock and electrically reproduced womb

The Merriam-Webster unabridged has this to say about the durability of happiness: "A state of well-being characterized by relative permanence . . . and by a natural desire for its continuation." And the Oxford English definition includes this indication of *where* happiness occurs: "The state of pleasurable content of mind . . ."

Dictionaries merely report how a word is commonly employed, and true to general usage, all the ones I looked at cited good luck, prosperity, and other forms of worldly success as the principle origins of happiness. This is not only how the word is used but also the general conception of how this "content of mind" comes, and goes. It is a "beautiful feeling" which we want to endure but is dependent on how outer things go. "Oh, what a beautiful morning. Oh, what a beautiful day . . . Everything's going my way."

But for how long do things go our way? We want a better car. But for how long will it be better? We want a better house. But for how long will it be better? And so it is with the better body promised by the spa and the better spouse promised by the magazines. Is it any wonder that we do not believe in lasting happiness even though we have "a natural desire for its continuation"? As we have set the thing up, happiness that endures is a decidedly unhappy subject, and for the sake of our own sanity we had best forget it altogether as a rational goal.

---

rhythms (I kid you not)—and drag out what was propping it up: Volume I of the Oxford English Dictionary. Since we have the teeny-print edition, I then had to locate my bifocals, but I knew it would all be worth it just to be able to quote a thing with Oxford in its title. And as you may have guessed, the first words I was rewarded with were, "Happiness: The quality or condition of being happy." A quick return trip to the baby's room revealed that the good people at American Heritage evidently found this British assertion about the nounal form so obvious that they didn't bother putting in a separate listing for happiness. Nevertheless, there are other dictionaries (although, inexplicably, not in the room where I write).

That is, unless we can find another source besides "everything going my way."

Is it possible to say, *"Nothing has to go right today,"* and still be happy? As a matter of fact, it is the only way. Because nothing *will* go right. As I'm sure you've noticed by now. It started again this morning, didn't it? A little something spills, certain people are late as usual, our hair is never quite right, and then there is the neighbor's dog. Is there any real hope of eliminating forevermore all noise, smells, poor workmanship, overpriced products, traffic snarls, and rudeness in stores? Then why get so caught up in the very nature of the day that simple enjoyment becomes impossible? As the song says, "You can't roller-skate in a buffalo herd, but you can be happy if you've a mind to." The key is "having a mind to."

The Grounds for Happiness

There is a mental state—it could perhaps be called the grounds for happiness—that passes gently and easily over the endless nonsense that litters the day. Like a gentle breeze, it refreshes everything but disturbs nothing. It is happy being itself. And being something, it has something to give. Its opposite is the mental state that is constantly getting entangled and pulled down by almost everything. Unhappiness is undisciplined, agitated, and above all, scared. Having no integrity, no calm inner direction, it takes its cue from whatever problem is perceived to be before it now.

The mind *can* be trained, yet in most instances our thoughts are so chaotic and vulnerable that we go through the day looking at everyone through a thick mental haze that blocks from our view what each person is at heart. Yet it is seeing the urges of the heart that makes us happy. Babies and very young children, for example, make us happy because we allow ourselves to see their basic innocence. In their case we are quick to see *because* we are slow to judge.

Although it is by no means inevitable, the ordinary efforts made during the mere passing of years can occasionally bring about a small measure of the mental stability needed to permit at least a little vision. That is why older parents, and especially grandparents, often enjoy children more than "the young and the restless." By the time we reach middle age we have sometimes learned enough to devote ourselves to our children and not just squeeze them in among a bewildering array of ego pursuits.

Children, like everything else of value, cannot be hurried. The pleasure that a baby or young child has to offer is as delicate and subtle as a sunrise. Sitting quietly in the hush of dawn, with nothing to do and nowhere to go, we hear the waking sounds of the earth and see the shifts in light and shadow that a more hurried mind will miss. Haste makes unhappiness. The love within you is very still. It is not physically slow; it is simply at peace.

It is silly to hold children up as models of behavior. They obviously do not come into the world equipped with everything they need to remain happy, or else they would remain so, but they do start with certain strengths, especially mental strength, which many of us have lost. A child can prove that it is possible to be extremely active, and interested in everything, and still be happy, provided that a single goal dominates the mind.

Gayle and I were asked to bring our son John to the first wedding we conducted, not only to the service itself (during which he comported himself reasonably well for someone who had been alive for only two years), but also to the formal wedding dinner that followed. The meal was to be at a "nice" restaurant, and so I asked the couple if they knew what they were letting themselves in for. "Oh yes!" they laughed. Even though Gayle and I know it is best to take children only where they can be their age, the wedding party was an unusually child-tolerant group of people, and so we decided to make an exception.

The table was formally set with a rolled white linen napkin inside each empty water glass. As a boy I had learned that at nice restaurants, unless one is eating bouillabaisse, one does not tuck one's napkin into one's collar, and in the case of bouillabaisse, one titters guiltily as the waiter applies the bib. But somehow I had missed the one about the proper moment to put the napkin in your lap. With an ancient fear I looked at it elevated before me. Any mistake now would be highly visible.

John pulled out his napkin, played tent for a few seconds, then put all his utensils into the glass.

I started to speak to him but, looking around and seeing no consternation, I held off.

He took out an imaginary box of matches and began "lighting" each fork, spoon, and knife. He explained to the whole table that this was a birthday cake and they were going to blow out the candles. As the glass was passed around he watched carefully for omissions and patiently pointed out such things as, "You missed the spoon," and made the person blow again.

All this was taken in great spirits, and so I began to relax a little and just watch.

The first course served was salad. It came garnished with olives. I happened to know that John didn't like olives, but whereas not liking an ingredient could ruin a dish for me, John saw that these sliced black olives were actually racing tires, and within seconds he had set up a drag strip on the tablecloth. (The right combination of black olives and white linen can simulate "laying down rubber" with remarkable resemblance.)

I will not go through the entire dinner in which the grated cheese became modeling clay, and so forth. Obviously John was operating within an exceptional atmosphere. Plus the fact that all young children know they have you at their mercy in any place where they sense you do not want to make a scene. Being self-conscious, you suddenly become considerably more tolerant and kid yourself that you are further along than you thought.

Children, if they are to interact happily, must eventually learn that most adults have very strong opinions about how water glasses, tablecloths, black olives, and everything else in the world should be used, and it will not make a child happy to buck this. We took a neighbor's four-year-old girl to a magic show last week, and the woman who had the seat next to her scolded her for squirming excitedly. "Little girl," she said loudly, "you are disturbing me!" Of course it was her own unquestioned outlook about how everything must be that was disturbing her. But it is pointless to fight these things. We simply told little Melissa to sit still, even though half the audience was composed of excitedly squirming children. That was all that was necessary. To have done more than was necessary would have made everyone concerned unhappy and would not have pushed the woman in a gentler direction.

It is their single vision, so free of the past, that children have to teach and not the particular way they act it out. Adults are not required to play tent with their napkin in order to acquire strength of purpose. Even children themselves express single-mindedness in different ways. A five-year-old might like to use fingers to make shadow figures on the wall, whereas a five-month-old will like trying to grab fingers as they move. Yet both are certain there is a way to enjoy fingers. Children are so noticeably decisive because they have made a single decision about everything. John, as almost any small child would have done, saw it all—the table setting, the people, the food—

through the lens of a single interpretation. Everything was there to be enjoyed, and he was positive it could be.

It is evident that the opposite occurs as we "mature." Each thing in the world begins taking on a separate and restricted function. Until that dinner a linen napkin had only one small purpose for me, and that not a very happy one. For most adults this kind of pettiness has already blanketed the world they see. I am sure you know people who simply do not cultivate relationships with anyone who would not serve as a step toward money or social advancement. For them, people exist only to use. This is an exceedingly unhappy way of seeing. Whereas in the eyes of the very young even an individual's physical deformity can be a thing of great interest and delight, or of no particular interest, but not a reason for judgment and unhappiness.[2] I recently saw some four-year-olds go into a pool that normally contained children their own age but on this day contained only adults with severe Down's syndrome. These four-year-olds had never seen Down's syndrome. In watching them play, and afterward in listening to their chatter, I realized they had not seen it today either. Since children are so observant, it is probably more accurate to say they had found the differences between themselves and the others in the pool too unimportant to react to or even comment on. The adults were having great fun, and to them that was what counted.

---

[2] Obviously this changes very rapidly as the child takes on the values of the world, and we have all seen older children be quite cruel about differences.

Thinking Coats the World

"There is nothing either good or bad, but thinking makes it so."[3] What a relief! Because as it turns out we can have very little control over things, yet we can have complete control over thinking. It does not follow, however, that the key to happiness is to fill our minds with "good thoughts" if by that is meant telling ourselves that everyone is nice and every occurrence a blessing. This is the way to inner turmoil because it cannot help running up hard against our basic honesty.

Thinking *makes* it so. Thinking coats the world. The world has surprisingly little effect on our happiness until it is coated and given meaning by us. When Jordan was five months old he liked sitting up better than lying back in his portable carrier, and so we began putting him in a walker, even though his legs were not yet strong enough to move it. One day Gayle had just gone into the kitchen when a friend came in the front door and heard a crashing noise in the bathroom. Fortunately she went straight to investigate and found Jordan flat on his back, staring curiously up from the bottom of a full bathtub. It seems he had picked that exact moment to start "walking," and as the bathroom had a sunken tub, he had fallen right in. Needless to say, she was horrified at seeing a baby under two feet of water. She pulled him out, called us, and as we dried him off and fussed loudly over him, we noticed that he wasn't in the least upset. We kept waiting for him to start crying but he never did.

[3] Shakespeare has Hamlet say the above words in an exchange with Rosencrantz in which the latter points out that Hamlet would not think of his country and the world as a prison if he was not ambitious. With his usual irony Shakespeare has the one who does not appear to see the obvious summarize it best. Hamlet: "O God, I could be bounded in a nut-shell and count myself king of infinite space, were it not that I have bad dreams."

In fact, when we set him back in the walker, he headed for the tub as fast as he could and we immediately had to take permanent safety measures. There was nothing in his thinking to tell him that lying underwater when you can't swim is "bad." But evidently the memory of his recent womb experience told him that the sensations were "good."

I know you have heard the expression "That's a comforting thought," but have you ever heard its opposite? A friend who is a neighbor of ours said something once that is the closest to this I can remember. Although his work is psychiatry, his passion is new cameras of every size and make. His wife and children are very patient with him about this, and whenever he makes one of his frequent purchases they always smile and seem sincerely pleased for him. One day we were over visiting and once again Bill brought out a new camera to show us. After admiring it and asking pertinent questions, we laughed and said, "How many cameras do you have now, Bill?" He seemed subdued for a second or two, then answered, "That's not a happy question." And indeed, as is so often true of kidding, it was not.

These expressions—"That's a comforting thought," "That's not a happy question," "There is nothing either good or bad, but thinking makes it so"—acknowledge the same fact. Once thought, an idea is part of our perception. In a sense it becomes the eyes with which we see. It determines what we pick out to notice and what we choose to overlook. The thought itself, and not its object, comforts and makes happy, giving support, hope, and self-confidence. Just as it is the thought and not the subject of the thought that takes comfort and strength away.

Yet this is an extremely difficult insight for most people to practice. We simply are not in the habit of looking just at thought alone, and so there is a profound tendency to confuse what we see with how we are looking. It is indispensable to your happiness that you not only appreciate but love the difference, for unquestionably it is a very friendly distinction. "How many cameras do you have now?" is not a "bad" subject. Another person might have liked toting them up. The unhappiness was in the intent of a question that concealed a very mild judgment, but a judgment nonetheless.

There are no discrete attacks. Criticism takes place in the mind and infects the entire mind with which we think. Criticism cannot be confined. Whenever we condemn we cloak the world with pain.

Several years ago Gayle and I were able to do little more than stand by and watch as the only child of a couple we know grew sicker and weaker from a congenital defect. The doctors had tried everything, and now the couple could only devote themselves to loving the boy and making him happy and comfortable, which they did exceedingly well and with all their hearts. Finally, just before his fourth birthday, the boy died.

This couple had unusual strength and resiliency. I have rarely seen anything like it. Their grief was enormous, and yet their focus very quickly began to shift away from their personal sorrow to helping other parents who might be working through the same shock and loss they were. At that time there were no groups in Santa Fe to which people in grief could turn, and so the four of us decided to start one ourselves. We put a notice in the paper, contacted hospitals and churches, and held our first meeting in a small conference room of the branch library.

I think all four of us knew that this was going to be a fundamentally grim and depressing activity. But we were wrong. As the sessions continued we were surprised to find that, although there was silence and crying and deep outpourings of emotion, on the whole these weekly meetings were remarkably happy and uplifting. I can remember more than one occasion on which, when people coming for the first time would stick their heads in the door, we quickly had to assure them that, despite all the laughter they were hearing, they had indeed found the "grief support group."

Gayle and I observed several dynamics in these meetings that helped us to a better understanding of happiness, but one in particular kept repeating itself with almost every new member. When the individual forgave totally, letting go of all grudges and bitterness, the grief itself would begin dissipating dramatically, but as long as some deep anger remained, the grief would persist, sometimes for many years, regardless of what other therapeutic measures the person took.

Many of these people had abundant reason to be angry. Their accounts of mistakes made by doctors and nurses, of insensitive behavior and remarks by relatives and friends, were sometimes so outrageous that the group would be left speechless. However, time and again we saw them come to the realization that if they truly wanted to be free of their grief, the question they eventually had to ask themselves was—despite the justification, and despite even continued provocation—how much longer did they want to remain angry over this?

Very simply, *you have no chance of being happy when you are angry.* Yet we are in a period in which anger is greatly honored as one of our most natural and useful emotions. In a thousand variations we hear the pronouncement made, "It's important to be angry." As long as you fail to question this current assumption, you will never know what it is like to go through one whole day in peace, for something will inevitably come up to justify your irritation. And the possibility of day upon day of peace will seem to you a cruel hope.

Because anger never occurs at the deepest level, it can be relinquished without hypocrisy. To see what you really want will clear your mind of superficial passions, and even of chronic bitterness. However, without preliminary ground-work, most people simply have not reached a place where they can quickly know their true feelings. For them the question is what do they do to make this possible.

As a first step it is far better to be confused than to lash out. *Do not permit the body to act out your desire to attack.* Stopping short of involving other people in your distress will definitely save you time. But of course that alone will not eliminate the surface layer of emotions. With even mild irritation you must turn quickly and watch the anger, otherwise you will continue to believe it is how you really feel. *To look so carefully at the anger that you see through it to your heart is to learn how to use the greatest corrective force there is.*

Ideas Do Not Leave Their Source

Most of us give lip service to the thought that happiness is a state of mind, but why do we fail so thoroughly to live it? The evidence supporting it is in plain view every day of our life. It is not that we haven't seen the evidence but that we reject it constantly. We are afraid that this trite little fact could deprive us of something so valuable that we relentlessly trade our happiness to retain it.

The truth that all criticism attacks the criticizer is difficult to accept because it appears to threaten our worth as a person. We believe that we are thought more highly of when we have seen to it that someone else is thought less highly of. It is therefore crucial to our image that our judgments leave us and attach themselves to the person who is our target. It would perhaps be possible to rid ourselves of such thoughts if we were to change our mind about an individual after condemning him, but even this we do not think we can afford because we also believe that we sustain our opinion of ourselves by *continuing* to judge. If suddenly we were to forget to attack, and recognize that everyone is innocent, where would that leave us? Indeed that is the question.

For so very long we have not allowed ourselves the smallest doubt that we have been mistreated and damaged. We can cite all who are responsible, what they did, and what they should have done instead. If the rules of behavior we have chosen to emphasize are a little easier on us than others, we rectify this by occasionally turning the guns of our disapproval on ourselves. This we call "admitting our faults," and we are usually careful to do it in the context of someone else's greater fault. In our upside-down way of thinking, it is who we criticize, and not whether, that matters. Yet in the case of unhappiness, attack thoughts are the *only* factor. Whether the target is ourself or others, some object or situation, the result is mental damage.

All thoughts are circular. However much we want to stand apart from our accusations, if we still believe them, they remain an irritant to our mind. As I mentioned earlier, this condition is not improved by acting out our disapproval. To inform someone of the faults we see does not weaken our belief in them. All that "ventilating" our judgments really produces, aside from a feeling of righteousness and a little bodily numbness, is the enervating sense that the problem is now beyond our control because we have spread it to other minds and drawn more egos into our unhappiness. It is true that by voicing criticism we "get it out," but it is not true that it is any less inside because it is out. If anything, it has been emphasized, hardened, and will stay with us longer, and now added to it is the sadness that always accompanies betrayal. We have attacked, however mildly, another human being, a person who, just like us, has tried very hard.

It is possible to be open and honest with someone without attacking him. It is also possible to beat pillows, scream into the wind, go for a walk in a nourishing setting, or do other physical things that may release bodily tensions and clarify feelings and still be dealing with our emotions *within ourself.* This form of "acting out" is harmless because it does not complicate the problem by stirring up other people or increasing the numbers involved.

The rule is, *do not allow the criticism to leave your mind; remove its source, and repair the damage to your mind quickly.* This entails no loss because until you have forgiven absolutely, you can only have the illusion that your disapproval is separate from you. And you *do* wish to act at once, for the simple reason that the longer you dwell on another's weakness, the more you infect your own mind with unhappiness.

By far the most difficult part of the guideline to apply is "removing the source." This is not because the procedure is complicated but because the habit of blame is deeply rooted. I once watched a friend work very hard, not for just a few minutes or hours, but for many months before she began to make progress in forgiving her parents,[4] even though they had been dead for years. By the time she reached forty she had come to realize that her bitterness over her childhood was so entrenched that, among other manifestations, she would continue having turbulent, unendurable relationships with men until she stopped looking at them from her past and seeing their every act through the lens of her father's behavior.

She worked out a daily program, the main component of which was to carry a notebook with her in which she wrote down any symptom of anger (frustration, criticism, irritation, ill will, etc.). At the end of the day she would read her entries,

[4] I have never known anyone to reach the kind of deep, stable contentment I have been speaking of until coming to see his parents as *completely* innocent and himself as undamaged by them. There are unquestionably other blocks to happiness, but this one is practically universal. Many of us think that because we have renounced our childhood, we have forgiven it, but of course we have not.

and with each one she would look in her heart for her genuine feelings about the person or situation that had provoked her. After a good six or seven months of this, along with the very pleasant changes in her internal atmosphere, she was able, for the first time in her life, to form a new, and this time, lasting relationship.

Most people would not persist as long as did my friend. If the change does not come quickly, the tendency is to dive back into the old way. This woman had come to recognize that so long as she continued to carry a residue of bitterness, so long as there remained even a small persistent grudge, her enjoyment of life would be vulnerable and unstable.

Shortly after her new relationship was begun she realized that a little of the old anger still remained, and so she immediately went back to work in the same simple way—comparing these surface emotions with what she truly yearned to be. This she did until she knew with certainty that she never again wanted to cherish another hurtful line of thought about anyone, including herself.

Forgiving Honestly

Forgiveness is an often misused and fearful concept. Frequently it is a type of arrogance by which we look down in pity on those who "need" forgiving. Used in this way it is mere attack. We also assume that certain behavior must accompany it: If we forgive someone we are going to have to spend more time with him. We must not fire an incompetent employee. We should socialize with our ex-spouse. This kind of reasoning is of course illogical. *To forgive you need do nothing; it is an act of the heart, not of the body.* And genuine forgiveness contains not even a hint of the supposed necessity to force the mind or to reason dishonestly.

The root meaning of the verb "to forgive" is "to let go, to give up, to cease to harbor." Seen in this way, forgiving is a very passive and restful activity. A premise of pure truth lies behind how and why it works: The mind is already happy until made to be otherwise. Whenever the unnatural use of the mind ceases, happiness is seen already in place, like the sun "coming out" from behind clouds.

The source of any critical thought must be removed before the damage it has caused to our mind can be repaired. What then is the source? As you can see in the case of my friend, if the source had been external, if it had been either her childhood or her parents, her plight would have been bleak indeed. Her childhood was now lost in time and could not be relived except in fantasy, and her parents were dead. Yet both those facts were irrelevant because, although the damage began in her childhood, it was carried on by how she was *continuing* to use her mind, and this was within her ability to alter.

When any judgmental train of thought ends, the damage it caused to the mind ends with it. That is precisely why this woman spent so many months quietly looking at her pain. She *wanted* to be informed of the extent her bitterness was hurting her each day because she knew that once she saw this clearly, there would be no question of motivation. Now she would do whatever was required to "let go."

We are unable to forgive because we do not yet want to. It is that simple. We want the evidence. We want to hold someone's behavior against him. But we no longer want this once we see what it does to our own mind. If you are ever to know a sustained happiness, you must first come to recognize the consequences of the ideas you entertain as welcomed guests.

It must be remembered, though, that true forgiveness is never dishonest. It is not some futile exercise in rosy self-deception. To the contrary, it is a calm recognition that below our egos we are all exactly the same. Yet we live in a time when the concept of honesty itself is being extensively and popularly misused, and in order not to become confused, we must see exactly what this self-indulgent version of honesty is.

Our ego demands loyalty strictly to itself, to its tastes and prejudices, even though these are never completely steady and are based on a pitifully small and distorted point of view. If we are to be righteous within its terms, we must be constant to what is temporary and petty. In the course of a day we are likely to be asked directly—or more often indirectly—what we think of a person's new coat, a certain colleague in the office, a movie, a meal, a political issue, or about the weather, or just how we are doing. The ego's ideal of honesty dictates that these overtures be responded to straight from our mood, that we must be "brutally" honest, even though we should perhaps word what we say discreetly and cover our little murders with amenities. Whereas in simple truth these everyday kinds of questions are almost never seeking anything more from us than acceptance and love, and since in our heart we know this, to react to them literally is merely dishonest.

We have a choice. We can consult our understanding and goodwill and respond from love or we can dredge up our current ego opinion and make that our "truthful" answer. There is no mistaking which choice the majority makes and why most people walk away from even the most casual of social contacts feeling a little anxious and guilty and slightly misunderstood.

Gayle and I both like to cook and we each have dishes that we think we do well. We had been married seventeen years before we realized that for all this time we had been making each other unhappy by believing that we had to give an "honest" answer whenever the other one asked, "How do you like it?"

"Too dull. It needs some green chilies and a little cumin."

"Yes, but I don't like to overseason everything the way you do. And besides, the children have to eat it."

"So why did you ask me if you didn't want my opinion?"

"I just wanted to know if you thought it had finished baking."

"It depends on how you define 'finished.' "

One night after another one of these pointless exchanges, we sat down and decided that we were going to eliminate this seventeen-year-old bone of contention once and for all. We made a rule. Unless it was physically impossible to swallow the food and keep it down, we would always tell each other that what had been fixed was just wonderful and, no matter how closely cross-examined, we would not back down. We expected this plan to merely eliminate a sore point, but it has actually provided a running joke that continues to delight us.

You always have the option of not consulting your ego.[5] We frequently choose this alternative when dealing with someone very young. We instinctively know that it is unnecessary to give children our opinion of their first drawings or to critique their innocent attempts at completing a new task. We do not even bother to see what our judgments are. Instead, we speak to the child out of our kindness and happiness. And it is our privilege to do likewise with adults. It is always *possible* to view anything—a new building in town, the life-style of certain groups, the climate, the time of day—from our core instead of from our personal history or current disgruntlements. Of course this implies an attitude only and not "nice" words.

Periodically John announces that *he* will do the dishes. He

[5] Unless of course the person really is seeking your ego position because the situation absolutely requires it. If for instance you are being asked by your spouse if you will be able to live happily in this particular house for sale, and you know that your prejudices against it would never allow you to, then of course you must say so, for to be a martyr would jeopardize the future peace of your family.

sprays, soaps, scrubs, rinses, in fact he does all the necessary procedures, it's just that he doesn't do them in the right order, and by the time he is finished there are remarkably few clean dishes and a great deal of water everywhere. Yet he is always proud of his job, and we tell him how proud we are of him, too, for truly we are.

It is a part of realism and sanity, and it is certainly a part of happiness, to look upon the world the way we allow ourselves to look at a child. Any child can be seen as annoying, and some adults have been taught always to choose this view. But most of us do not. We see the blamelessness in the two-year-old even though it says "no" to everything. A little baby remains sweet and absolutely pure in our eyes even during a diaper change. If we could but take this gaze and turn it upon the world we would not have to do one thing more to be continually and deeply happy.

Our so-called truthful way of looking pervades every waking hour and can easily set the tone of an entire lifetime. It is surprising how bitter many people become. Our morning chores, our job, our drive home, our kids, our evening pastimes are either being viewed with sympathy and perspective or in the harsh but apparently virtuous light of "honesty." The simple fact is that a gentle vision makes a more gentle world in which to walk.

Mired in the superficial layer of our emotions, we can feel quite certain of the carelessness, selfishness, callousness, and even viciousness of another individual. And we may in fact have guessed correctly about this person's ego characteristics. Yet where did being right take us except into a deeper blindness? Indeed we all have an ego, but our petty side, our shadow identity is no better than anyone else's. Even in this we are equal.

Each of us is so much more than a mere ego, and this evidence for a higher yearning can be seen when thought is still and gentle. One of the oldest books in the world, the *I Ching,* points out that "stillness is the mountain." When we view ourselves and others from the vantage point of a quiet mind, we see how small indeed is our negativity, a mere shadow hiding out of sight of the rising sun.

Our Fear of the Present

The judgment and agitation and the pointless mental chatter so common to our experience comes from excessive interest in the past and future. Another word for quiet is "now." Only one thing keeps us from seeking the steadier ground and broader view afforded by the present, and that is our anxiety over what we will find there. When a person has spent a lifetime avoiding looking at something, he is tempted to conclude that there must have been good reason. This is a temptation you have probably not escaped. But even though your position may be time-honored, it is hurting you nevertheless.

Our fear of the present, which is exhibited in our unwillingness to stop and look, will always hold us back from opportunities or hurry us beyond reach of them. Mentally we are in the habit of oscillating between a state of anxious anticipation and small discouragements, like waves that break against a beach, accomplish little, and then turn back on themselves. When we act we practice a kind of martyrdom or else pursue a thing that, when it comes, is without real significance and enduring satisfaction. A rushing after, a turning away. Only the form varies, but the basic pattern remains undisturbed. Anything, anything at all, is preferable to remaining mentally in the present.

Even though we have stumbled over the same fact all our lives, we have not yet acknowledged it. Yes, we know the words that describe it, but we have not stooped down and taken this fact into our hands and gazed at its overwhelming brilliance. Perhaps it is because we sense that if we were to do this, we would never again be the same. Yet how harmless, how completely innocent, is the fact that the present is real.

Our life makes contact with us at the point known as now. That is the place where it breaks out of time and into reality. To the degree that our thoughts are lost in past regret and future scheming, we are not living, in fact we are very nearly dead. This is not a sin but it is definitely unhappy. Our actual life span is composed of an unbroken series of now's, and its quality is determined by how well we have learned to respond to the present. Most of us do not even see it yet.

For just a moment, please, allow me to be very direct. I want to ask you a question. When will you stop fighting your appearance? When will you enjoy your child? Will there ever be a time in your life to drink in what your friends have to offer—it seems so little, but have you received even that little? When will you first feel a breeze passing over your cheek? Will there finally come a meal in which you will taste, really taste, your food? Just where are you going anyway? All you will ever discover about the future is that it remains the future—and so why do you still turn it over and over in your mind like some delicacy? This life of yours is not an easy habit to break, but do you really wish to continue missing almost everything of value only to end up on your deathbed wondering why you never took the time to love?

We no longer have time for games. Let us be done with guilt and duty. There is a song to sing. There is life to live and people to enjoy. In your heart you know that something lies beyond all this pettiness and chaos. It really is possible to live in this world and still be happy. Far more than that is possible, but let us begin with that.

We are speaking here of your *approach* to life. You are not yet approaching it because you have not yet recognized where it lies. Where is happiness found? You have a thousand assumptions about this you have not yet questioned. You are currently *living* these assumptions. Almost everything you think and do stems from them. And that is the way it has always been. If this book is to be different, you must understand one thing: It will take enormous effort for you to walk past your ordinary way of doing things. And yet, once you have decided to make the effort, and have committed yourself completely, all of it will eventually become surprisingly easy. Martyrdom, drudgery, testiness, suffering, tension have nothing whatsoever to do with the effort you must make. There is no organization to join, no doctrine to subscribe to, no person or book to follow, no cause to give money to. A decision must be made. It can be made now. It is simply this: "I will begin."

And what must you begin? You must try to be kind *now*— not appear kind, but *be* kind. You must make the effort, no, the struggle, to be happy now—and not first gain what you need in order to be happy. Some people have an experience, such as a narrow escape from death, in which they suddenly see the importance of opening their heart to the present, and for a time they are transformed. But so often this fades and is lost, and they are left not really knowing why it passed. This must not happen to you. You cannot just add what I am talking about to your life. It must be your life.

Your goal to be happy, and kind, and at peace, will allow for no secondary aim. You cannot hope to bring your life to peace and also take time out to be irritated. Irritation does not add to your chances for happiness. Of course you will make mistakes, in fact you must lose your fear of making them, but your life purpose will now be so firmly rooted in your heart that anytime you recognize an error you will unfailingly return to the only thing that matters. And what is that?

The words are so flimsy. An experience is needed to give them substance, and consistent effort will bring you that experience. Just a slight glimmer at first. A kind of happiness you had forgotten was possible. At the start of your journey it will seem to come and go as if by magic, but gradually you will begin to recognize its independence of all the happenings you thought were prerequisite. And then the moment will finally come in which it will dawn on you: "Nothing has to go right for me to be happy. People do not have to behave themselves for me to love them. I am free."

CHAPTER III

Getting Started

Stopping Is Starting

The world is like a dog guarding a meatless bone. It gnaws on concepts and remains empty. The great neglected need in this era of clashing opinions is the need for direct experience. Once an individual experiences a fact he stops arguing about it because he no longer needs to convince himself. But before this simple change can take place, he must step back far enough to see the fact plainly.

For many years I have worked with people in crisis.[1] Time and again I have watched even those who are desperate go right ahead with an approach they know in their heart will not work. A kind of blind fear takes over, and they convince themselves that there is nothing left to try. So they stick with failure

[1] Batterers and battered women, rape and mugging victims, parents in grief, suicidal adults and adolescents, alcoholics, etc., in individual counseling, through groups, and on a crisis line.

to the bitter end. They have lost their natural instinct for knowing when to stop and regain perspective.

As I began to do more counseling involving less dramatic circumstances, I noticed that the same dynamic prevailed, even with the most minor of problems. The difficulty was almost never sustained by what the person was blaming. Solution was blocked by the mere failure to pause.

Here is Edward Bear, coming downstairs now, bump, bump, bump, on the back of his head, behind Christopher Robin. It is, as far as he knows, the only way of coming downstairs, but sometimes he feels that there really is another way, if only he could stop bumping for a moment and think of it. *(Winnie-the-Pooh)*

There are many times—far more than are recognized at first —when we have gotten so caught up in the day's problems and events that only by pausing and intentionally stilling our thoughts will our awareness expand enough to take in all the ways we are limiting our options. This is a book of experiences as well as ideas, and the first experience we will attempt is to see what happens when the bumping stops.

EXERCISE III-A

Perhaps you believe that you already know the benefits of pausing, but I can assure you that unless this practice has become as second nature to you as breathing, you have not yet *enjoyed* the benefits sufficiently. Once you have recognized the cumulative effects of this practice, you may find that you want to begin scheduling breaks throughout the day, but it is not necessary to concern yourself with this now as there will be exercises presented later that will introduce this procedure in a simpler and more gradual way. For now your objective is just to take a couple of days to experience some of the happy effects.

1. Notice that the day comes in segments, with little beginnings and endings to each. Also notice that the mind refocuses with each change of bodily activity. I am not speaking of whether a task you have started gets finished—that particular sense of things is a result of anticipation and expectation. No matter how thorough or incomplete each activity turns out to be, the day still proceeds as a chain of events rather than as a continuous stream, and our mind makes a brief transition or adjustment in going from one activity to another, from sleep ending to the act of rising, from making the bed to getting dressed, from getting dressed to eating breakfast, and so forth. Notice, too, that there is a natural stopping point during this instant when the mind is shifting gears. It is "natural" simply because if done happily it can facilitate and smooth this shift in the focus of our concentration, as well as provide many other pleasant and more lasting benefits.

2. For at least two complete days take advantage of as many of these transitional periods as you recognize by merely pausing and stilling your mind for a few seconds. Of course do not take one of these breaks if ever the circumstances are such that you could not help worrying about the consequences, because the aim of the break is to become more conscious of the present.

It is generally easier to settle the mind when the body is still, so either quietly stand where you are at the time or, perhaps even better, sit with your eyes closed. Only an instant or two is needed.

All you wish is the sense of your mind slowing and settling down, somewhat like coming to a stop at an intersection and allowing the car's engine to idle for a moment. How you attain this is not important, but you do want a genuine break with the way you have been using your mind up until then.

If you already know some means of stilling thought, it is fine to use any of these; if not, you might try doing no more than to think gently for a while. Simply let your mind drift easily and happily, and avoid pursuing any one thought. If this does not appeal to you, try listening peacefully to the sounds around you. Or slowly repeat these words to yourself: "My mind is quiet. I am still now."

3. If for the course of these two or more days you will be as conscientious as possible about shifting your focus to peace between events, you will certainly become aware of some unexpected benefits. Any of these that you notice, record in your notebook (see Preface).

The Work of Happiness

Have you ever, as I have, watched absentmindedly as you chose the wrong key and yet continued trying to insert it in the ignition or front-door lock anyway? We were not thinking. Or more accurately we were thinking rather than paying attention. It is not that we didn't know which was the right key, but in a kind of reflexive, almost hypnotic way we picked one we often use rather than the right one. The analogy is obvious: Everyone has the key but very few are using it. And the key is our undeveloped mental focus.

You must understand, however, this is a book on the key to happiness and not to great income, super health, the right friends, mental powers, model children, or all the other idols the world raises above the simple and deep enjoyment of today. As probably every child who has ever attended any kind of camp knows, you must "row, row, row your boat gently down the stream." And if you will maintain this pace, and this direction, you are guaranteed to be merry four times to every three times you row. There is definitely a way to walk through the world in peace, but attempts to change the nature of the world itself are not helpful.

If we row gently, even the rowing becomes part of our pleasure. But row we must. Pain and tedium are not required—they actually hinder—but nothing worth having will come to anyone without concentration. What makes most of our work so arid is the impossibility of the task we set before ourselves. And this is also true of the work needed to be happy.

We insist that everything be done at once, never to be undone. We think that somehow, with a casual reading, with one good meditation, with the understanding of a few little concepts, with the mastery of one or two spiritual practices, our life will transform and we will arrive. We actually believe there is a way it could happen in just this manner, and consequently we insist on seeing our way *through* before we begin. In short, we believe in magic. So naturally our first efforts leave us feeling tired and defeated, and very soon we want no more of it. And all because we expect too much of ourselves.

The world's motto is "Do little and expect much," whereas the key to genuine success is *work hard but expect very little.* It is *in* giving, not *from* giving, that we receive. Expectations merely delay because the focus of our effort is misplaced. We forget how hard and long we have worked at being unhappy and how painstakingly we have learned the rules of misery. The reversing of our steps can go far more quickly, but still the undoing must be done step by step.

The Unhappy Use of Questions

A true answer is often unsophisticated, obvious, even corny. The difficulty we all have, and we have plenty of it, comes in our reluctance to take what we do see and live it. We want to know in advance every detail of our future course, and we think we are due as well an exact accounting of the results before we start. Since this is impossible, we never start. *If you want to get there, begin* is a rule so unusually simple that most people have immense difficulty learning it.

When I was in my early twenties I started a real estate firm in Dallas. I took on a partner, and after a year or two of business it seemed to us we were not growing fast enough, and so we began seeking an investor to capitalize an expansion. Someone suggested we contact a particular Dallas business-man described as both wealthy and compassionate. That indeed was the combination of qualities we were looking for. He agreed to see us, and we gave him the details of our plan and asked if he would be interested. "You are intelligent and imaginative young men," he said. "And your plan seems sound. But I won't invest because I sense you haven't learned one basic lesson—do not spend money you don't have."

My partner and I decided he was not compassionate and quickly sought another investor, whom we succeeded in finding. In short, it took us five years to climb out of the financial hole we got into as a result. "Do not spend money you don't have" was too simple for us to assimilate, and it is only recently—some twenty-five years later—that I have become simple-minded enough to begin to understand it.

We frequently take something as obvious as this and ask endless questions about its application and ramifications: What does "have" money mean? In the bank? What about accounts receivable? Must I always carry cash and never use a credit card? Is it right to lend money to others? And on and on. The unhappy part of us will not receive a simple answer. It will question it to death so that it can carry on with the same pattern that is causing all the difficulty. Only in the calmness of our heart can we receive what we already know and go forward.

On a far higher level than spending practices there is the old familiar truth "as the sowing, the reaping" or "to give is to receive." In other words, to be at peace yourself, give peace to others. To feel loved, love. To be happy, make happy. This is very simple and is a part of all the world's inspired teachings. But it can be accepted and understood only by a mind that is not agitated, otherwise the tendency is to become mired in a thousand considerations: "Does this mean I must agree with a person who is trying to cheat me?" "Should I tell someone I am not angry when I am?" "If I give physical possessions away, will I get more?" "What about my rights; am I supposed to give those away too?" The sole intent here is *not* to apply the answer, and that is the outcome this kind of question always succeeds in bringing about.

We must become questionless. Worry has no practical value. It is a wholly useless and delaying activity. It does *not* protect us against making mistakes. In fact, it clouds our perspective and scatters our concentration and makes us more prone to error. Naturally one does not jump from extreme to extreme. To remove fear does not imply foolhardiness, and to remove worry does not imply carelessness. An absence of fear in the present leads naturally to an absence of fear later. If we are at peace now, we will not make a mistake now. And we will apply a good answer in a good way.

The Heart—The Ego

The objective of the next exercise will be to begin experiencing an increased sense of the difference between what I call in this book the "heart" and the "ego." The heart is your deepest mental level, your core. It is the seat of your true feelings. It is your center of calmness from which anything in the world can be viewed without interference from irrelevant anticipations or the influence of old sore lessons from the past, that is, without interference from your ego. The heart is your store of gentleness, and you will not act unkindly, either to yourself or others, when you proceed under its influence. With a little work it is definitely possible to have a growing sense of when your perceptions are coming from this place of quiet as opposed to when they are ego oriented.

The alternative to our heart's desire is our conflicted and unstable ego preference. I will be using the term "ego" more in an Eastern than a Freudian sense, and to some degree this is also how it is used in everyday conversation. In expressions such as "So and so has an ego problem" and "There are a lot of big egos in this room,"[2] the implication is that a fake identity has been assumed and that an unwholesome influence is being projected. In other words, the people with "big egos" are not being themselves, and the effect on them and others is unhappy.

The ego is our shabby self-image. As such it is almost pure fear. It is the cornered, crazy, arrogant, agitated part of our mind, which, in its misery, is always attacking us or someone else. Like an imaginary playmate, it can seem quite real and autonomous, but this *imaginary identity* we have established in

[2] Whenever any ego is "big" enough the nature common to all egos becomes more apparent.

the world does not hold our true feelings about anything and is therefore a very unhappy aspect of ourselves to turn to for guidance. Our ego can of course be "honored"—and this, in a very roundabout way, may eventually weaken it—but it is my experience that there are far faster and simpler ways of shaking off this mental dust we have picked up over the years.

EXERCISE III-B

All the body's emotions can be triggered by fakery, as any child who has gone through a carnival fun house can tell you. What most people are not aware of is just how often this happens in daily life. Not every thought that passes through our mind is our true opinion, and not every emotion the body feels is representative of a profound self-purpose. Just as "honoring" an imaginary playmate does not give a child a true friend, so "being yourself," if this means trying to be your highly unstable ego, will not put you in contact with what you genuinely feel because there is no consistent self in an ego. Our self, our essence, is experienced in a ground of calmness.

There are countless examples of how the body is continually being tricked into an inappropriate emotion: a shadow scares us, a drink makes us hostile, cloud cover depresses us, a crying baby angers us. If it all stopped there, perhaps no real loss of happiness would occur, but what so often happens is that we take the feeling to heart. And so, for example, while sitting in a waiting room we pick up a magazine and read an article on a subject that we had absolutely no interest in just seconds before, but suddenly we have been "made" angry over the issues raised and, without fully realizing it, we carry this irritation around with us for several hours, and many other lives are affected.

We have an experience. We feel an emotion. This much is

simple. And at the level of learning most of us have reached, it is unavoidable. But what comes next is avoidable. We then *remember* the experience and thereby continue regenerating an emotion that is incompatible, perhaps even destructive, to the new situation we are now in. I know a young girl who loves to watch the giant construction cranes, which are a rare sight here in Santa Fe where we have so few tall buildings. But her father, who on most occasions has no difficulty joining in on her fun, cannot sincerely share this particular enthusiasm because of a story he once heard about a crane collapsing and crushing many people. He doesn't know for certain if it is true, and his little girl actually heard the story at the same time he did, but for him it remains a sufficiently real picture to pollute the present.

What I want to emphasize is that we behave as though we do not have an alternative to this kind of dynamic. We believe that we have been "made" angry (scared, depressed, sad, jealous, etc.), and there is little we can now do about it.

Possibly a good place to start seeing through this fallacy would be with some relationship that is a bit difficult. A surprisingly large percentage of our mental activity is spent reviewing what happened between us and some other person, and very little attention is given the relationship at hand. Even the individual who stands before us now is more remembered than seen.

1. Recall a verbal exchange between you and another person, a conversation that still seems unfinished, or one that remains puzzling or in some other way continues as an irritation or merely an embarrassment. If you can, pick a scene that still comes to mind and is not a happy line of thought. Write only enough to identify it. A word or short phrase is fine.

2. Take a moment now to remember (but do not write) what the actual words, gestures, facial expressions, and general tone of the encounter were. Include as much of the clothing, sounds, surroundings, movements, and so forth as you can, but do not attempt to be perfectly thorough. Simply recall as much as you are able to without strain.

3. After you have dwelled on that kind of detail for a moment, write some brief descriptions of how you would revise the scene if you could. For example, what do you wish you had said instead? Are there some ways you could have come off better?

It is essential to record at least two versions of how it would be different if you had it to do over again, and if you can put down three or four this will be even better. As you write these notice that your ego does not have a consistent answer in mind. It is conflicted as to just what, if anything, you should have done differently.

4. Close your eyes, relax your body, and allow your mind to be lazy, to have not a care in the world. Just sit back and be comfortable and think comfortably for a time.[3] And please do not be in a rush to finish. Do this now, and when you are through go on to the following paragraph.

Describe in writing any resistance you may have felt, especially in the beginning. Did this mental rest period seem silly? Were you fearful (tense) that somehow you were not doing it right? Did you feel slightly ridiculous for following someone else's instructions? Perhaps you were so afraid of being manipulated that you did not follow them. Write down this kind of reaction. (If you did follow the instructions and there

[3] Several of the upcoming exercises include this kind of stilling-of-thought step. With any of these please feel free to use whatever means you wish. For example, if the suggestions made here about thinking lazily are not effective for you personally, use one of the alternatives given in III-A. Do not remain undecided, because you will never find a perfect technique. Just choose one that brings you some degree of stillness.

was no resistance to speak of, skip the written part and go to #5.)

5. Again, quietly rest your thoughts for a few seconds. Then recall the conversation once more, only this time stay with your feeling of relaxation and comfort as you do so. Remember it in peace or, more accurately, remember it *from* peace. For the moment, assume that all you wish to come of your review is an increased sense of well-being. In doing this it is important that you not try to change your memory of the scene. Simply remain calm and relatively happy as you recall the way it was. In so doing you will see more clearly that a memory cannot dictate your present mood unless you choose for it to. You will also see that how you feel is not the direct by-product of anything that once happened in the world. Both of these lessons are hard to learn in any thorough or deep sense because they undercut all the cause and effect relationships we are used to relying on.

6. Once you have succeeded—to any degree—at remaining inwardly comfortable while making your review, you will then be ready for the final part of this exercise. It is not necessary that you feel consistent peace during the review. In fact, this is probably not possible. But if there is even an instant or two when you feel comfort while looking at a scene that ordinarily makes you uncomfortable, then you will know better what actually "makes" you. When this has happened, slowly write the following statement several times: "Nothing pushes my buttons except me. I am not a robot; I am free."

If you don't like the way this idea is phrased, please feel free to make up your own rendition. The point is to put into words, that you can call upon, the simple truth that you are not a victim. We are controlled by the past only when we are not conscious. *To become conscious is to enter the present and thereby break our mental link with the past.* The peaceful repetition of a true idea in words we like is one way of doing that.

Watching Thought

The goal of the first exercise was to provide a small experience of the effects of mental stillness. Stopping is essential if perspective is to be maintained, but stopping in itself is merely a negative, a not-continuing. Stepping back is the first step, but we must step back into stillness or very little will change. Mental stillness is an attribute of the mind that can be felt and employed, and in the first exercise it was used as a means of preparing for future—and letting go of—past activities and events.

Our mind includes more than just stillness, or we would not suffer. Before we will come to know a stillness that is unshakable, we must first prove to ourselves that we can choose it on at least some occasions, and then expand the number of occasions. Thus in the second exercise stillness was used in a new way, to eliminate one of the primary origins of unhappiness, recurring thoughts. In practicing this perhaps you also gained an increased sense of the ego (mental agitation) and the heart (mental stillness) as sources of experience. The third and last exercise in this getting-started chapter will represent a major progression in the application of mind-training principles. It is not a unique approach, nor will it take the place of other needed procedures on this level. Its power lies in the range of its effects. Whereas the first two exercises dealt with specific ways of utilizing an attribute of the mind, the target of this last exercise is the overall condition and integrity of the mind itself.

Strictly speaking, we have only one mind, but that it is split is painfully clear. It is not only feasible, it can be quite helpful to view our lower mind from our higher mind, to look carefully and in detail at our ego from the standpoint of our heart. And it truly is not difficult to do this, even though there are levels of attainment.

When you are inwardly calm, provided that the calmness is gentle and happy, you are "in your right mind" and are automatically in position to do much good, especially for yourself. Your goal should never be to "integrate" all the contents of your mind (it is best to keep the pollution in one place) but you do wish to extend your sanity into the ego part of your mind.

Please be assured that this is possible. Depression, irritation, anxiety, jealousy, guilt, and all the other forms of mental misery that we so quickly accept as inevitable, do not *have* to remain coiled to strike. A strong mental state is yours if you will merely undertake, easily and with patience, the steps necessary to attain it.

The first step needed to heal our mental split is an increased awareness of the split itself. Sometimes our thoughts strengthen and comfort and other times they enervate. We are split between happiness and unhappiness, and we have interchanged the two so frequently that we are deeply confused as to what genuine happiness feels like, and blind to the major themes of our thoughts, even though these themes alone set the tone of our life.

As individuals we carry an individual mental pattern with us at all times, and yet most of us have no real knowledge of what it might be. We believe that our mind is simply as it is and we cannot escape it: This is just the house we live in. Unfortunately it was designed by someone else. And even though its rooms are cramped and confused, and the walls despairingly bleak, its arrangement must go unquestioned.

If you are ever to be free you must learn to track your mind as an unknown animal. You must come to know its habitats, its stopping points, where it always wanders into trouble, and what the places of rest and nourishment are that it invariably skirts. Your mind is doing no less than determining the way you experience life, yet you cannot change even one detail of this unless you know what that detail is.

EXERCISE III-C

When doing this exercise it is very important not to allow a sense of fighting yourself to develop. You are not attempting to manipulate your mind but merely to watch it carefully in order to increase your knowledge of its thinking habits. Once you are more familiar with how you get yourself into trouble, you will naturally want to begin the necessary adjustments and corrections. And there will indeed be a time for this. The danger is in undertaking it too soon.

When working with our own mind we all have a tendency to judge it and jump to conclusions about how it needs to change. But remember that when you feel judgmental in this way you are criticizing your mind *with* your mind, and all you accomplish is to enlarge the split. The mind is helped by *extending* sanity, and never by attacking insanity, even though the attack may be quite moderate. It is for this reason that the practice of watching thought, because it is entirely gentle, includes an enormously powerful corrective force. *To watch is to extend.* The watcher (our heart or higher mind) enters what is watched (our ego or small-mindedness) and transforms it the way light streaming through an opening curtain transforms a room that was deep in shadow. So if ever you are uncertain whether it is now time to correct in a more direct way, remember that you will not hurt your progress by waiting to act and continuing to watch.

1. Once a day, for just ten minutes, sit quietly and look at the thoughts you are having. Do this conscientiously for one week.

Since your wish is merely to increase your awareness of what you are thinking, do not decide beforehand what ideas should or should not be there. If you already have opinions on this, see if you can suspend them for at least the duration of each practice period. Before you begin one perhaps you might say to yourself, "I am not perfectly certain what is a good or bad thought. Therefore, I will look at my thoughts as if seeing them for the first time." Repeat this decision not to judge yourself as often as needed.

While practicing, the attitude you want is similar to one you may have had as a child when you would lie on your back and watch the shapes clouds took. There was neither approval nor disapproval involved, just relaxed interest. You are merely on a discovery mission.

At the conclusion of each period record anything of interest that you have noticed about your thoughts.

2. Beginning the following week, for fifteen minutes once each day, watch your thoughts in the same relaxed manner. As you identify any idea, list it under one of the five headings suggested below. Continue doing this as diligently as possible for two weeks.

You may want to write the thoughts out in detail or merely describe each one by its central subject or theme. Either method is fine.

Please feel free to add or subtract categories, but once you have decided on what they will be, try to stay with these for all fourteen days.

As you probably noticed while doing #1, the mind tends to quieten when watched, and so it may take a few moments for thoughts definite enough to categorize to begin coming. Should you start to feel anxious about the duration of the stillness, you could try recalling what some very recent thoughts have been, or you might even pick a few subjects at random to think about, but do return to allowing your mind to be spontaneous whenever possible.

Upon consideration a thought may appear to fall under more than one classification. If you find you are being delayed by this question, merely place it under the heading that seems to dominate that particular thought. Ask yourself which of the five characteristics weighs most heavily and class it accordingly. The goal of the exercise is not mere accuracy in categorizing, but a more acute awareness of the individual ways your thoughts spoil your enjoyment of the present.

It may not become clear to you until you are well into this book that when you think in any of these categories you are making yourself unhappy, but please do recognize that it is not necessary to believe this in order to do the exercise. Once you have trained yourself to be aware of when your mind is attacking, thinking fearfully, or leaving the present, you will see the effects for yourself. Should these effects begin to be obvious to you in the course of this exercise, it would definitely be best *not* to force yourself to stop thinking along these lines. To do battle with your unhappiness actually strengthens it. Increased awareness is increased sanity, and as your sanity grows there will naturally be less insane activity within your mind. The principle of correction advocated by this book is age old: It is more practical to light a candle than to curse the dark.

JUDGMENT/ATTACK

(Your attacks and judgments might include such thoughts as revenge fantasies, feelings of personal inadequacy, imagined arguments, comparisons and categorizations of other people, analyses of your own behavior.)

WORRY

(This category might contain: attempts to understand why something happened; concerns over what you have done or are leaving undone; small worries about your appearance, diet, car, weather, etc.; nagging background questions such as whether you are doing this exercise right.)

FEAR

(Worry is a question whereas fear is experienced more as a fact. For example: fear of predictable consequences from something you have been ingesting, such as becoming violent, activating an ulcer, etc. Fear of physical danger to you or others from driving too fast, not locking up at night, etc. Vague fears of general catastrophes: earthquakes, inflation, exposure to disease. Fear of inevitable changes in the course of your life, i.e., fear of loss of reputation from retirement, of loneliness from divorce, of abandoning others by dying.)

PAST

(Among other thoughts, this list might cover: Recalling past successes. Remembering embarrassments, mistakes. Reenacting former provocations. Rewriting past conversations. Nostalgic sadness over the old days.)

FUTURE

(These are common future-oriented ideas: Speculating on what might occur. Longing for some situation to change. Planning before it is necessary. Rehearsing upcoming conversations. "Watching the clock.")

3. At the close of each week read over the thoughts you have recorded. Write down any new insights you have had into your mental patterns and describe any changes in your overall state of mind of which you are fairly certain.

CHAPTER IV

Beginning the Day

Reacting Blindly

Have you ever hypnotized a chicken? When I was a boy I lived part of each year on a farm. At that time chickens had not been domesticated to the degree they now have and these rather wild birds fascinated me. When fried chicken was planned for dinner, the hen that had been chosen to fulfill this brightest dream of all loyal chickens would, in the course of the day, find herself without a head. But this was not an immediate tragedy, because such is the nature of the chicken that it can run around quite well without a head, at least for a time.

The roosters were also slightly beyond belief. They apparently had only three goals in life: to eat, to fertilize eggs, and to attack anything that moved. Of course these are not uncommon goals, but what was uncommon was the rooster's single-minded determination to pursue them. I have known a cock to be knocked cold with a grain bucket, come to, and instantly attack again, and to continue this until the villainous egg gatherer had left the coop.

Thankfully I was never assigned the task of either fighting roosters or wringing hens' necks, but I was allowed to hypnotize as many chickens as I wished. The hardest part was to catch them, for in those days they could fly quite well. After that the rest was simple. You merely hold the chicken's chin flat against the ground and with your finger or a stick draw a line straight out from its beak. It will watch the line form in the dirt, and even though you release it, so fixed is its attention on the line that it will stay frozen in position as though it were still being firmly held. Once its attention turns to itself (at your urging or in due time), it realizes it is free and runs off.

There is a good parallel here to our own experience. As long as we are preoccupied with how others comport themselves, we are locked into our own self-styled hell, yet the instant our awareness returns we cannot help realizing that we are free to feel the way we wish. Even though this is an accurate statement of cause and effect, a means is needed to change it from a description into an ability.

If we continue the same reactions toward the world that we have always had, we will remain its victim, and our chronic feelings of discontent will merely deepen with age. The key is not to change our reactions. That approach is interminable. Instead, we must continue to notice them but decline to take them to heart, and thus we will cease altogether being some bit of paper tossed by every worldly breeze. Reactions use the past as a guide instead of the gentle preferences that come from peace. We will never be free of our erraticism so long as there is some aspect of the world that can manipulate us at will, because this part of what is outside of us will take precedence over our longing to be of reliable value.

Please do not misunderstand me. Declining to react blindly does not mean that we are now beyond being shocked or deeply saddened by a tragedy, or that we neglect needed repairs, or refuse to shop in advance for our meals. Anticipating our peace of mind and convenience, and doing in the present what needs to be done to protect them, is not coming under the spell of events. Blind reactions do not flow from the practice of viewing the day calmly. Looking at things honestly and quietly leads to well-considered overt acts as easily as it does to waiting patiently. Therefore, let your first reaction be stillness.

Our life merely reflects the unity or division of our will. Either we decide life or it will decide us. In one choice is strength, and hope based on vision, and growth; in the other there is only a spreading impotence. All too often isolation and physical misery dominate the closing months and years of a lifetime. They descend slowly, like a vast and final curtain on a play that never reached a denouement or even meant a thing to anyone. Because a decision was not made, life just happened, and the loneliness and bewilderment of the ending happened too. It was inescapable because an alternative had never been sought.

The Power of a Decision

If a decision about life is possible, and indeed it is, there must be something outside of it, or at least outside of life as we ordinarily view it. If the way you think about your day determines the kind of day you will have, *you* must be more than your day. The mind that decides to decide, gradually moves into that realm which is more than a day, more even than a single life, and far more than our daily peck of troubles.

The ability to decide is merely the ability to give attention. Whether we realize it or not at the time, we have *chosen* to look at whatever "has our attention" and have decided to turn away from its opposite. "To be in the kingdom is merely to focus your full attention on it," says *A Course in Miracles.*

Even though the mind exists, it can imagine itself as anything, and quite obviously does. The basis of these fantasies, and that which gives them their appeal, is always an unquestioned judgment. When the mind stops judging altogether it assumes its natural function of love. Love has no singular, small, unconnected target, for nothing is outside of love because it *wishes* nothing outside of it. These words are easily misunderstood and are almost meaningless without an accompanying experience. However, every experience is preceded by a decision, a deliberately chosen focus.

Letting your day dictate your mood *is* a decision. "Indecision" is a deliberate choice that the status quo continue, that there be still more versions of what has always been, that nothing new start now. *Confusion about what to be in life is disbelief in love.* So it must be remembered that to decide your day is not to declare war on events. If try as you may you still do not know what to do, it is indeed best to do nothing.

Deciding to have the kind of day you want will not give you special powers and advantages over those who do not yet know enough to decide. And the kind of choice I am speaking of will never call for you to wring from other people their compliance by nagging or outreasoning them. If you try to decide against certain circumstances occurring in your day, you will lose; but if you peacefully and kindly plan how to bypass their usual impact on your emotions, you will win.

Even to want personal advantage is a joyless state because of the sense of estrangement it entails. By *consciously* choosing to be happy we leave the battlefield altogether. Why would we incessantly skirmish over how things should go and people should be if we knew that the great field of peace surrounds these tiny places of war and all we have to do to enter it is decide that we would rather be happy than right? In order for this to occur, the hypnotic hold of the battlefield must first give way to a greater interest.

What Do I Have to Do Today?

In the first two chapters we discussed a little of the theory of happiness and started practicing it in general in Chapter III. The next three chapters begin our application of these ideas to a typical day. However, if you have not yet completed the first exercises, you may not entirely understand the purpose and receive all the help afforded by the exercises that will be included in this chapter. The *effect* of remaining unaware of your thought patterns must be seen before any real progress toward sustained happiness can be made. If you lack motivation enough to do the first three exercises, perhaps it is because you believe that you are already fully aware of what you think. If so, may I suggest that you test this premise.

Set an alarm for a random time, and when it goes off later in the day, stop and ask yourself if you know what you have been thinking about for just the past ten minutes. If you will do this two or three times for only one day you will recognize how deep is your habit of allowing your mind to operate in the dark. Then the only question will be, Does it matter what you think?

Possibly you believe it is important to know how you spend your time when you are at work, and you consider yourself a person who is "time efficient." Maybe it matters to you where your money goes and your bank balance seldom surprises you. Perhaps you also keep track of what you put into your body. Yet I am sure you have heard other people exclaim, "How could I have possibly gained this much weight? There must be something wrong with the scales." Or "We had so much money; how did we spend it all?" Or "I haven't even started; where did the day go?"

I want to remind you again that there are not just a few individuals who end up asking themselves "Where did my *life* go?" Of course the answer will be "You do not know because you never loved it enough to look. And because you didn't look, your life wandered aimlessly and went nowhere."

This is indeed an option. But certainly it is not a necessity.

For over ten years a singer, composer, guitarist friend of mine had performed in several groups, including two of his own, and although his hopes had run high his success had been moderate. In order to achieve a more stable income for his family, he eventually became a building contractor, and he also started a small side business of wholesaling insulated glass. Since his priority was constructing new houses, he devoted very little time to the glass, and one day his wife asked if she could try her hand at it to see if she could increase the extra income it was bringing in. Within a year and a half she had built it into a million-dollar-a-year business.

So busy was she in the new offices they had to build behind their house that her husband was the only one available during working hours to buy groceries, clean house, and care for their two girls. This was unfair to his partner in the construction business and so he sold back his interest and suddenly found himself with no job description but "house-husband." His in-laws and many other people who knew him thought that he had merely become lazy. He started staying up late watching TV, drinking too much coffee, and had other familiar symptoms of depression. But he quickly recognized what was happening and asked his wife for help. She joined him in seeking an answer because she was wise enough to realize that this was also her problem and therefore her equal responsibility.

Together they sat down and completely rewrote their priorities. They decided to put their relationship first, because without peace between them their children would not feel loved. Their girls were placed second, but only in the sense that they were an inseparable part of the relationship and an extension of their love for each other. Everything else—friends, bills, house cleaning, appointments—came after the happiness of their family.

Who then should do what? This they realized was not important, and so they divided duties according to their separate strengths and preferences, with the surprising result that almost nothing of their past routine was altered. She continued to run the business and he the house. The one important change was the program they worked out to alter the overall tone of the day. Here is an idealized version of their plan, and I include it, not to recommend its particulars, but as an example of one of the themes of this chapter, namely that the daily purpose of everyone is the same, only the way we execute it differs.

1. To the family his new job title was "Bearer of Peace." His function was to prepare the atmosphere in which the four of them would dwell. He was the bringer of comfort, harmony, order (simplicity), and restfulness, and his goal was to see that each thing that surrounded his family—the car ride to and from the girls' school, the evening meals he prepared, the beds he made—reflected peacefulness. When questioned about what he did for a living, he was to give a simple, pat answer so as not to fall into his habit of joking in a disparaging way about his duties.[1]

Her job description was "Bearer of Love." Throughout her

[1] A recurring problem for all of us are these questions we get about situations that are difficult or impossible for us to talk about. For example, long after we have stopped grieving over the death of a loved one, some individuals may continue to ask, "How are you *really* feeling?" Or someone may inquire about an employee we had to fire or about a health problem we do not wish to discuss. There is a particular kind of flattery that I sometimes

business day she was to try to do all things as a gift to her family. She knew that realistically only love would sustain her family, and so she would attempt to conduct her affairs with kindness and fairness, and whenever she forgot to do this she would quickly forgive herself and begin again, because the quality of love she expressed to her family would be unavoidably tainted if she was judgmental of herself. In the evening, before she came back into the house, she was first to clear her mind of worries and excitements so that what she brought to her home was truly nourishing and good.

2. When they awoke in the morning their first thoughts were not to be about what they had to do but rather about their affection for each other and their family, and about their purpose for existing. They would orient their minds toward the present instead of toward yesterday's mistakes or today's upcoming events, and before they discussed what needed to be done they would sit down together and allow their hearts to join and their love to encircle their family. This was to be for only a few minutes, but it was to come before breakfast or phone calls or anything else that could sidetrack them into the mindless hurry of the day.

---

receive after giving a talk that is very hard for me to respond to, and yet I also do not feel comfortable being silent.

Under these circumstances a pat answer will often save one from becoming confused or from overreacting. A set response is not a form of dishonesty but a form of simplicity. Its purpose is to get you out of a difficult situation quickly and unmemorably. Thus it should be very gentle and, if possible, satisfying to the person who has brought up the subject.

Never attempt to indirectly point out the mistake the individual is making, for so often the inquiry, the criticism, the compliment is well meant, and if it is not, what is gained by attacking back? When someone asks how she has been feeling since his death, a woman I know talks briefly about what a wonderful man her husband was. I answer the flattery by thanking the person and then saying some nice things about the audience. My house-husband friend found that when he answered "I'm a house-husband and I just love it" no one wanted any more details.

3. As the day progressed it was not unusual for them to become a little tired and discouraged, and they knew from experience that, if not dealt with, this could result in their being irritated—she with her employees, he with the girls—and so they scheduled into their day "a new beginning" in which they came together and, with eyes closed, remembered their real purpose. They put behind them any mistakes they had made that morning in order to give themselves a better chance of enjoying what was to come and to be in a mental position to respond without anger.

4. They found that the "new beginning" period fit best into their day just after lunch. After dinner they scheduled another time together. This was to be an activity for just the two of them, and it required that they get someone to watch the children for twenty minutes or so. It was to be something purely restful and enjoyable, for example a walk along the arroyo beside their house or a pleasant drive somewhere, but not an activity that would be diverting such as going to a movie or eating a meal.

During this period they were to practice being each other's absolute friend. They might talk about neutral subjects or even about how things were going with each of them and with their family, but they were to defer any subjects that were merely anxiety producing. This was emphatically not to be a time to criticize each other but a time to understand and to come to one another's support. (I should add that they eventually found that it was not necessary to give "practical" advice to each other, but only to ask for the other's help in a general way. She, for example, might tell of having to refuse credit to an old friend, and he would not feel called upon to pass judgment on this, or even to understand why, but only to be accepting and appreciative of *her*. It has also been Gayle's and my experience that when one of us tells the other of a problem, that to answer with a suggestion often causes confusion, and sometimes annoyance, and is not as effective as simple support and unconditional love.)

Although this couple did these things together, this general program could also be carried out by a solitary individual. Often it is not feasible to ask another to join in. The essential point is that they took a new "job," one that covered everything they did and that assigned a single purpose to it all. *A life that encompasses multiple directions goes nowhere.* A quiver may be impressively full, but it can never do more than impress. Be simple and straight. Be a single arrow shot from the bow of peace.

This couple's life did not run smoothly merely because they wrote out new job descriptions. In fact it did not run particularly smoothly, at least at first. The transition from multiple aims to a single purpose takes sustained effort and great concentration, and they made, and continue to make, many false starts. However, the difference in their level of happiness is now quite noticeable and, as a natural result, their days are becoming decidedly easier.

About three weeks after they had begun their new program, my friend's sincerity was put to the test. A helicopter landed across the road from his house, and he took his girls over to see this unusual sight. When they arrived two familiar figures were standing there. My friend—formally an aspiring singer—introduced his children and himself to Glen Campbell and Roger Miller, and they all stood there and chatted for a while before he took his girls back home.

A few moments later, with visions of the big time dancing in his head, he found himself back in his own living room, babysitting and darning his wife's dress. Needless to say he was depressed. And he remained that way until he asked himself bluntly if he wanted to try to make it as a singer one more time. He saw that this was not an issue of right or wrong. It would be perfectly all right for him to take up his musical career again, and probably someone adequate could be hired to perform his domestic duties, but was this what he truly wanted?

Is It Natural to Be Conflicted?

He decided to change nothing in his life, but in itself this is unimportant. The peace, however, that his clarity brought him is not. It takes a great deal of practice for us to be able to ask ourselves a simple question and, without guilt, without anxiety, come to a decision about which we are completely sure. Most of us decide in conflict, act in conflict, and think this is the way life must be. All mixed feelings arise from a sense of having more than one self, and on the surface this appears to be the inevitable outcome of our personal history. Since we have had many opposing experiences, it seems natural that we would be divided about almost everything.

If you take food as an example, you can see how this dynamic develops. Very few children escape, on the one hand, a series of running battles with their parents over what, when, and how much they should eat,[2] and on the other hand, being presented special foods as a reward or as part of a celebration. Usually these "wonderful" foods are the very ones over which

---

[2] A good parent will realize that there are alternatives to these daily wars that ruin mealtimes for everyone and can color an entire childhood. Most children can do quite well on remarkably poor diets, and even though the parent should unquestionably make the diet as wholesome as possible, it must be remembered that anxiety and chronic unhappiness are health-affecting also. Often children are not as hungry by evening as adults and it is frequently unrealistic to expect them to eat their major meal then. We know how hard it has been for us to abandon our eating preferences, so why wage these battles with our children over precise manners and over tasting every last thing just because it was fixed?

issues had been made on previous occasions. The resulting lesson that the child learns about a surprising number of things is, "I want it but I shouldn't want it."

As if this was not enough to cause confusion, thrown in are inconsistent messages from TV, schoolteachers, and friends about what foods are nutritious ("make you grow up tall and strong") or, in the case of TV ads, give you all variety of magical attributes. As the child becomes an adult, inevitably there are bad experiences with food along the way: food poisoning at a restaurant, taste reactions from overindulgence, unexpected weight gain from a change in diet, allergies, indigestion, plus the constant glut of contradictory articles and pronouncements on exactly what should always be and should never be eaten, until finally a single attitude toward anything edible has become an impossibility.

Up to this date I have either heard or read stern warnings from one or more experts against the following foods, all of which I had previously been taught were "natural" and completely safe: tomatoes, potatoes, eggplant (and other nightshade plants), avocados, any *raw* vegetable, bell peppers, all nuts, milk (in fact, all dairy products), beans (except green), beef, shellfish, commercially raised chickens, eggs, vegetable oils, whole or refined wheat, dried, cooked, or raw bananas, any fresh fruit or fresh fruit juices, and carrots "in excess." I can't recall having read anything against rutabaga or okra, but then these are not hot topics of conversation and I am sure that by their just being mentioned in a book the necessary research will now commence and these two vegetables will be stripped of their cloak of innocence.

Our daily decisions concerning food are just one illustration. Almost everything else about which we make decisions—picking out the "right" presents to give, shopping for a car, choosing a spouse, deciding how much time to spend away from home, knowing when to step in and direct our children and when to step back and let them learn for themselves—could easily be shown to hold vast unconscious conflict for the average person. Possibly the only thing we can still do without conflict is have a diarrhea attack. When that happens we seem to know exactly what to do and there are no second thoughts.

By merely having had previous experiences around anything we are rendered divided as to how to approach whatever choice we think is called for. Our habit is to *quickly* find some grounds for a decision; to act; then, as the lessons from our contradictory past push toward the surface of our mind, to worry at length about what we have just done. And all of this seems not only normal but unavoidable.

Setting Your Purpose

Before this subjective mess can be cleaned up, a single life purpose must take the place of variable conflicting goals, for it is these goals that provide the grounds for incessant mental activity. A slow mind is content and is a definite improvement, but only a still mind is genuinely and deeply happy. To reach this state you must come to have one, whole, all-encompassing reason for being alive, and this will be an experience of the heart and not the mere grasping of theory. All I can do is assure you that such an experience awaits you and give you one or two good ways to have it, but by no means will these be the best ways.

A major breakthrough has taken place when one becomes willing to work in a specific, formal, daily way, for this means that the answerless question "What is the best way?" has been put aside out of love of the destination. Hopefully you are like me in that you have already changed your "way" enough to recognize that the "quest for truth" is one of our ego's favorite delaying tactics. The truth is true, and it is so obvious that it can be heard from the mouths of children. Let us stop looking for still one more way to say it and begin the daily practicing of what we already sense is good. Do we know that it is happier to be kind than to attack? Then let us be kind.

The single daily purpose that everyone shares can be stated, and has been given down the years, in myriad forms. The phrasing is not important but it will be very helpful if you can say it in a way that is simple and clear, and in a form that pleases you, even though from time to time you may want to change the words.

It is never required that this purpose be expressed in spiritual or religious terms, and because of the unhappy experiences some have had with this kind of language, it would be a definite hindrance for those individuals to use it. Any words that are repugnant or even mildly disquieting should be avoided, but, again, the exact way it is expressed is not perfectable. *There are no right and wrong words since what is true applies to everything.*

Even though my last few books have been spiritual statements,[3] I sometimes prefer writing and speaking in nonreligious terms. However, I do most of my thinking in words that are deeply devotional. Certainly devotional wording is not needed, but many people are like me and do love this at times, and one of the most commonly used statements of a daily focus that I have run across is what has come to be known as "the prayer of St. Francis." I have seen it written in several

---

[3] My first three books—*Notes to Myself; I Touch the Earth, the Earth Touches Me;* and *Notes on Love and Courage*—contain almost no religious vocabulary, but the next three—*There Is a Place Where You Are Not Alone; A Book of Games: A Course in Spiritual Play;* and *The Quiet Answer*—are spiritual statements. Of the latter, *A Book of Games* is on the same subject as this book.

forms. This one is perhaps the simplest, and unquestionably the least religious:[4]

> Today, let me be an instrument of peace.
> Where there is hatred, let me sow love;
> Where there is injury, pardon;
> Where there is discord, union;
> Where there is doubt, faith;
> Where there is darkness, light;
> Where there is sadness, joy.
>
> May I not so much seek
> To be consoled, as to console;
> To be understood, as to understand;
> To be loved, as to love.
>
> For it is in giving that we receive.
> It is in pardoning that we are pardoned.
> And it is in dying to self
> That we are born to eternal life.

For some this prayer is impossibly demanding. It seems to be asking them to become instantly egoless, a saint who walks the earth in absolute purity. But if you know a few of the details of St. Francis's life, you understand that the prayer states the yearnings of his heart and is assuredly not a description of what he was able to achieve each day. Our ultimate goal, even our daily goal, can indeed be perfect—if we are certain to be patient enough with ourselves to ensure a steady and consistent advance. We are expecting too much of ourselves if we think we can go even a few hours without making

[4] There are many books that contain expressions of a life purpose. The following three do nothing else, and each includes hundreds of such statements written specifically for daily use: the second volume of *A Course in Miracles* (Foundation for Inner Peace, Tiburon, California 94920), and two pocket-size books published by Hazelden (Center City, Minnesota 55012): *Twenty-Four Hours a Day for Everyone* and *Day by Day.*

mistakes. Please remember that discouragement, even when it comes in the wake of striving for perfection, is the love of unhappiness, because that is what it turns back to as its alternative. All you can do is the best you can.

EXERCISE IV-A

Our job this day is to become part of the answer to the world's immense and protracted suffering rather than continuing our ancient task of being part of the difficulty. How very few there are who make life easier on other people! For the most part we needlessly complicate the lives of those around us. The sum of our effect is an added degree of hassle and worry rather than relief. If we have been honest with ourselves we know that we confuse and tire even our own children. In the ways we usually relate to those around us, we are basically a burden and at best we are unreliably so. What I am asking you to do now is join with me in my attempt to become more of a comfort.

I know from many reinforcing experiences that you will not bring this off if you don't take all the time you personally need to set this purpose clearly and firmly in your mind first thing in the morning. This step cannot be slighted. You are kidding yourself if you think you can wake up and fill yourself with worries about what you did yesterday and concerns about what has got to be done today and still not be a source of concern and worry to those you will encounter. How can we possibly bring comfort to others when our mind is scattered among a hundred ego-gratifying goals?

1. Write down all that you can remember of what you do physically (not mentally) just after you awake. Put these in the order they usually occur. Do you first lie in bed a minute or two with your eyes closed and "think"? Or jump up immediately? Yawn and stretch? Then go to the bathroom? Once in the bathroom do you first look in the mirror? Weigh? As best you can remember, record in detail whatever is your most common routine for this first fifteen or twenty minutes.

2. For the next two or three mornings watch your behavior carefully and add anything you left out in your list above. Do not as yet catalog mental activity.

3. Beginning the first morning after, have your notebook beside your bed and start recording the ideas that accompany each separate physical activity. You may not realize it but you are in the habit of thinking certain lines of thought as you look in the mirror, while other lines accompany brushing your teeth. For example, just after awakening you may keep your body still while your mind quickly surveys it. You are taking account of how you feel, and this roving of your attention over your body is so rapid and automatic that you may never have noticed it.[5]

If it is not feasible for you to record each of these mental connections to walking to the bathroom, taking a shower, opening the refrigerator door, etc., record as many as you can. Note the others carefully as they occur and write them out as soon as possible.

Continue this every morning until you believe you have thoroughly identified your usual mental accompaniments to your first twenty minutes' activity. Even a full week devoted to

[5] I am still very much in the habit of watching my first thoughts, and I recently discovered that every morning I have been toting up the number of hours' sleep I managed to get. (John sometimes wakes us to discuss on-the-spot dreams and can't possibly imagine our not wanting to hear every detail.) Now that I have dropped this anxious and pointless practice, I notice in its place the little sense of increased freedom that release from an old fear always brings.

this would not be a waste, but continue it for at least three days.

4. Once you feel well informed as to how you begin your day —both physically and mentally—you are now ready to improve on it. Hopefully #4, #5, and #6 will become the basis of a very happy lifetime habit. However, unless you take time to first see the tone you usually set, and how you set it, you will know of no real reason for correcting it, and although you may make some efforts at beginning your mornings differently, these will be halfhearted and will eventually be discarded.

Just before lying down to sleep, formulate your purpose for the next day. You could pick one from the three books I mentioned in footnote #4, or put an idea into your own words, or choose from the ones listed below. How you arrive at it is not critical, but be certain it is a purpose that will cover everything, and one that can use anything that happens to its own end.

If, for instance, you were to choose "Today I will judge nothing that occurs" from *A Course in Miracles,* you can see that no matter how outrageous the occurrence, it will still serve your aim of not judging it. In fact, the more outrageous it is, the more interesting might be the challenge of applying your single goal. Whether this would be true for you or not, I can promise you that to take on the job of judging nothing will give you all the mental work you could possibly want for one day, and that if you were to succeed even for a few scattered moments, it would be one of the happiest days you have yet experienced. I realize it may not be obvious why that should be true, but if you will make a very sincere effort at setting and carrying out a single daily aim, for just a few weeks, you will unquestionably experience enough to see for yourself that what I am pointing to is there. And then perhaps you will want to take up this lifelong practice so beneficial to your happiness.

Here are a few more examples of the kinds of unifying thoughts you might use. Only one such idea should be practiced per day, and often there is a deepening effect from continuing it several days.

"I will do all things in peace."

"I would rather be happy than right."

"The answer to every call for help is gentleness."

"I will follow my peaceful preference."

"I am happy to be wherever I am."

"My interpretations are my world."

"Nothing has to go right today, because peace is my decision."

"What do I want this to mean?"

"The key to happiness is to think gently."

"To comfort is all I seek."

"Happiness is the choice I must make."

In your notebook write the purpose you intend to remember your first morning.

5. When you begin to wake, immediately start repeating your purpose (or some phrase or two from it) over and over in your mind. The night before you might memorize what these words will be and in the morning let them come from your heart.

By waking in this manner you will begin moving past an ancient habit of unconsciously setting multiple, conflicting goals. There are many ways to do this, but to repeat a single honest thought is an excellent means of experiencing some of the effects of clearing away the mind set you will ordinarily awake with.

6. After your period of repetition, sit up and begin building your determination to follow your purpose throughout the day. Although this need take only a few moments, do not start your usual activities until you know that your purpose is clearly set and that you are sure it is this you want above all else.

Do not tell yourself what conduct your purpose demands of you. You are setting a mental tone and not fantasizing outward reactions, and so it will be more in line with your aim to allow your actions to flow naturally from your attitude. In this respect your morning decision is to leave yourself alone.

Do not, for example, use your quiet period in the morning to rehearse what you should say to others. Instead, picture the kinds of things that are likely to happen today and see yourself responding completely from one whole disposition, a temperament that is as gentle and free as it is certain of its way.

Picturing the tone you wish to carry throughout the day is a fast and extremely effective method of orienting the mind toward happiness and of building a reserve of strength that you can quickly fall back on whenever your happiness begins slipping away.

7. (SUMMARY) *Ask yourself who you are and what you want.* You cannot repeat this question too often. Be certain to take enough time out of your life to see the answer clearly and to recognize that it comes from your heart and not from one of a thousand conflicting authorities in the world. Then consciously, deliberately, decide to be what you want to be. And each time you forget, remember. In this way you will gradually come to know your self, and what every prophet, saint, and sage has said since time began will dawn on you as true. You will know what you are a part of. And this will make you happy.

CHAPTER V

Going Through the Day

Routing Around Mistakes

In the early stages of retraining your mind it is to be expected that you will frequently forget the purpose you set in the morning, and that it will stay forgotten for fairly long periods. This will not hurt your progress provided you begin again as soon as you realize what has occurred. Like an angry child, the ego's stock response is to knock over the whole tower of blocks because one or two fell. The tendency you therefore must watch is to count the day lost because you have already made several obvious mistakes.

You may even have been aware of a mistake at the time you were making it, tried halfheartedly to check yourself, and then "willfully" continued being wrong. None of that will matter if, as soon as you see that you are once again strong enough to do so, you start the day over. *It is not making a mistake, but dwelling on it, that will delay you.* Look at how far you have come rather than how far you have to go. Your motivation is up to you.

The unhappy part of our mind thinks that self-criticism is virtuous, a form of humility and a worthy indication of "being honest with oneself." It is forever engaged in trying to understand and trying to explain. Yet to attempt to understand a mistake is simply to make another mistake. You will have eliminated one of the most pervasive hindrances to growth when you learn to react to every error, no matter what its degree or persistence, by merely acknowledging it and beginning again.

A major help in this direction is routine. A simple, settled daily pattern will allow your momentum to build more quickly because a good plan can route you around foreseeable entanglements. By having no clear idea of what you wish to do you will be inclined to be hesitant about almost everything, and the situations that have called to your unhappiness in the past will continue to do so because they are still not receiving your full attention. The day will happen *to* you and its only meaning will be in whether you like or dislike what has just occurred. You will have put yourself in a position where all you can do is await the outcome, and since very few moments are perceived as pure outcome, you will spend most of your life waiting.

Within a day approached in this indecisive way there *will* be a greater number of unexpected and unusual occurrences. Many people think they like to view these as adventures, but you must realize that even if you are excited you will continue more or less a victim of the general course of things, circumstances will remain heavily weighted, and your happiness will be contingent. Because of its desire for chaos, the ego likes to believe that vulnerability to being caught off guard increases freedom. Yet freedom is not really found in abandon.

Everyone's day has some routine, but often it is merely a pattern that has grown up unexamined and is an aid to nothing in particular. It is not happy to incessantly make rules about how life should be (as so often parents do with children and continue to do with themselves), but if the basic plan of your day has been simply and intelligently set out, you are relieved of many shallow decisions and it will be far less difficult for your mind to know quiet.[1]

Your body will demand less of your attention if you will allow for such obvious factors as how regularly you must eat not to tax yourself, what foods you personally should avoid because they consistently make you anxious, and how much sleep and exercise you require in order to feel good. If a type of TV program, having lunch with a particular person, phone calls at certain hours, house guests, too many social engagements, or any other activity obviously stirs you up to the point where concentrating on your purpose for the day becomes difficult, your life *can* be adjusted so that many of these unproductive little wars are sidestepped.

It is obviously not the function of this book to lay out a model daily routine, even if such were possible, which clearly it is not since individual needs vary so greatly. To even mention the desirability of coming up with a plan that avoids obvious pitfalls runs the risk of strengthening our ancient penchant for external solutions and our appetite for rules and strictures. There are no external solutions, except temporary ones to external problems, and of course unhappiness is not an external problem.

If the true purpose of your routine is kept in mind, it will not become a little god that everyone around you must bow to.

[1] There are many ways to organize the mundane side of your day, and almost any of these will do some good, because the more choices that are automatic, the freer your mind will be for the deeper mental processes. One system that Gayle and I use is set forth in *Sidetracked Home Executives* by Young and Jones. With great humor the authors explain how to organize all routine decisions such as household chores, remembering birthdays, planning meals, maintenance and repair, etc., through means of a card catalog.

A rigid routine makes no sense. Your firmness should lie in your resolve to be and make happy. You can have consistent behavior or you can have a consistent mental state, but you cannot have both. Your daily plan is there to make life easier on you and must therefore be able to accommodate shifts in circumstance. If, for instance, some morning your scheduled quiet time would be an inconvenience to a member of your family, you will not achieve your true goal by insisting that this person wait in distress while you practice serenity on time. Simply do it as soon as you can do it in true peace.

Eliminating Stimuli

The Eastern mystical tradition of withdrawing from ego-provoking stimuli, although misinterpreted in the West as turning one's back on the world, is nevertheless a precise antidote for one of our most common and devastating mental pollutants. Relationships founder, families split apart, and health deteriorates in the churning aftermath of overstimulation, and yet the effects of excessive activity on the internal state still go essentially unrecognized.

Being preoccupied with surrounding conditions, we are consequently influenced by them, and as long as these stimuli have sway they cannot be ignored if we are to have tranquility enough to concentrate. It is irrelevant that people and circumstances should not be able to distract us, if in fact they do. Even though we are still vulnerable to much of the world, we are at the point where we can minimize its effects on us, and we can do so far beyond what we conceive is feasible when we first set out. Your possibilities for cutting back and simplifying are enormous, and will actually appear to expand as you proceed.

Without ever meeting you I can tell you one hard fact about

your life-style: *You are doing too much.* Even if you consider yourself an indolent person, you are being overstimulated and need to step back. This statement sounds absurd because of our habit of characterizing activities such as sleeping, watching TV, eating, sitting, taking long baths, chatting on the phone, etc., as "not doing anything," meaning "not producing anything,"[2] and yet *every* bodily activity produces a precise and lingering mental disruption, however mild. These stimuli can and should be carefully selected, and their number reduced, but obviously they cannot be eliminated entirely since the body is always doing something.

Some activities call more to your ego than others. This is the simple truth that will set you free. It should be clear, for example, that starting your day with a quiet period will entail less ego involvement than rushing madly about. But it will entail some. Short of ascending out of the world altogether, there is really no final and perfect attainment in this area, and yet substantial gains await anyone who is willing to recognize that a simple, clutter-free day makes it far easier for one to be tranquil, kind, and present than a day chuck-full of "meaningful" activities. How meaningful can an activity be if it is not done with happiness?

Perhaps it has already become as apparent to you as it has to Gayle and me that unless we carry our core of peace into the task, the task itself does nothing for the world or for us. Rather than one's duty being to add more and more hollow deeds to a life already so scattered that it is in fact heartless,

[2] The typical unconscious judgment is even more specific than this. Any activity that does not lead to money is looked down on. It is very difficult for most people to clean their own house or care for their own children for any sustained period without becoming annoyed and depressed. The reason for this is that the prevailing attitude of our time is that unless there is the possibility of monetary gain in the end, our time is being poorly spent.

each individual's actual responsibility is to cut back to the point where a few things can be done with true grace.

Your happiness is like the first tiny green shoot of a new plant. It is fragile and vulnerable to incursions. Unless you give it space to grow, it will wither away, and this has already happened too many times in all of our lives. *Do not interfere* and your happiness begins increasing in strength.

All that is necessary to see at this point in the exercises is that you tend to be happier, more at ease, and more truly compassionate when you have fewer contacts with the world. The wife and three children of a family we know were recently visiting relatives in Washington. One afternoon, just after the grandmother had taken a roast out of the oven, their five-year-old girl accidentally pulled down the bowl of hot grease drippings over her face and chest. The father flew from New Mexico and joined the family at the hospital, and after weeks of operations and convalescence, they all found themselves driving back home, in severe debt from the costs and still very uncertain as to the amount of permanent scarring their daughter would sustain. And yet that day in the car they were happier and more peaceful than they had been perhaps in years.

Before the visit the family's life had been hectic, and of course it had remained so during the long emergency, but driving home there was suddenly nothing to do, and the natural, almost inevitable result was an immediate surfacing of love and peace despite the considerable pall which still hung over their lives. When home was reached and life resumed as normal, just as naturally as it came, their happiness began to vanish. The only difference in this very common tragedy is that they saw what was happening and took a step to reverse it. This is the corrective exercise they used, and it is the first in a progression of four steps that will be presented in this chapter, each of which builds on the foundation of the last.

EXERCISE V-A

Make a list of every contact you have with the world. And cut back on those that it would be peaceful for you to cut back on.

A typical list might include these activities among many others: 1. An hour and a half of background television before leaving for work. 2. One or two phone calls. 3. The drive to work. 4. One or more radio news breaks while driving. 5. The job itself. 6. Going to a restaurant at noon. 7. The drive home. 8. More radio. 9. Stopping to shop for groceries on the way. 10. Also stopping for gas three or four times a week. 11. Once home, making or receiving two or three phone calls. 12. Watching an average of three or four hours of evening television. 13. Having to run to the 7-11 two or three nights a week. 14. Inviting friends over once or twice a week. 15. Going out with friends once or twice a week. 16. Two or three parties a month. 17. Two or three meetings a month. 18. Seeing an average of one movie every weekend. 19. Shopping and errands at the mall twice or more every weekend. 20. Ten or more phone calls and ten or more hours of television every weekend.

Note that these activities include mostly those times when your choice is to come into contact either directly, or indirectly, with other people (besides your family). And of course many of these encounters are good and necessary and certainly should not be eliminated. It is the overall volume of busyness that you wish to turn down so that your mind will have time to hear its own joy.

At first glance it may seem that nothing you are doing can be touched. But if you will be very honest with yourself you will see that this is not true. Let me cite for you only a few out of actually hundreds of cutbacks Gayle and I have made over the last two years. I realize that many of these most people would not even *want* to make. The point is merely that almost any simplification is possible.

We have reduced the number of incoming phone calls from approximately twenty a day to about ten a week; we have organized our shopping and errands so that our trips in the car are probably about one twentieth of what they were two years ago; although we still try to help where we can, we are no longer members of any organizations; we now watch no television except an occasional "Scooby Doo" or "Sesame Street" with John; we have finally extricated ourselves from those "we owe them" kinds of parties and dinners; except for other children, we seldom have house guests (there was a period when we seldom did not); we now go new-car shopping (a long-standing insanity of ours) only when the old one is literally falling apart; and by changing our diet we have radically reduced visits to the doctor.

As a consequence of these and numerous other simplifications, we have amassed a fortune in time that we lavish upon our children, meditations, long walks, and other what might be called "heart-oriented" activities. My income is now about half what it was before I started declining most speaking invitations, but my new riches in loving and being loved make any comparisons to the enjoyment level of my life a few years ago downright silly. Cutting back is certainly not all there is to growing happiness, but like clearing weeds and preparing soil, it is a critical first step, and, quite strangely, a step that is often neglected or passed over in the name of one's "duty"—as if being harried and irritable could add to the peace of the world.

Giving Up Useless Battles

Once you have cut back on what you can, what do you do about all that is left? The current desire for spiritual advancement and new-age attainments has had at least one unfortunate result. Many are now delaying their progress by insisting that they are beyond their true level of growth. They try to force an appearance, an empty image of what they think enlightenment looks like. Somehow they should not be afraid of a dark house; they should remain unaffected by crowded or angry places; their latest system of diet should not be making their tummies gurgle or their children's faces break out; the fur of a tiny kitten should not cause them to sneeze; and when they go camping nature certainly should not make them itch.

To deny our fears and fail to recognize that activating them always has mental consequences, sets us up for a string of little defeats throughout the day. Perhaps common sense is not sufficiently exciting, but it does take us further than pride.

The best way to rid your day of the turmoils that regularly plague you and yet seem so unavoidable is to walk around them in some gentle way. *You don't have to "learn to deal with" anything.* Certainly it may be simpler to do so under certain circumstances, but there is no specific characteristic of the world that requires your mastery. Unless you understand this your progress is likely to be very sluggish indeed.

Just think for a moment how absurd is this concept of needing to "cope" with everything that goes on in the world. Yet most people believe they must overcome the circumstances that have arisen in their daily life because it will be good for them in the future to have done so. Perhaps if there were only a few worldly conditions this ideal would make sense, but the problems that *could* be "faced" are legion, and I promise you they will never come to an end.

It should be obvious that it is *happier* to walk gently than with bloodied feet. "The easy way out"—that phrase so profane to the ego—is attended by kindness as well as peace. Nothing worth having is gained through martyrdom, for it is not possible to attack yourself without attacking others. Therefore, your goal today is not even to overhaul your personality. That is part of the violent approach that has kept everything the same. You are merely attempting to allow more of your basic nature to surface gently, and to do that it is desirable to have a way of living that does not distract you from that purpose.

Do not hesitate to turn and look straight at what usually happens to upset you. This is quite different from trying to explain your mistakes to yourself. Whatever it is, there is a way past it. Actually there are a hundred ways, and you will see at least some of them if you will set aside your self-imposed restrictions, take time to look at what is going on, and not be too picky about which means you use to put the problem behind you.

EXERCISE V-B

1. Start an ongoing record of upsets. It would be good to continue this for two weeks so that weekly as well as daily patterns can have a chance to surface. Write just enough to identify the incident.

When you become irritated or frustrated you can be sure that you have forgotten your purpose, no matter how justified you believe the anger is. The justification aspect will only mean that you are conscious of what you have presently elevated to a position of greater importance.

Begin this exercise now by recording any recent disturbances you can remember, then add to this list in the following
weeks. Consider any gradual as well as sudden loss of happiness as an "upset." During your morning period of preparation (Chapter IV) you will reach a certain level of happiness,
which of course may vary from morning to morning. Use this
level as your guide for the day, and very briefly describe the
circumstances that cause you to fall below it. Is it in rushing to
get to an appointment? After making a large purchase? During
a disagreement with a friend? While on the phone with a relative?

Even though eventually you will be interested in patterns,
for the first week record even those upsets that seem once-in-a-
lifetime. You will come to see that at least some, if not all of
them, are not. In an attempt to shift guilt we try to perceive
every difficulty as uniquely caused in order to hold our habitual involvement in the shadows. Guilt is a totally useless reaction, but it is not without consequences to believe in it, for it
effectively blocks correction and keeps our mistaken approaches intact. So of course we can always plainly see a new
person to blame or a special set of circumstances to justify our
irritation, but seeing these does not exclude the possibility that
our pattern of participation is the same.

2. After the first ten days of recording upsets, you should be
ready to write your initial plan. It will not be perfect, and
please do not try to make it so, but you do want to begin
proving to yourself that there *are* steps that can protect your
state of mind and that you are capable of taking at least a few
of them at this time.

Review your list of disturbances and mark one or two that
keep reappearing.

Take up one of them at a time and review the pattern. In
order to look at it honestly you first need to relax thoroughly

and let all prejudices that you have about this subject slip away.

Before deciding on your plan of correction you also wish to view this pattern with freshness, and so you might try writing a brief description of it with the objectivity of, say, a scientist or lab technician. Describe it as if it were occurring in someone else's life.

3. Once again, calm your mind and body, and while looking honestly at the problem ask yourself, "Is there something I want to do about this? What might I try that would have a chance of making things better?" Then write down a few options that you could carry out easily, just a first step or two that would be within the range of your present willingness.

Be quite specific, but do not try to come up with answers that will solve the problem perfectly and forever. All you want are some measures that would make it easier for you to remain happy. It does not matter whether they are mental or physical, but it does matter greatly that you not limit your options when deciding what they will be. If it would help to begin by listing some totally absurd solutions in order to loosen your thoughts, then by all means use this trick or any other that will help you not be narrow-minded. Put down the silly as well as the practical steps that occur to you. Repeat this with each pattern you consider.

4. After first carrying out the remedies you have planned for any of the patterns of upset, record, not the results, but the effects that the actions you took had on your state of *mind.* Whenever you side with your heart (your honesty and calmness), you automatically have direct benefits mentally—whether or not a dramatic change in outward circumstances occurs.

5. For this last part of the exercise assess your overall gains with each pattern you have been working on, and continue with additional steps if they are needed. *Any problem, however chronic, is finite, and only a finite number of steps is needed to walk past it.* If you will persist, the day must come when this pattern will be behind you. Either it will no longer matter or it will seem solved in practical terms.

Once again, avoid anxiously casting about for solutions. *The mind is of little use when it jumps around.* You want only to take another step or two. Therefore, consider easily and happily what these might be and record them before following through.

The Ego's Use of Goals

The great common door through which most forms of negativity enter is premature expectation. If you will watch carefully (since these thoughts are usually unconscious) you will see that from the moment you get out of bed in the morning you start exercising the ancient human habit of deciding in advance how some little thing must go in order for the day to be a happy one, and as usual the day becomes perverse and refuses to go along. "I must have Uncle Sam's Cereal" (and yet, unknown to you, your spouse has just spooned the last little flaxseed into his or her admittedly cute mouth); "I must have a long soak in the tub" (and yet in the middle of it your child calls you to come see the wonderful thing the cat threw up on the living-room rug); "I must leave the house by 8:00"; "I must drive to work in twenty-five minutes"; "I must get my favorite parking place." In a downward spiral we carry our frustration from one activity into the next, and the only thing we can rely on is having the same nagging sense that somehow life shouldn't be this way.

Even though we can do much in the present, a surprising amount of our frustration is over what we cannot possibly do anything about. It has already happened, or it is something that will never happen, or it may happen but cannot be acted on today. And most of the questions we ask other people do no more than cause this same kind of useless distress.

The specific habit of going through the day absently setting the terms of our happiness may appear to be a type of thought that is different from frustration, but actually it is only a more focused form of fear, one that is concentrated on the immediate future and therefore seemingly more practical. And so you swing your feet out of bed and the first thing you look down on is your spouse's underpants. "I must mention that," you say to yourself. "This will not be a happy marriage until that stops." (And yet you've been mentioning it for the past twelve years.) Or you notice that the floor needs sweeping. "The Steens are coming for dinner. I've got to take care of that before I leave for work." (But in rushing to fix your breakfast you drop the last egg, and by the time you've cleaned between your toes, not only is there no time left for sweeping, but you also have to forgo the french toast you had your heart set on.)

Have your heart set on peacefully doing whatever you are doing now. Because, remember, nothing will go right today. And if it does it will merely scare you.

The things that truly need to be taken care of *will* be taken care of if you remain in the present. But you must not incessantly question yourself about what those things might be because to do so makes you lean out of the present and become significantly less efficient. Even more to the point of this book, it makes you dissatisfied not to do well what you are doing now. Simply carry on with the activity this moment that would appear to add most to your peace later on, and while you do it be as happy as you can be in the doing. *Your ability to be happy grows inexorably from your repeated attempts to exer-*

*cise it, despite how unsuccessful you may think you are each
time.*

Stop frequently and ask yourself if this is what you want to
be doing. At least ask yourself if this is how you want to be
feeling. If you are about to begin a new activity, stop and ask
yourself if this is what you want to do next. Never be afraid of
your heart's preference because, unlike your ego preference, it
will always answer for the present. It will guide you from
where you are and not fill your mind with pointless longings.

You wish to run your life on the track of your own will and
eliminate once and for all the vague feeling that there is somewhere else you would rather be. Nothing has gone wrong with
you. And you will clearly see this if you take the time to know
your own heart.

The Ego's Definition of Now

*The ego's idea of staying in the present is to continue what-
ever it is doing at all costs.* Remember that your heart's desire
is to do what you are doing happily and well, and it is *not* to
prevent interruptions. Your ego will react irritably to anything
that thwarts the pursuit of its chosen goal, even though it has
never stopped long enough to see if it likes it. Even a flicker of
frustration is a reliable signal that you have fallen into this
trap.

Why does everything have to be finished? Why does every
movie and TV drama have to be watched to its depressing
conclusion, every Christmas card answered, every party attended until someone else leaves first, every attack endured
until the last bitter word has been thought of? True happiness
is infinitely flexible because it is geared to an inner state that
can always be controlled and not to the world which never can

be. There will always be interruptions, and this must become unimportant.

Unquestionably it is essential not to be scattered ourselves even though we live in a world that is thoroughly disjointed. We should know what our priorities are and refuse to confound ourselves by needlessly jumping from one pursuit to another.[3] We think "This will eventually have to be done, so I might as well do it now." But that particular category is open-ended. We walk into the bathroom because the time has come to get ready for bed, and with the new all-organic unwaxed floss dangling from our teeth, we peer wistfully into the mirror hoping for a brighter smile. But all we see is a three-day accumulation of toothpaste splatters. Quite dutifully we set the floss down and march to the kitchen for the Glass Plus. There we notice that someone has left the milk out. When we open the frig to put it back an evil-smelling aroma engulfs us and an hour later we have half the food we own on the floor and we still haven't found what has gone bad. However, while we are at it we do manage to sponge off the shelves and rearrange all condiments according to height—once again proving how much Homo sapiens love to start projects they can't finish just when it's time to sleep.

[3] Your ego (your habit of being unhappy) will push any practical thought to a distressing extreme, including this one of not being easily distracted from your priority. The priority itself can be pursued in whatever ways please you most. If it is important that the house be cleaned, you would not, as you pass by your desk, sit down and start answering letters because letters are not your priority. However, this does not mean you must finish the countertops before you pick up the living room, or that while picking up the living room you shouldn't stop to straighten a picture, since all of this would be part of your priority. I personally like cleaning in a random way, whereas Gayle enjoys proceeding task by task. Think of whatever you are doing as a gift to your happiness and you will not go wrong. Your single "purpose" in life is genuine happiness, and your worldly "priority" is whatever serves it best in the present.

The Ego's Answer to Conflict

Possibly you can see that by asking yourself if what you are doing is what you want to be doing, you are apt to look more honestly at whether you wish to continue being conflicted about it. Conflict causes us to be always a little late and never to quite complete the things that truly should be completed. So shut your eyes and say, "I am balancing the checkbook. This is what I chose to do. If I rush through this trying to get to the TV, there is no way I can be happy now." And, surprisingly, the task is done more quickly despite the time taken for this pause, and it is certainly done more happily.

To barge ahead is the ego's way of resolving conflict. Since our ego is merely our insane belief that appearances are everything, to it this tactic seems perfectly logical, for if we are *doing* something, we do not *appear* to be conflicted. Therefore, rush into activity, engage in conversation and fill the air with words, seek a hundred different remedies at once if you are sick, busy yourself with something, anything, if you are depressed, but whatever you do, do not rest a moment in peace and consider your heart's desire. Because, to our ego, pausing *appears* to signal indecision.

Despite its enormous drain on our energy, tension does not get us what we want. We want to be fully alive now. We want to know love, and how can we know it if we feel conflicted about what we are engaged in? Tension is a signal that we have set a goal which slights the present. If we are under stress we have unwittingly assumed that something in the future is more meaningful and that the present is merely a thing that must be gotten through first. This is a dangerous attitude to practice because we are teaching ourselves a faulty approach to the very thing we cannot escape: now. The only day we will ever live is the one we call today, and the one lesson worth learning is how to walk through today in peace.

EXERCISE V-C

1. Starting with the period just after your morning quiet time and continuing on through to the start of your mental preparation for sleep (which I will discuss in the next chapter), look carefully at how your day usually goes. What are the low points, and when is the lowest point of all? Write out your general impression of these now, and include your best guess as to what times of day they usually occur. Supplement and correct this in the days to come. If you did Exercise V-B thoroughly you should be able to identify these periods fairly quickly.

In Exercise V-B you were attempting to become more conscious of upsets, and especially recurring upsets. Here you want to observe how these are regularly grouped within a single day. For example, it is quite common for there to be a series of small agitations every morning. Most people are not reasonable in how they start the day. They have never sat down and worked out an intelligent morning schedule. Consequently they are invariably caught off guard by something and begin the day in confusion, behind time, slighting their own bodies' needs and often running roughshod over other people's feelings. Even if they have had an early meditation, they end up throwing away most of the stability they gained because for them morning is not a time but a transition.

Once you begin to see that there are predictable periods when most of your setbacks occur, and that there are other times when almost nothing upsets you, you will know with greater certainty that you are not so much a victim of circumstances as you are of your own moods, and you will begin to discover easy ways to avoid the moods that set up these recurring letdowns.

2. Even though the graph of each person's vulnerability to upset varies, sometimes so sharply that there are occasionally true "morning people" and "night people," for most of us the little discouragements accumulate as the day progresses, so that by late afternoon our minds are distracted and more susceptible to unhappy emotions. This dynamic is by no means unavoidable, and a routine that anticipates it can be of great help in preventing it.

Take what you believe to be the lowest period of your day and schedule a small break just prior to it. If your job or other circumstances make this awkward, plan it as close to your time of vulnerability as possible. If from, say, three o'clock on you are typically judgmental and tired, and if it is not feasible for you to stop at two or two-thirty, then perhaps you could set aside a few minutes at the close or beginning of your lunchtime. How easily you are able to schedule this and how consistently you remember to take it will depend on how important you think your goal of happiness is. It is that simple.

Record in your notebook the time each day you will be taking this break.

3. During your break mentally divide the day into two days. Declare the old day over and done with and the new day beginning as of now. Be firm with yourself that your purpose is not to continue carrying with you the things that have already occurred. Recall your actual purpose for the day and set it again as if for the first time.

You will probably need to give some incident special attention in order to let it go. If so here is a visualization you might try:

- Picture, one at a time, the people involved in what happened earlier and, for a moment or two, mentally surround each one in light. Do this until you feel your grip on what you are still carrying with you loosen a little, but do not try to attain a perfect release. If the incident involved only you, picture yourself once again going through it, only this time surround yourself in light as you do.

For most occurrences this surrounding procedure should be sufficient to release your mind from the previous "day's" disturbance, especially if for the rest of the day you will repeat it each time any version of the original scene returns to thought. Your simple decision to out endure your ego gives you the means to let go of a distressing memory and return your mind to peace, but in order to accomplish this you must have ready and in place another response to which you can immediately turn your thought whenever your ego invites you to think about what went wrong. These follow-up responses, since they may need to be repeated often, should be something short and simple.

An unconflicted motive heals the mind, and that is why you will eventually find that during your break to do something as uncomplicated as surrounding in light is all you need do. However, in the beginning stages of learning mind-clearing you may require something a little more complex or of longer duration in order to feel that you have been thorough. If so, here are a few possibilities to choose from, and still more will be included in the next chapter.

• Sit on the edge of a chair or bed and lean completely forward, letting your arms and head dangle toward the floor. Slumped forward and totally relaxed, feel everything that has happened to you "roll off your back" and drain completely from you.

• Slowly drink a glass of water and as you take each sip picture the water cleansing you of all accumulated negativity.

If you scan your body you may notice that a grievance or some other form of past disturbance can be felt in a particular spot: the pit of the stomach, the temples, around the shoulder blades, etc. If you are aware of this, think of the water going to that location and washing away the memory and its discomfort, and finish with a visualization of a complete cleansing of all parts of you.

If you feel a need to repeat this or any other exercise, it is of course fine to do so. Be sure though not to torture yourself with goals of perfection.

• Surround in light not only the people who were involved in the disturbing incident but also every *object* in the scene. See each separate thing you focus on as innocent. Say "That is just a chair. It is completely innocent." "That is just a phone. It is completely innocent." "Those are only the eyes of a face. They are completely innocent." Do this with *anything* in the scene that catches your attention as you review it.

The Use of Doubt in Forgiving

It is often said that we can forgive but we can't forget. Yet to forgive in a way that restores our happiness we must fail to keep recalling, and this is decidedly *not* a hopeless task. An idea is quickly relinquished once it is recognized as meaningless. Imagine the private lines of thought that might follow an announcement that, after a close count, a particular candidate for President had won, and how dramatically they would shift if later the nation learned that in fact that person had lost. Who would continue pursuing a pointless thought after it had been seen as such? So let us consider a little more fully why it is pointless to harbor a criticism.

This much should be clear: You will not know peace while using your mind to attack. Even if the attack is against yourself. When the mind focuses on a failing, including an imagined failing, it is imbued with the sadness of that subject.

There is no joy in perceiving another's weakness, although our ego argues that the comparison is good for it, for the ego indeed lives off the blood of these comparisons. Contrary to this unhappy belief, the *experience* of seeking out and treasuring guilt is consistently miserable, and we continue seeking it only because of the sorry hope that next time the darkness we pinpoint in another will add light to us, even though this kind of boost to our self-esteem has always collapsed.

Our ego can, and often does, use its own version of forgiveness as a way of attacking still further. We may approach the person directly and in effect say, "I want you to know that although it wasn't easy, I have finally forgiven you for what you did." Or we may carry on the attack mentally: "Surely God will forgive him—perhaps in two thousand years?" We may even explain to ourselves *why* the person did what he did, but we never question our impression of *what* he did. Yet it is the "what" that must be let go of if our mind is to be free of pain.

Grievances arise from not having all the facts. As has been well said, "To understand all is to forgive all," but it does not follow that the answer is to try to increase our understanding, because no matter how much we increase it we will still not understand *all.* Perhaps the more preliminary insight is: *To see our perfect ignorance is to exonerate others from imperfection.* "I do not know" is the door to mental release from separateness. When we acknowledge that the grounds for our point of view may be faulty or distorted, we automatically begin relinquishing our point of view. Blame simply cannot be established in any final sense, nor can innocence be effectively *argued,* and so the only sanity is to stop thinking about what others have done instead of conceitedly trying to "understand" why they did it.

If we have a strong personal opinion about anything, we are wrong. The only real issue is happiness. If we are making others happy we are right—not of course appeasing their ego, but truly adding to their peace. Yet if we are making unhappy we are wrong, and *our treasured opinions never make anyone happy,* not in the deep, restful sense of that word. The one stand to take is peace—firmly being it, and consistently extending it. Any stand that does not offer genuine peace to another is not justified, and will never be justified, no matter how many people we get to say they agree with us. We all do the best we can, and herein lies our innocence. What more do we need to "understand" than this?

To forgive is to turn from the past out of a strong interest in the present. This is what very young children often do so easily. They are not more virtuous, they are simply much more interested in playing with their friend now than in dwelling on what he did five minutes ago. As adults we have logic to aid us. We admit that we are not qualified, and thus we are incapable of judging. For indeed this is a fact. "Who am I to judge?" points to a miraculous truth that should be guarded like an antidote to poisoning. Sit quietly and say, "What happened is not worth thinking about because it is beyond me to understand it perfectly. I therefore choose not to dwell on it. And because I am serious about this, I am now willing to use whatever means I need to stop."

EXERCISE V-D

This upcoming step can become one of the most basic and prized tools you will have for restoring your mind to happiness. Some form of this is needed by everyone, until possibly the most advanced levels of learning are reached, because a way must be found to *quickly* extricate ourselves from mental misery, unless the very rate of our progress is to become a dispiriting factor.

1. The habit you wish to begin cultivating is to break from the situation the instant you realize that you have lost your peace. This may mean getting up from the table, pulling off the road, excusing yourself from a conversation, or merely putting the eggbeater down and standing in the kitchen a moment with your eyes closed.

Whenever you recognize that you are less than happy, do whatever you need to do to symbolize to yourself that there is something more important than the worldly activity you are engaged in, and that one thing is your state of mind. Perhaps this exercise seems radical to you. "Radical" means what goes to the root. So indeed this step is radical.

Very few people realize how important symbols are when attempting to reestablish communication with their own mind. Our bodily actions keep our mind informed of our true priorities. If you see that you are not happy, yet continue right on with what you are doing, your mind will resist any tampering with its confusion. But if, for example, you pull your car off the road, call for quiet, and talk directly to your mind, what is said gets through now because you have your own attention. A recognizable gain in serenity is the result, not because sitting, closing eyes, etc., are somehow "good" activities, but because for most of us they are strong symbols, just as for example dropping to one's knees in prayer is within many religions.

If you had diarrhea you would break with almost anything. Is your happiness as important as diarrhea? What are you willing to *do* to bring peace to your life? If you had diarrhea you would let the phone ring, you would give up your place in the eight-item check-out line, you would not answer the front door, you would miss the end of "General Hospital," you would interrupt your breakfast and let your toast return to room temperature. But what are you prepared to do if you lose your peace?

Before you will ever know what it feels like to go through

just one day totally unafraid and completely happy, you must first be willing to look honestly at all the things you currently put before your need for a consistent mental state: Needing to be on time? Needing to interrupt and make your point? Wanting "to get ahead" in business, and even on the highway and in play? Having to pursue a sexual object? Dreading to offend? The list goes on and on, but the truth is that no room exists in most people's lives for a different kind of priority, especially one so gentle as happiness.

2. And what do you do once you have stepped aside? Surprisingly enough, it doesn't matter, as long as you concentrate in some calming way and bring the pieces of your mind back together. So perhaps you will talk to yourself from your heart and remind yourself what is truly important. Maybe you will use one of the visualizations or letting-go procedures from this book. Or just be still and blank for a moment so that you can settle down and "come to your senses."

Not much time is needed. You may be surprised to discover that your sudden absence is rarely commented on or even noticed. Expressions such as "Hold on a minute" and "Be back in just a sec" are so often heard that almost no one pays any attention to them or to the sudden departures that follow. The ancient needs of bowels and bladders have already paved your way for many unsuspected meditations.

3. Entire days are frequently lost to confusion, discouragement, resentment, guilt, bitterness and other versions of unhappiness, only because one small stirring of the ego was neglected and grew into an engulfing mood. This exercise has no assigned number of days because you *do* want to find some easy, reliable way of quickly restoring your peace and happiness. Breaking with the situation is one way simple enough to use for a lifetime.

CHAPTER VI

Letting Go of the Day

Many people will see the relevance of starting the day with the proper orientation and of then following a reasonable plan for dealing with habitual patterns of daily distress, but it may not be as obvious why getting ready for bed is important enough to merit a separate chapter. Everyone knows you just brush your teeth, put on your Snoopy nightshirt, pull up the covers, and turn off the light.

It is not an overstatement to say that if at the end of the day you were to prepare your mind properly for sleep, and on awakening returned your thoughts to the same state, you would need do nothing more to assure your eventual mastery of the rules of happiness. There is of course no reason to confine yourself to this one form of effort, but the manner in which you fall asleep and rise to start the day is so essential to your mental well-being that in itself it could truly be considered a yoga or "way" of happiness.

The Weight of the Past

The means of unhappiness are the accumulation and retention of a past. One reason that very young children are so noticeably happy and have such seemingly impossible energy is that they have very little past to drag behind them. They come into the world unencumbered by experience and free of anxiety about the implications of what has already occurred. It is difficult to get most two-, three-, and even four-year-olds to answer any questions at all about what they did while they were away. They are so interested in "What are we going to do now?" that the past seems an obvious bore in comparison.

At the little preschool John attended when he was two and three, there was always an after-lunch snack prepared by a rotating list of parents, which the teachers and all the kids would sit down and eat together. In those days Gayle and I were concerned that John was not eating enough, and so after picking him up from school we would not only carefully inspect the almost untouched contents of his lunch box but would quite casually ask what the snack had been that day, hoping to discover if he had at least eaten *that*. The first few weeks he simply said he didn't know, but when he saw that this answer did not put an end to it, he began answering, "Noodles." And "noodles" it remained until we finally realized that he had such little interest in the subject that he probably did not remember.

Children are quickly taught to carry the past with them by questions like these, and even to fear it by such warnings as "Don't do that. Remember what happened last time?" so that by their teens or early twenties, and sometimes much sooner, a complete mental turnabout occurs and the past is thereafter put above the present as their main concern.

The life goals set by most adults are motivated by the fantasy that their "accomplishments" will become a "permanent" part of their past and therefore of themselves. As will be discussed more fully in the chapter on jobs, our usual assumption is that our identity is everything we have done, and not how we are this instant. That is why many people find it difficult to complete a personal transformation while remaining in close contact with those who have known them for a long while. So often our old acquaintances just can't see that we are truly changing; they are convinced we are the same, and so they get angry when we do not respond the way we always have.

Our great fear of mistakes also comes from this assumption that our past behavior is more real than our present mental state. Whatever error we commit appears to be incorporated into our identity, remaining plainly within our history for all to see, not a correctable mistake but an abiding sin. Inevitably there is a mishap or lapse or personal failure and from that point on we are an ex-alcoholic, ex-mental patient, ex-batterer, ex-shoplifter, our premiums are higher because once we had a wreck, or we have great difficulty getting a loan because there was a period when we were unable to meet our bills. In light of the honor it pays the past, all these correlations appear quite just to the world, for how could one rightly praise past accomplishments without also cherishing guilt?

Emphasis on the past produces fear of the present. That much may be obvious; however, what is not often recognized is that all forms of fear transport psychological *weight* into the present. There is no such thing as "idle" worry. Worries do not idle; they grind. Fear presses upon the body as well as on the mind. By the time most of us reach the so-called golden years —the culmination of our efforts to build the best past we could —we have become so weighted down with all the miserable lessons we carry with us that we are in permanent depression and despair, as a visit to most homes for the elderly will show.

There are a few individuals who escape this, but it is not by accident.

Another showcase of worldly happiness, the romantic relationship, breaks up or enters a stage of repressed futility when the *history* of the relationship becomes about all that the two people can see in each other. Once again, very few escape this. One can walk into a restaurant and with surprising accuracy pick out the "old" married couples by the noticeable lack of love between them. I am sure you have had the experience of hearing people you know well talk about their spouse and then on meeting and getting to know that person discovered that they were blind to many of their partner's good qualities. The reason you could see their spouse more accurately than they was that to a large degree you had no choice but to see that individual *from* the present. *People are never now how they have always been.* Even though the amount varies, some growth and flowering is steadily occurring in each life.

Our perceived defeats weigh us down, and yet what we think of as our victories can be equally as smothering. Life can later become very difficult for those who had great physical beauty when they were young. And a body can appear to be a curse when its athletic gifts are spent. Past presidents of major corporations, former politicians, old actors and actresses know well the feeling of now being looked at as if a freak. For us to succeed, someone must fail, and once worldly success is ours we are not suddenly exempt from the worldly law that brought it.

To have a hold on us this misery must be mentally reentered daily, and the doorway we provide is our preoccupation with what happened. *There is very little that can hurt you once you learn how to release your mind from what you have unconsciously picked up during the day.*

Releasing the Residue of the Day

The process of taking on the weight of the past is unmistakable even within a few hours. Very early in the day something fails to go as expected and a slight discouragement is carried unnoticed into the next activity. As a consequence the new activity is not performed satisfactorily and an additional worry is set silently into place. As the day progresses, a mounting sense of bleakness and weariness becomes unavoidable, all of which is so noticeably absent in very young children because their reigning interest in the present allows them to dismiss each event at its close. A state of mind this simple cannot be recaptured at once, but it can be attained deliberately. To this end there are two tools that can be very helpful. One is the kind of break discussed in Chapter V, which you schedule into the course of the day to release what has accumulated within the last few hours, and the other is a major period of relinquishment at the close of the day.

The particular methods you use to clear your mind are not critical, but how unconflicted you are about wanting to is. If you truly wish to let go of the past you *will* find ways to accomplish this. When you sit down to commence one of these practices, if you are not clear about its purpose or satisfied that it is all you want to pursue for the next few moments, what technique you use, or how long you engage in it will matter very little. You simply will not achieve meaningful results. So the first rule is to be certain that you know what you are about to attempt and why it is personally important to you. Then begin using one of the methods described in this book, or something else you have found to be useful, and when the day comes that you feel its effectiveness starting to wane, do not hesitate to try another technique. All remedies eventually lose their efficiency because trust has not been placed in something perfect. Therefore, do not let this fact discourage you; the number of approaches still available will be too numerous to exhaust.

One of the ways we are currently letting go of the day is to picture a rocket (we used to picture a hot-air balloon, but it took too long to get it out of sight) containing a special electromagnetic time capsule (as you may know, when you have a five-year-old boy, you succumb to this kind of talk). With our eyes closed, we silently go back over the day and imagine anything that may still be burdening us being dumped into the time capsule (specific mistakes, guilts, embarrassments, grudges, excitements, triumphs, as well as fears or longings about the future). After we have emptied ourselves of every scene or person that was cluttering our thought, we switch on the magnetic force of the time capsule and imagine it drawing out of us anything we missed. During this final purging process we count down from 10 to blast off.

I'm not sure where Gayle sends her rocket. I aim mine into a black hole, never to be heard from again. If one of the concerns I am releasing happens to be something that will need attention in the future (say, for example, I remember that the chickens are low on scratch—which, incidentally, they are) I will send that particular worry into high orbit where I can't see it but can get it back when the time comes for me to act on it.[1]

The object is to lift everything from your mind that is of no use to you, now that you are going to sleep. The side benefit is that the ego is lessened in the process. A surprising number of our unhappy personal experiences reappears in the form of

[1] I have a friend who suggests a simpler approach of imagining putting these bits of unfinished business on a line out of sight and then hauling them in the next day when you have a moment to devote to them. This eliminates splashdowns and ocean rescues.

reactions within any given day, and so to relinquish the day is also to let go of a portion of the ego itself and thus make a small but permanent gain in happiness. It is precisely because of this side effect that the simple nighttime practice of forgiving all that has occurred is so profound.

EXERCISE VI-A

I would like to suggest that until it becomes a natural and consistently effective practice, you break your evening meditation into three or four specific steps. In #1 I will give some general rules on how best to prepare for it. I will describe techniques you can use to let go of the day in step #2. In order to eliminate sleep problems and rest more deeply, it is often good to include a moment in which you set your purpose for sleeping, and that will be discussed in #3. And then with #4 you can conclude your pre-sleep period by establishing the mind set into which you wish to wake. All of this does not have to take more than a few minutes and therefore should not be a delay to sleep or in any significant way lengthen your day. In fact, you will find that this simple practice will sweeten your sleep, and will have enriched your sense of rest and well-being upon awakening.

1. You should schedule this quiet period of relinquishment as close as you reasonably can to the time you will fall asleep and try not to do anything that might agitate you afterward (phone calls, news, planning, arguments, etc.). Unless of course you are bedridden, it is better not to attempt it while lying down because your concentration will tend to be divided. Three or four minutes often suffice, but there will be many days when more time can be well used.

2. Quietly review the day, and then make the effort, consciously and resolutely, to let go of anything that is the least bit disturbing. Do not expect to achieve a sense of complete release, but it is always possible for you to reach a feeling of certainty that you have done the best you can.

In order for this step to be carried out adequately, it would be advisable for you to employ a specific visualization technique or a formal verbal or physical procedure, like those described in #3 of Exercise V-C. I have already told you about one Gayle and I use; here are four more to select from.

• Picture *as you* someone for whom you have great respect reenacting the incident you are attempting to release or, if you like, going through the entire day. See yourself back in the same circumstances but now as some dear friend, as a loving relative from your childhood, as a being of light, or whoever else symbolizes purity and innocence to you. Do not ask yourself how this other person would have *behaved,* but merely think of yourself possessing this individual's perfect gentleness, while you imagine going through the episode once again. Look through your guide's eyes of peace, feel your guide's acceptance and forgiveness, and then allow yourself just to see what happens this time through.

• Hold in your mind the individual who has done something that disturbs you and pretend that you can now see all that this person has gone through since birth. Allow yourself to imagine the kinds of circumstances that he had to endure at home, at school, and so forth that would explain his behavior and make it completely understandable. Do not try to discover the facts, or kid yourself that you can guess them, but merely relax and have a fantasy of what *could* have happened that would certainly make the way he acted inevitable.

• See the individual standing before you, and in your own way silently bless this person. Or, if you prefer, choose from the following statements:

"My ego is no better than yours, (name)."[2]

"You merely made a mistake, (name). You did the best you could. I forgive you out of love of what you will become."

"This is truly not important. In a hundred years there will be no one who even remembers it."

"In your heart lies the innocence of the child you once were." (Picture that child.)

"I want a peaceful mind more than I want grievances."

"I would rather be happy than right."

• My grandmother had a way of releasing things that I looked down on as an adolescent, but now I can appreciate it and frequently use it myself. There were many tragedies in her long life, and whenever I would see her during one of these periods she would often appear completely unaffected. I would ask her how she was doing, knowing all too well the answer. As always she would say, "I'm not worrying about it. I've turned it over to God."

Be certain that you do not try to explain away what others have done or try to reinterpret their behavior in some insincere way. Forgiveness will not be accomplished in this manner. It is not seeing that what they did is somehow okay that will allow you to release it, but recognizing that attack thoughts are impractical. They make the mental atmosphere in which you must dwell chafing and hostile. Nor is your aim to shift the blame back on yourself. During this concluding meditation for the day you wish to restore your mind to a gentle state regardless of what this individual, or you, or anyone else, has done. You wish to construct a genuine place of peace where you can now take your rest from all the day's stresses. The one sure

---

[2] This statement is true of all egos. The ego can be weakened and eventually relinquished, but because it is incapable of love it cannot be improved.

way to do this is to empty yourself so completely that ease and freedom are the only residue.

3. Although insomnia leads the list, there are any number of other sleep problems that plague the average person: restlessness, indigestion, fear of the dark, recurring dreams, oversleeping, grinding one's teeth. This is not surprising since most people are habitually conflicted about sleeping. Often there is a lingering sense of tasks unfinished or a vague feeling of some moral responsibility going neglected. With others the fear is more general: a growing realization, now that one more wasted day is passing into night, that the dreams they had for their life will never be realized. And so as the hour approaches for them to get some sleep, the nagging feeling arises that some nebulous something should be set right, and that it is not right to sleep when there is work to be done.

More often the person is not aware of these emotions but merely feels a little restless and begins futzing and puttering and once again not getting to bed on time. The delay is not even devoted to what most needs to be taken care of. It is just more waste added to a day of waste.

Whenever there is a pattern of being late you can be sure you are conflicted about what you are doing. As with sleep, the answer is not necessarily to eliminate the activity, but to become clear about what you want to do. You do not wish to take these formless fears into your sleep, and it is unnecessary to do so.

After you have let the day go and have released your mind as best you can from all cares (#2), take a moment to see that your sole purpose from now until tomorrow morning is to rest both mind and body—and that you have no second purpose. Tell your mind that it is now off duty and there is nothing further you wish it to engage in. Resolve to gently bring your thoughts back to a peaceful repose every time they wander into some disquieting consideration. Decide that you will not concern yourself with what you can do nothing about, for there is one good thing you *can* do, and that is to rest.

Time is a luxury, so be lavish with the time you provide yourself for getting ready for bed, for repose, and for doing your morning tasks. Do not crowd yourself on either end.

While in bed your aim should be to rest your *mind,* and not to force your body to sleep. You wish no war of any sort. Your nights can be enjoyable, and they will be if you concern yourself with what you can presently accomplish, which is to rest your mind by using it more peacefully.

You are not wiser in the middle of the night than you will be in the morning. You will not make sound decisions about the future if at the moment you want to do two things at once—rest *and* worry. Should you suddenly think of something that will soon require attention, if you need to, put out a reminder, but do not engage your mind in the problem.

If you see that you have begun a disturbing line of thought, do not complete it. Simply interrupt it, and gently, without self-censure, return your attention to more relaxing pursuits. Think about something that will not stir you up. *Any thought that contains love has a calming effect.* So think about the funny things your children have done. Or imagine yourself gardening if that is what you love. Remember the antics of a childhood pet. Or picture yourself in some wonderful spot where you would love the present and would easily have no cares.

Be certain not to limit yourself. Anything, mental or physical, that you find restful is perfectly all right. Perhaps you would enjoy silently saying a mantra, an affirmation, or simply some comforting words that come to you at the moment. One chant that I have sometimes repeated is "All released; all is peace." I don't usually think these words in time with my breathing, but when I do I say the first part as I exhale, thinking of anything at all I need to release, and as I inhale I say the second part and breathe in peace. An application that I find very useful is to slowly list the people or circumstances that may still be bothering me. For example:

"I release my car; and all is peace."

"I release you, (name); and all is peace."

"I release my (stomach, hair, back—whatever part of my body is troubling or embarrassing me); and all is peace."

"I release (name of politician or foreign country); and all is peace."

"I release my life; and all is peace."

As I mentioned earlier, I personally love to think in devotional terms, and this is especially true at night when I am falling asleep. I know that some readers will share this sentiment, and so here are several personal examples of a more religious approach.

• Some variations on the above mantra:

"I drown in God, and breathe in peace."

"I release the world, and dissolve in God." (I picture myself dropping from the world into a sea of light.)

• I sometimes enjoy reminding myself of this metaphysical concept:

"The world has been answered. I can go to sleep now."

• It is often comforting to address my mind, or my body, as if it were a little child:

"Don't be afraid, little mind. Be still. Be calm. Let go now and rest in peace."

"There's no place to go. There's nothing to do. My Friend is with me, and all is well."

Because the newsbreaks and many of the ads and programs appeal strongly to the ego (justified anger, acquisitiveness, fantasies of revenge, physical specialness, tragedy), most television fare can be agitating on an unconscious level and is not the best way to get back to sleep or even to "unwind" before going to bed. Television tends to set the wrong life purpose as well as very subtly stir up the body. There are happier alternatives.

For instance, much more control can be exercised over books. It is possible to discover many authors who can be relied on not to jar their readers, and some people find that, if they are unable to sleep, reading a little while in a book that is gentle to its characters will often settle their mind to the point where they can sleep. Even if this is not the outcome, it provides them with an alternative way of resting.

I have no idea where I ever picked up such a silly idea, but for most of my life I would not allow myself to read anything that was not edifying. Reading gradually got to be such an unpleasant activity that the day came when I realized that I had probably not read a new book of any kind for over four years. Gayle, on the other hand, finished a new English mystery every three or four days, a practice I not so silently looked down on. But now it was inescapable that although she had "bad reading habits" I had none. I was a self-made illiterate in a world that abounded with good books.

One day I casually asked her if she had read anything recently that she thought I might *enjoy.* She said possibly I would like the James Herriot books. She was right. So at age forty-five I discovered, for the first time in my adult life, the sheer pleasure of reading, and I now read more books in one year than I had read before in twenty. But for all that, I can no longer drop titles at sophisticated parties. Most people there are not impressed with my literary references to (my recent discovery) Georgette Heyer. They smile painfully and head for the croissants and Brie on the other side of the room, which, as it turns out, allows me to leave all the earlier and pick up *The Reluctant Widow* where I left off.

Rigid rules, like mine about edifying books, are blind to change and do not make happy. The only one that will serve our happiness is the rule that still serves the present situation. Behavioral guides can indeed be useful, but only as long as they are tentative. The present must be treated seriously if we are to remain reliably kind. And there is no happiness without kindness.

One final exercise that I sometimes find restful is to mentally list every sensation, thought, and emotion I am aware of, and there are of course thousands of these available. If I am having an especially difficult time keeping my mind in the present, I may even number these as I go along: #1, John's snoring; #2, the pull of the sheet against my neck; #3, a passing thought about full moons; #4, something mumbling in my stomach; #5, the cry of a night hawk diving for insects; #6, a quickly dismissed question about the protein content of bugs. . . .

A common refinement of this exercise is to mentally watch the body breathe without attempting to change it.

The reason this type of practice works is that agitation, anxiety, excitement, and other unhappy emotions require a past and future in which to operate. Remove these by resting the mind within the present, and mental tranquility becomes automatic, for peace is the very fabric of the mind and therefore its natural state.

Let me reiterate that the mistake most people make when trying to deal with a sleep problem is that they panic, look around for something to blame, and start a mental battle with their sheet-hogging spouse, the clock, their child who needs attending during the night, their pillow, last night's cooking. Obviously it does not follow that one should never try light stretching, aspirin plus a short soak in a lukewarm bath, a truly boring book, a glass of warm milk and honey, a weekly massage, herbal teas, a late-afternoon exercise period, a consultation with an authority, or any other simple external remedy about which there is no strong personal fear. To assume greater responsibility for one's body, especially when this is unhurried and unforced, makes any bodily problem simpler, and a calm and intelligent willingness to try things is always a part of responsibility.

Never fight yourself. Never deal directly with the ego—yours or anyone else's. For you will merely strengthen it by increasing your belief in its autonomy. Children do not get rid of their imaginary playmates by cursing them. What is imaginary leaves when what is real becomes more interesting. Your ego (your imaginary identity) is best first seen clearly and then left behind. It is merely a place of no peace, and to start a slugging match with it will always appear to strengthen its hold on your mind. Just begin turning from discord to harmony in some easy way. You do not have to quickly do something simply because you feel a certain emotion. Let the jealousy, the depression, the guilt be, and take one or two sure steps in the direction of the restful side of your mind.

4. The final part of your brief preparation for sleep is to decide how you will awake. Most people decide when but very few decide how. Yet it is how we live our life and not what activities and people it consists of that determines the depth of our enjoyment. Once this is understood, our growing need to be always changing things begins to dissolve.

The reason it is not a good idea to wait until morning to choose how you will awake is that during sleep the mind enters an almost pure ego state. In a sense, sleep is dreams about a dream; it is twice removed from reality, and so when you awake it will take an effort on your part to shift into your saner mental regions. This is made easier by knowing in advance what the first thing is that you plan to do with your mind.

In Chapter IV I suggested several possibilities of what form your first efforts might take. What I want to stress here is that because of the dominance of the ego during sleep, your purpose is already set, and you must reset it if you wish to avoid taking the same multiple conflicting values into your day that you had in your dreams. Obviously there can be moments of insight and sanity during sleep, and occasionally these are so powerful that the mind wakes in a lifted state, but these moments are not as frequent as many people like to believe, and yet their belief is not without consequences because it tends to deny the negative momentum that the mind has built up by morning. This is not something to either fear or fight. Simply notice that a question about a dream never comes *completely* to rest. Therefore, be questionless, for this is your right. Do not waste time trying to understand; turn instead to the light of happiness so that it will be light and not questions that you carry with you into the day.

As I stressed earlier, in all endeavors, including even repose, try hard and expect very little of yourself. The world attempts to live the opposite rule, and although it is always undergoing some promising new change, it has never once moved close to happiness. This need not be your lot, for when you focus on the means and not the end, on your effort and not its outcome, on the present and not the future, you quietly shift from slight outer accomplishments to immense indwelling gain.

CHAPTER VII

Your Job

Cutting Back on Problems

In the next three chapters we will take a look at some typical areas of concern. Have you ever made a list of "typical areas of concern"? I would advise you to set aside many hours because the list may extend into the night and out the other end. I realize that "job," "money," and "possessions" are quite arbitrary, so please think of them as mere examples, for unless you do you will quickly realize that I have left out many favorites.

It is not entirely inappropriate to impute favoritism in our choice of problems. We are all collectors, and our personalities are just the display cases. We think, talk, and act problems. Secretly we often do see the insanity of other people's choices, but as to ours, they are "real concerns," and we feel personally attacked should anyone fail to adequately toast our problem du jour. And yet so trivial are most of our cares that it is usually impossible for us to remember what we thought was important only last week. The happiness of an entire family can be shattered by just one argument, and yet often by the next day no one can recall the incident that started it all.

Have as few problems as possible. This policy will serve you well. Our ego does need some things to gnaw on but it does not need every size chew stick made. So, kindly, do not add these three areas to your personal list of worries. It is just fine to love your job, to have no money problems to speak of (the ultimate criterion), and to not identify with your possessions. In fact it is quite possible (and a good exercise) to make a thorough list of your problems and to check off a few as no longer of real interest. You will be surprised.

It is also possible to draw in the boundaries of your ego's concerns. This concept was new to me until a few years ago, but Gayle and I have since been working on it with very good results. We decided to put limits on our worries. Only our family and its paraphernalia are now permissible. Things like the economy, other people's religion, the mysterious decision-reaching process of the city streets department, and newcomers' tastes in landscaping are now mentally off bounds. We have even given up trying to reform our parents (at best an act of fantasy), much to their relief. However, since it is good to keep the agitated part of the mind harmlessly engaged, questions such as what is the most natural dishwasher soap, is our dog gaining too much weight (I say yes), does the cat need a friend, and is there truly a school worthy of our children are legitimate trains of thought, provided we do not get too loud about them. After a couple of years of team effort we are happy to report to you that the mind is very amenable to this form of training.

Except for the exercises, which have general application, do not take the next three chapters too personally, unless of course you have the difficulties in these areas that most people do. Pick through the various points presented as you would through a box of assorted chocolates (when everyone has left the room) and see merely that the concepts you and I have been discussing are indeed simple enough to use in any area of your life.

Your Job Reveals Nothing About You

I don't recall how old I was when I discovered that if I answered "architect" instead of "fireman" to the question "What do you want to be when you grow up?" I got a much more satisfying reaction from adults. I still remember vague feelings of guilt about not knowing what an architect did, but at the time that did not seem to matter. Today's five- or six-year-old is likely to answer "I haven't decided between palmistry and astrophysics," although there are some kids who can be quite firm about "doing charts."

All of this is probably very harmless because children seem to enjoy this little game as much as adults do. But just a few years later the same question can become terrifying if teenagers feel pressured to set out on the impossible task of trying to second-guess what high school specialty or college major will best prepare them for the future course of their life. Most parents ought to know that the young person's distress over this is not without foundation since so few of us have ended up doing what our education supposedly prepared us for, yet some of us still persist in requiring teenagers to exercise this rather silly form of precognition. It is of course fine to choose a major, but no one should have to kid himself about its implications.

Thinking that appearances are everything, the ego naturally concludes that "you are what you do." During our middle span of life the seemingly affable question "What do you do?" really means "Are you somebody?" and most of us think far too much about how to word our answer should some stranger at a party ask us this question, even though if we just took a moment to look at our feelings we would see that we really don't care what a stranger thinks of us. It is only our ego that attempts to judge, and being quite blind, all it can see is other egos. This common social line of attack and counterattack has so very little to do with what people are at their core that you would think it would be self-evident that a person's means of earning a living reveals only the most superficial and insignificant information about what he or she is, and yet the issue of career has become a source of great unhappiness.

It is now generally assumed that anyone is capable of doing anything. "Why then," our society asks, "have you settled for work that is mediocre?" We should somehow be more creative, more humanitarian, more productive, more something. So tangled up with our job are our feelings of self-worth that businesses, if they want their fair share of good employees, must periodically spend time rewriting job titles to make the same work sound more impressive. We have actually gotten to the point of disliking people for not doing more than they do, and we ourselves cannot sidestep the disgust, however mild, we think we have managed to reserve only for others. Surely it does not have to be proved that all of this is quite insane. And yet, if you wish to be happy, you must free yourself completely from this point of view. *You are not what you do; you are how you do it.*

You will not think better of yourself by engaging in a selection of those activities currently considered to be impressive. Nor will you recognize your worth by avoiding them. You will know that you are good when you consistently bring goodness to all you do. If the job is to straighten and clean for a small family, your work is no less holy than, for instance, that of a personnel manager who hires and fires hundreds of employees for a large corporation. We have such silly ideas of what is important work! For example, what more far-reaching activity could there be than devoting oneself to helping a child be happy and unafraid and to develop into a gentle, kind adult? How many people will this one child touch within a lifetime? Is seeing to this little person's happiness really less significant than composing music, throwing pots, being socially active or "living up to one's earning potential"?

Your Career Forms Behind You

Most people have never stopped to ask themselves exactly what it is they are seeking in place of a good life *now*. There simply is no such thing as a career. People talk about pursuing a career as if all the turns were already mapped out and their destination set there waiting for them as solid and immovable as the town civic center. Except for the straight line of automatic promotions within organizations such as the armed services, a few large corporations, and some branches of civil service, none of us advances to our goal with a predictable precision, and even within the fields where this appears to happen a closer examination shows a nest of entangling exceptions, including the employee's health and will to endure, exigencies of location, family demands, government allocations, and the goodwill of superiors. It is not realistic to think in terms of "arriving at the top of your profession." There is no perfectly defined profession and no true top.

Our trail through life can be seen only in retrospect. It *does* all add up, but not in advance of the steps taken. If each small step is guided by the present instead of by a hodgepodge of fears about the future, we can discern a lovely wake flowing from the actions we have taken, including even our mistakes. There is a beauty, a just-rightness, within the course of every life, but so often the individual is blinded to it by constant worry and second-guessing.

The only thing you can know for sure is whether you feel at ease in the present about a step that is possible to take today. No one can adequately define all the consequences, see all the people this step will affect, and accurately determine whether the ramifications will be fair to everyone eventually touched by them. You merely delude yourself if you think your vision is that free of distortion. Why then attempt to resolve interminable future implications when it is simply not possible to do so? Instead of the fantasy of a glowing future, why not settle for the very real possibility of a satisfying present?

Nothing Has to Be Decided in Advance

When we attempt to translate a fantasy into a worldly event, the result is a different order of reality. Like most people, I have run through many such fantasies in my life. My mental pictures of what it would be like to become a sculptor, ranch hand, secondary schoolteacher, real estate broker, guidance counselor, construction worker, psychologist, circuit lecturer, and a few other false starts were so unlike the reality of the work I ended up engaged in that it is really very funny to me now that I thought I could imagine in advance what my life would be like within these various fields.

A fantasy does not give firsthand experience. That is why no matter how informed we think we are, we do not know beforehand what will make us happy. Nor is there any reason to know since it is the degree to which we have developed our capacity to enjoy the present that determines our happiness and not our job classification. This does not mean that very little care need be taken in choosing one's way of making a living, for of course care should be taken. It means only that our freedom from conflict over whether today to ask for an interview, enroll in a class, question someone within a certain line of work, or buy a book or two on a particular field is a more reliable basis for making a decision than our fantasy of an entire future course of action that will entail hundreds of separate choices. Our desire to anticipate every move we will make for broad periods of time is nothing more than our present wish to struggle, and it is simply not necessary to indulge this form of false humility. All we ever need do is take the obvious steps before us today and let our sense of direction clarify as we proceed.

There is also a strong tendency within all of us to get ourselves into a difficult situation and then think we must see it through to the bitter end. Trusting in fantasies instead of our present perception of how things are going is a major contributor to this pattern. To decide beforehand what kind of job we deserve can cause as much unhappiness as deciding what kind of child we have a right to, as many parents unconsciously do. In their mind is a constantly escalating standard of acceptable manners, the proper height, an adequate IQ, sufficient social skills, a pleasing appearance, and so forth. Inevitably the child fails in some respect and feels their disapproval. Disapproval is irrelevant to appreciating children and working with them toward their, rather than our own, feelings of well-being. And just as with a child, a job must be looked at, taken as it is, and given time.

Relax into your destiny. Giving something time is quite different from forcing yourself to see it through to the bitter end. Let each workday come to you. Watch it approach without suspicion. Expect happiness from yourself, but expect nothing from the job. Approached in this way, happiness is a possibility in any situation. Take each task as it comes and do not constantly peer over it to the next task. Don't rush to complete it, or rush toward some hour on the clock. We need not stay on guard in order to see that a job is not working out, but we do have to let down our guard to enjoy what we have pre-defined as "work." We may not be able to change the task, but we are always free to change our definition of our function within it.

Finding a Job

Our discussion so far may seem insensitive to the many people who sincerely want to work but cannot find employment. This is obviously an extremely complex and difficult question, and the factors within these cases can vary so dramatically that any generalizations I make here would be unfair in light of at least some people's plight. So of course there are countless exceptions, and yet I believe a few things can be said that apply to some of those who find themselves in this predicament.

Many people—far more than consciously realize it—make themselves walk a very narrow path in finding work. For instance, there are entire categories of jobs they will not consider because of a certain self-image they believe must be maintained. Other occupations go unexplored because of their conviction that society, the economy, the present controlling minority, big business, or some other generalized enemy should not be forcing this kind of choice and they must stand alone against this outrage, even if it means their family's well-being. "I won't work for a company that . . ." "I won't live in a place where . . ." "I won't take orders from a boss who . . ." and yet it does not have to be that way. Clearly we should never do what is morally intolerable, but so often this is not the real issue. We think we must be right at all costs.

Another hampering bias is directed, curiously, at ourselves. *Most people tend to look down on what they do best.* This is merely further evidence of our aversion to what is easy and simple. Our areas of greatest strength are usually the ones to be given the harshest scrutiny, and of course if you look for fault anywhere long enough you are sure to find it. Instead of doing what we know how to do (which often is also the work we can do most peacefully), we assume that the higher pursuit is to enter a new field altogether, especially one that fits the current definition of "meaningful" work. Seldom is it sufficient to simply earn a living. Better to have an erratic income and be able to give the impression that we are sacrificing ourselves to set the world straight.

Unfortunately our friends are sometimes the ones most likely to distract us from our own quiet knowing. As a general rule you will be less confused and consequently miss fewer opportunities if you will decide for yourself whether a job fits your present needs and not even open yourself up to conflict by discussing decisions you are in the middle of. Strengthen your mind by reminding yourself that *you* are in the best position to know what you should be doing. And after you have started a job save yourself the pangs of doubt by talking as little as possible about the inevitable problems that accompany a transition of this sort. Few people can resist an opportunity to sow confusion. So do not give them one. Do not be afraid to stay close to your heart, to keep your own counsel. *Do not be afraid to know.*

Another cause of defeat, although far less conscious, is the unexamined premise that the job choice one is making is permanent. Out there awaits some eternal and just-right niche, and the only real problem is locating it. And yet, *there is no right job.*

"This is right" implies "this is permanent." It shouldn't, but it does. Who could believe he had finally found the right job or, worse, was "guided" or "led" to it and still feel perfectly free to quit at the end of the first day? Given this approach, it should not be surprising that most people's major concern is to avoid making a mistake. If you believe in the existence of a right job, you will also look on all other jobs as "wrong," at least for you.

Do you see the position this puts you in? Since there is a job that is best for you, most of the work that comes to your attention is a potential mistake and your life is now like walking through a mine field. Should you already have a job, you cannot help harboring the suspicion that you chose wrongly. We think we can somehow believe in the preexistence of a right course of action in one area of our life and yet not believe in it in every other area, and because this is impossible most people also suspect that they married the wrong person (which means, of course, they have the wrong children), bought or rented the wrong place to live in (so the neighbors aren't what they should be), and probably ate the wrong cereal for breakfast this morning. I don't think any of us has managed to escape this outlook entirely.

No more absolute and awful tyranny reigns than our own fear of being wrong. We have a simple choice. We can try to avoid all mistakes or we can relax. In seeking a job it is good to drop the notion that the universe has hidden away some haloed position just for you. Now at least you will not be haunted by the vague feeling that somehow you are not going about this job-finding business in the correct way. There are a thousand correct ways because there are a thousand peaceful ways.

Do not remain in fear. Very often if someone attempting to avoid the wrong job will accept just any job, a more pleasing position will appear shortly thereafter. There is no magic to this. The elimination of fear is the beginning of vision, and to give ourselves a broad range of options permits us to see opportunities we were blind to before. It is not uncommon for an individual who is unable to find a paying job to take volunteer work or to just begin helping someone for free and suddenly have a salaried position, or sometimes several at once, become available, much like the classic example of the couple who cannot bear children, decide to adopt, and instantly become fertile.

Once again, this phenomenon is not the mystery it first seems. So often the cause of our problem, whatever it may be, is fear, and the willingness to act in a simple, direct way will begin lessening it. The precise external results are not predictable—an adoption does not automatically render a couple fertile, and volunteer work does not consistently manifest a paying job. Nevertheless, openness to starting and continuing the small steps involved in walking around a problem will eventually result in leaving the problem behind. Overt manifestations of willingness reduce inner conflict, and an unconflicted mind can step over any hindrance.

How to Make a Decision

The making of decisions has been touched upon several times already in this book, and in the upcoming exercise I would like to bring together the points that have been made because it is so common for people to become hopelessly confused when faced with questions about their livelihood.

Decisions come far more rapidly than is at first realized. They are in fact continuous. Thus our individual choices are not as important as they seem. Yet our *approach* to making all decisions is vital for it lays before us the terrain we must travel. This isn't to say that some decisions are not more life-affecting than others, for in terms of how they influence the outward course of things they are indeed. They are not, however, more happiness-affecting.

It is not necessary to have one way of deciding what color potatoes to buy and another way for choosing a job. It is actually this hidden belief that a more perfect answer is required for a larger question that initiates the turmoil we get ourselves into. Regardless of how dramatic the circumstances surrounding a question, all we need is an answer that *comes* from peace. Perhaps the one difference in how choices about work, divorce, operations, money, moving, and other anxiety-riddled subjects should be made is that more care must be taken to see that they are done in the *same* way, because the temptation is greater to fall back into the more familiar habit of deciding fearful questions fearfully.

Our usual approach to choosing what to do is immediately to begin considering alternatives. This reaction is so imbedded in us that it is difficult even to raise doubt as to its practicality. If it were no more than a calm reviewing of options, it would cause no harm, but it is not calm, and it quickly *eliminates* good options. It is merely the cramping activity of being afraid, and I hope you understand that a sustained effort will be needed to break this habit.

After just a few moments of considering alternatives, the mind becomes scattered and incompetent. The reason for this is that there is no end to what can be taken into consideration. The potential here for scaring ourselves is great, and since we are naturally anxious to escape this mental discomfort, we frequently make a second mistake: We act in the face of our conflict. Because it has that look about it, we call this "being decisive."

A decision made in conflict will produce conflicted results, whereas one arrived at while in a gentle and restful state of mind will (even though it may not result in a particular ego-gratifying outcome) never disrupt the core of happiness within your life. Once you develop the habit of deciding all things with your quietness, your life—including employment, relationships, health, finances—will begin to smooth out and simplify. You will not magically be placed above others, but the outward circumstances of your life, which your decisions affect, will increasingly accommodate, rather than sabotage, your desire to be happy.

To make good decisions you must learn to focus on your state of mind and not on the unanswered question. As long as your attention is on the question, your mind remains unfit to choose in the interest of your happiness. And, once again, this is not "harmless" because your experience is a continuous outpouring of your mental environment.

EXERCISE VII-A

Copy the following seven steps and carry them with you. For at least one week use them whenever you recognize that you are trying to decide anything or solve any problem. By then you should know them well and can continue developing your own sense of this process. Deciding from peace will eventually become automatic, but much work with the steps involved is needed first. It is perhaps best to practice with the smaller everyday choices before you use this procedure with major life-affecting ones.

1. When you see that you have a question, stop. Do this *before* you begin considering alternatives and their ramifications, because soon after you start this kind of worrying, your mind becomes fear dominated and it will be more difficult for you now to go back and make an unconflicted decision.

2. Settle and still your mind. Use any mental or physical trick that helps. You do not have to attain some mystical state of calm, but you do have to take enough time to be certain that you are as peaceful as you are able to be at this moment.

3. Look very closely at the problem. Take your time and make sure that you see all parts of it clearly. Remember not to scare yourself by imagining consequences that could result from various solutions. In fact, do not think about answers at all. Just examine the problem calmly and thoroughly.

4. First making sure that you are not limiting your options in any way, look into your heart and ask yourself if there is anything you want to do about this problem now, today. Trying to decide before it is time to decide will do no more than pollute the present.

5. If there is nothing you wish to do, or if it is not yet clear what you want to do, decide to wait. Never be afraid to wait. But remember that waiting *is* a decision, so be certain to do it without conflict.

6. If you see that there is something you would like to try, carry it out easily and happily and do not reconsider. Instead of attempting to judge whether your decision was right, recall that your mental state was sound when you made it and questionable now that you are worrying.

7. If what you try does not sufficiently lessen the problem, simply repeat the steps and try something else. If you will keep doing this—deciding from your peace what you wish to do in the present and acting on it with certainty—you will eventually put the problem behind you. This is as inevitable as light dispelling darkness.

Developing an Instinct for Where to Be

As you go about seeking a job do not make the common mistake of presuming that there is a way to plainly *recognize* the position that awaits you, for this can result in your at-

tempting to rely on magic through a kind of divining of signs:
By miraculous coincidence the regular receptionist is absent
and in talking to the substitute receptionist you discover that
this person's mother has the same unusual first name as your
mother. "Ah," you think, "this is the job I'm meant to have,"
and during the interview you blow your chances by saying so.
Or, knowing that your reasoning was not perfect or the
"signs" not complete, if you do get the position you remain
fearful that this may not be the one that was being indicated,
and this uncertainty hinders your performance and may even
get you fired.

You will be taking no risk, and you will definitely increase
your happiness, if you will assume that wherever you are now
you are supposed to be, and whatever work you are doing is
"right." Then do the job at hand honestly. No gain can come
from dampening down your spirit or from feeding your mind
reasons to continue doubting. And doing something well never
blocks, but only increases, your ability to discern that the time
has *now* come to move on, should that time come.

So often we believe that in order to turn from something we
must first find fault with it. If we quit we must denounce our
former employer; a friend must become a disappointment before we can stop being romantically involved; a spiritual organization or teacher must be shown to be dangerous if we feel
like moving on. But why should our participation make something good and our leaving prove its inferiority? *A happy person enters and leaves in peace.*

None of this implies that there are no genuine indicators as
to whether you should give a particular job a try or leave the
one you are in. A sense of comfort about the people with
whom you would be working is often a very reliable form of
inner knowing. But it will not tell you how far you will advance, how long you will be employed there, or even whether
you will be hired in the first place. This sense is not mystical

but rather the beginning of true intelligence. It is a feeling something like this: You see that your mind comes to rest when you think of this place and these particular people. It is *not* a feeling of excitement about your prospective good fortune. Nor is it even a "liking" of the people or the facilities. You merely find that you are *comfortable* with the thought of taking this job. It is an adequate job for now.

This calm instinct about people and places can of course be applied to other circumstances besides employment. To do so will not provide objective knowledge about the world, because an uncomfortable situation for one will not be so regarded by another. Nor does this sense of things entail analyzing and discussing personalities. And it most definitely is not the sad accumulating of what some refer to as their "shit list." I am speaking of the ability to see things as they are in the present and not the tiring habit of avoiding certain people or establishments because of something disagreeable that once happened. It is simply a very natural realization of whether a particular relationship, a certain place, a specific kind of situation will make it easier or more difficult for us, personally, to be happy.

Such understanding is not fodder for gossip, nor are diehard rules of behavior formulated as a result, because this same calm knowing is sensitive to the changes constantly occurring in individuals and in places. Once it is developed it is an extremely valuable sensitivity that can gently guide you to where you wish to do your banking, buy your groceries, your gas, what restaurants you want to frequent, and all the other contacts with certain people and locations that may figure heavily in your daily routine. *If where you place yourself over and over is disturbing, it is unlikely that the overall happiness of your life will remain unaffected.*

EXERCISE VII-B

As you go about running your usual errands for the next week or two, mentally (and whenever feasible, physically) pause once you are within each place—store, laundry, service station, friend's house, church, bank—and very gently ask yourself, "Is this a happy place?" Do not give yourself a verbal answer, but carry the question into the place the way you might wear a new pair of glasses.

Be conscious of any tendency to form the answer from your memory of what has taken place there in the past, or from whether your eyes like the "class" of people, decor, etc., or what the cost in time or money is to you, or a hundred other factors irrelevant to the overall atmosphere into which you have just walked. You wish merely to be sensitive to the degree of ease or discontent, peace or anger, good or ill will, in other words, to the degree of happiness that surrounds you.

Immediately after you leave, stop again and ask, "Have I just left a happy place?" Do not answer the question in your mind, but let it come to you quietly in its own time. Once you believe you have seen the answer, if you find yourself either promoting or talking against this place to others, I can assure you that you have seen nothing as yet, because the kind of vision I am speaking of is not a judgment. Nor is it a decision about what is wrong or right for other people. It is only a simple recognition of what is best for you at this time.

If you realize that a place is not happy, this of course does not always mean that it would be easier on you to not frequent it. For example, it will not make you more content with life to abruptly stop visiting your parent or child even though you might see that this relative's home is unhappy and that it is difficult for you to be there. Nor does recognizing the pervading mood of a place imply that you now have reason to fear it. By becoming more aware of the atmosphere you have chosen to enter, perhaps you will now take the time to clear your mind of all conflict so that as you walk into this place you will bring your ease and enjoyment with you and, as you leave, you will carry no emotion that could chip away at your happiness.

No Purpose Is an Island

Careers and jobs are ordinarily thought of as forming a separate island of purpose within the day. This makes any grandeur, any unifying theme to one's life, an impossibility. It would seem that it would be feasible to limit oneself to just a few purposes, for example, to have a nutritious meal in the morning, to pursue one's career during the day, in the evening to be entertained, and to get a good night's sleep. But as a value, fragmentation contains no self-limiting guidelines. If you are like most of us, a typical segment of the day is more likely to go like this: You have come home from work and you see that you are out of toilet paper. It's an hour before the evening news and you calculate that you can just make it to Alpha Beta and back. You pick up the keys and walk to the car. Now, as you get in and turn on the ignition, what is foremost in your mind, what is your purpose in life, what is your "job"? Is it to idle the car long enough to eliminate the risk of wear to the engine? Or is it to put the car in gear immediately to cut back on the risk of being late for the news?

Your inner conflict is almost unconscious, even though there is a slight but perceptible undercurrent of guilt as you choose saving time over prolonging the life of the engine and bolt from the driveway. Or a little stab of anxiety as you just sit there idling the car while the seconds tick away and the first and most important segment of the news begins floating away from you like an ice-cream cone held uneaten in the sun as you pass pleasantries outside 31 Flavors with someone whose name you can't recall.

If your spouse is with you, and if his or her ego position on this differs, a thought critical of you such as "How did I marry someone so cheap?" or "You've never liked this car because I'm the one who picked it out" flicks through your spouse's mind practically unnoticed, but not entirely unfelt by you.

At the first intersection you wonder which way you should turn. Is your aim in life now to protect your self-image? For if it is, you should not turn right and go to Ralph's Food Market, even though it's ten minutes closer, because the last time you were there you told Ralph you were never coming back. This time the "wrong" decision might even draw a comment from your spouse.

As you drive to Alpha Beta should physical safety take precedence over making the lights? Perhaps a brief argument breaks out in the car over this one. "You ran a red light again, dear." "No, dear, I didn't. It was yellow as I entered the intersection." A long silence, and then quite innocently you ask, "Were you able to get an appointment with Dr., uh, what's-his-name, you know, dear, your ophthalmologist friend?" Because suddenly the meaning of life is to be right.

At last you are in the Alpha Beta lot and your one goal in life is to get the parking place nearest the entrance, but as you turn to back into it someone pulls in ahead of you, even though you clearly had the right of way. You are so angry about this that—for the moment—this grievance is more important than the latest war that was just announced on your car radio.

The point we are forever missing is that life is always "for the moment." While we stay lost in what is already over and done with ("They moved the toilet paper. Why is this store always reorganizing its stock?") or in what is yet to be ("The news is in twelve minutes and as usual there's no checkout person at the express lane.") our life stays patiently in the moment waiting for us to recognize it.

The unhappiness of this entire situation was caused not by Ralph, or the lights, or the speedy parker. It was caused by the same mental state that continues to torture us as we wheel into our driveway, just missing the neighbor's bull terrier, only to find that the news has been preempted by a funeral special.

We are upset, and yet we have so many "jobs" that we don't even know if we *want* to watch the news. We have never paused long enough to look into our heart to see.

Hopeless Mistakes

There are no permanent mistakes. If something begins in a mistaken way, and perhaps everything we do does to some degree, it does not have to remain a mistake. Nothing remains a mistake forever, but the moment it transforms into a spurt of learning is up to us. It is important to remember that changing the original form of what we suspect was a mistake (by quitting our job, reshaping our body, moving, trading in our spouse) is *not* an essential first step. We are not learning what is a good or bad outward form for things to take; we are already weighed down with this kind of confusing lesson. Our advance in learning, which will take us to another level of happiness, will simply be the transfer of a gentle lesson, already recognizable under some circumstances, into new areas of our life.

Naturally this does not imply there are no changes that would make things a little easier for you, because of course there are a thousand changes that would. However, your level of happiness will be unaffected if all you do is make changes. Unfortunately most people's first response to a feeling of discontent is to start rummaging around in their lives for what is wrong. Since nothing there is perfect, they quickly find fault with something, and trying to change it becomes their sole focus. In fact, some form of this syndrome constitutes the bulk of activity in most people's lives—either hurrying around to fix the latest perceived affliction or turning away in resignation because it is probably hopeless.

Happiness becomes a much simpler matter once we realize that it starts with a strong, whole, peaceful state of mind and then, very gently, extends outward. If a change is undertaken it is because it may make our way a little easier and not "to set things right." If we begin in a worried, agitated state, the changes we make carry with them an air of anxiety and defeat. All we see is that they, too, are not perfect, and once again we start our disjointed search for what more can be rectified or else we turn away and suffer a little death.

"Make your living with your left foot" goes the ancient Eastern wisdom. Don't let your livelihood be the aim of your existence. Do your job well, in fact do it magnificently, but do not take it out of context and make it the end you seek. If you wish to be happy, your function must remain the same under all circumstances. You carry with you an atmosphere—one that is strong and whole or one that is fragmented. Since this is your choice, be conscious of which you carry. Let not circumstances choose for you or you will always feel scattered and to some degree unreal. The reason you may seem of no contribution is that you are probably contributing very little from your heart—events seem to snatch away the best of you before you can extend it.

Please allow me to repeat one suggestion. Decide on one all-encompassing life purpose. Do this today and your way will instantly become simpler. Why are you here? Do you know what your job is *for*? What would you like it to be for?—because that is what it will be. Let your work be for your life, for your relationships, for the world, for all of you. Most people have never stopped to ask why they bother to go on doing *anything,* and consequently nothing they do is ever for the same thing twice. Make your job happy by making it the same as every other part of your life.

CHAPTER VIII

Money

Of all the topics upon which the mind can dwell, money is one of the most miserable. "I could use some more money" produces a dull distress in almost every heart. In the West it is a thought as unsettling as "Does what I'm eating have sugar?" Few have remained untouched by all the contradictions and guilt that swirl around the subject. Most of us can't even go out and purchase a few vegetables without feeling a tinge of self-disgust for not having driven the extra miles necessary to buy them for less. Or if we did go out of our way to get the "better value" we have fleeting thoughts of how tight we are or how uncharitably we use our time. After all, Mother Teresa wouldn't waste her day trying to find carrots at three cents less a pound.

What Is Money For?

The world sends out two basic messages about money. First: Nothing is more desirable. And second: Isn't that a shame; it really shouldn't be that way. So always we want more of it, but always it remains tainted.

I remember very well an early realization of just how unhappy a preoccupation with money can be. It was pointed out to me when I was still quite young that I had three wealthy relatives, and questions of who would inherit, and how much, were often discussed with overtones of great excitement. And so my daydreams began. Even a very young person can quickly recognize that these thoughts offer no refuge. To fantasize about this kind of thing you must wish for someone to die and for others to be out of favor. Then of course there are the guilty considerations of whether you deserve to have a lot of money come to you in this way, which, as it turned out, was a worry I need never have bothered myself about.

Possibly you have seen firsthand how insensitively people can act when property is being divided: picking and squabbling over the deceased's furniture and jewelry, and in the process forming grudges and personal shames that can be carried for a lifetime. But this is just one of the numerous pathetic outcomes of our inordinate fascination with money. There are the tactics many are tempted to use to get a promotion, the unkind way we parade our purchases before friends, the years we absent ourselves from loved ones in pursuit of. . . . In pursuit of what?

This is the central question that goes unasked about money. What is it for? We believe that we never have enough, that somehow we must get more, and that we will be content only when we have more than enough. But how much is "more than enough"? And does that concept even have meaning? The fact is that our desired destination is so vague that there is no way we can ever reach it.

My sister-in-law told me that a friend of hers called one day and asked if she would like to go with him to meet "a really wealthy man." On their way over she could see that her friend was very excited. "This man makes over twelve million a year!" he said. Clearly he was unimpressed with the two and a half million a year he himself made.

The point is not that money is somehow bad, but that the desire for money contains within it no stopping place. And yet nearly everyone has need of at least some money. And so the failure to ask "What is it for?" can lead to still another unhappy predisposition: the belief that money defiles, that it is at best a necessary evil, and that to give up as many symbols of prosperity as possible somehow makes one a better person. Specifically this point of view may include notions that it is a "higher" approach to life not to consider salary when selecting a job; that to resist putting money in tax shelters, investments, or even savings is less self-seeking, less spiritually stultifying; that having a large wardrobe, owning a "luxury" car, or living in an affluent neighborhood are reliable signs of personal shallowness. This outlook is commonly pushed to the point where now all purchases must be made with inordinate concern, and only out of the strictest necessity. Anything brand-new, such as a new car or TV, is automatically viewed with suspicion. It can even be applied to the amount of food one eats or hours one sleeps—less of both indicating the more spiritually minded individual.

To ask "What is it for?" puts money back into context. Money is simply a means, a medium, a way. If we stop to worship the road that leads to a desired location, we never arrive. Likewise, our progress ceases if we pause to detest it. Many people make a similar mistake in expecting something from particular days of the week or times of the year. The Christmas season, Saturday night, their birthday, the equinox, or some other number on a calendar is given importance in itself, and subconsciously they bide their time awaiting some undefined acknowledgment from the universe. But on this day, as on every other day, the earth revolves and the sun sets without incident. The highest number of suicides occurs around Christmas, and I know from my work on a crisis hot line that many people who feel suicidal at this time of year have had, once again, a great expectation dashed. Although they are unable to see this, it had to be dashed. The twenty-fifth of December is incapable of *doing* anything. And so, too, is the number on a bill or stock certificate. It is bloodless, lifeless, *and* totally innocent. It's just a number.

Unlike people, money is what money does. These little metal discs and slips of paper are merely a way of obtaining certain externals, but not the only way, and their helpfulness or hurtfulness cannot exceed the tiny range of things they can bring to us. There have been countless songs and jokes as well as essays, sermons, and books on what money can't buy. And this is indeed helpful to recognize. So much of the disappointment brought by the pursuit of or flight from money comes from associating it with irrelevancies such as self-respect, future peace, locating a person who truly loves us, being a winner, or in some other way feeling more satisfied than others.

The Fear of Money

There are so many wealthy people who are deeply unhappy that this realization can lead to the assumption that to find ways of renouncing money decreases our chances of being miserable. It is true that, just like anything else that sets us apart, having enormous wealth makes life more difficult, and yet how could merely reducing our financial options bring to us some-thing of value? The ancient wisdom that the love of money is behind much of the evil of the world is true. And so, too, are hate and fear of money. Can quitting one's job and turning instead to grubbing, scrounging, and groveling bring peace of mind? Those who do usually become so obsessed with ob-taining simple necessities that their minds drown in the world rather than rise above it. Seeking more than enough or less than enough cannot set the issue of money to rest. Only the lessening of fear around this entire subject will help.

A good overall rule might be: *Money is not important; there-fore, do whatever allows you not to be preoccupied with it.* Many problems in life can be resolved by our accepting a daily solu-tion instead of continuing to chase after a permanent one. For example, there may be a permanent answer to dental hygiene but most people would rather brush their teeth every day than to search for some final resolution. They are not in conflict about this and so the time spent in front of the bathroom sink is not a burden. Many who know in their hearts that they are alcoholics hold themselves in misery by insisting there must be a way for them to continue drinking. Possibly there is, but those who decide that from now on they will attend, for in-stance, an AA meeting every night settle the question and go on with their lives.

Likewise, a job, even though it can consume half one's wak-ing life, is an excellent way of diminishing anxiety about where the necessary funds will come from. Most of the other alterna-tives people turn to, such as get-rich-quick schemes, marrying for money, gambling in various forms, and skirting the law are far more fear-provoking than simply going to work every day. Of course it is possible to obtain all the money one will ever need virtually overnight, but short of inheriting it, this is so contrary to the general course of things that people usually spend as much time trying to get rich quickly, and not succeeding, as they would at a regular job and more time by far worrying.

In recent years the yearning for a way of life that is good and positively affecting has grown enormously. Many now find themselves wanting not only to be of help but to be of help in a more direct and consistent way. Along with this desire, which in most cases is sincere and deeply felt, is considerable ego involvement, and so at the same time there is a widespread belief that runs like this: "If you will just relax and trust a little, somehow it will all work out. And if perchance it doesn't, you will see that this, too, was a good thing."

That bit of wisdom is actually true but it is not true on the level of experience to which it is being applied, because what is implied here is that there are ways, especially mental or mystical ways, to have all our worldly desires met without following the usual worldly procedures. In fact, it is often part of this belief that the requisite inner state may be jeopardized if you *do* go by the rules. Consequently we now see many people living without economy, keeping inadequate or no track at all of their income and expenses, possessing no clear idea of where their money is going, or, as mentioned before, even giving up their jobs altogether and waiting anxiously for the universe to care for them. And there may even be a period in which they claim that all of this works wonderfully well. Discounted are the times they must scurry about for money or, in some cases, sustain an almost nonstop fear about the future.

One cannot hope to stabilize one's life if there is an inherent pattern of fear already set up and going unquestioned. The realities are that *a daily sense of economy is more conducive to peace than a daily sense of waste.* It simply cannot add to our happiness to destroy what we think of as real. In order to reach the depth of happiness that tranquility can bring, the question of how our needs are to be met should not be approached in a wishful manner. To conduct our affairs so that we feel secure about our income and our spending practices seem wise and good will not possibly hinder our capacity to develop a higher trust or to flow easily with life's circumstances. The simple fact is that *a stable source of income is less apt to spawn mental conflict than an unstable one.* This is not a call for sacrifice and scrimping, nor does anyone need to become mercenary. Rather it is a plea for simplicity and intelligence.

There is no magic to money. The problem of earning and keeping money can be resolved without resort to mental trickery and the interminable study of occult rules. The universe does not have to be entreated, nor manipulated, in order for us to be at ease in all our financial dealings. But it must also become clear that *we cannot separate ourselves from our money problems* because financial chaos activates the fearful part of us and thereby constricts genuine happiness.

Money is a problem in perception, and the ultimate solution to any financial difficulty is for us to view it with enough honesty so that our mind can focus calmly and see what to do. Once fear is eliminated, or sufficiently lessened, there is no problem that cannot be solved. That is quite different from saying "There isn't anything you can't get to go the way your ego wants it to go." By "solve" I mean "make happy." Options are always present to make any area of our life happier for us to live, and they will be seen as we release our mind from anxiety.

The Chronic Pattern

As was pointed out earlier, the world's two controlling attitudes about money are that it is wonderful and it is evil. Although these are contradictory, they are only different sides of the same misplaced emphasis, and very few people have escaped being infected by both views. The usual way we act them out is that we strive to get more and more but feel guilty about what we have obtained and unconsciously attempt to rid ourselves of it. Until a fundamental shift in emphasis occurs, the pattern will usually remain unchanged regardless of the amount of money that comes our way.

With the people you know very well perhaps you have noticed that certain individuals tend always to be on time or always late and you can often predict their arrival within a few minutes. For example, those friends who usually come twenty minutes late will remain fairly consistent even though their excuses each time may vary widely. The circumstances they cite are manifestly not the governing factor. The value they place on time determines how they use it, and this will not change until the value itself changes.

This is equally true of spending habits. A young couple starting out will quickly form a pattern of retaining a certain percentage of what comes in or of being a certain percentage in debt. This ratio will not vary by much even though their earnings may increase substantially over the years. If suddenly they receive a financial windfall, their financial "system" will begin digesting it, and as soon as this is completed—and it can be finished off in a remarkably short period—they will be back to the same pattern of indebtedness (or percentage of surplus) that existed before.

Although the form it takes can change at any time, *the desire level for externals remains the same until desire itself is questioned,* and this is true whether the wanting is for ever more money or for ridding oneself of money. Almost always it is for both, and the degree by which these two wishes cancel each other out determines whether the individual is always a little short, a little ahead, has needless surfeit, or just breaks even, none of which is either good or bad. The problem is not in the particular outcome that these conflicting attitudes produce but in the valuing of money, either positively or negatively, for its own sake.

Money by itself has no importance, and to think that it does will always cause some form of money-oriented problem, just as the valuing of time in and of itself generates problems in how time is spent. Remove anything from context and trouble begins, and if you have a recurring money problem you can be certain you are doing this. Just seeing that much can be of help because you will not be so quick to blame a certain person or special set of circumstances for why the problem has occurred *this* time.

What then can be done once a pattern of this kind is established? The following exercises should help.

EXERCISE VIII-A

In a moment you will be asked to dissect your particular financial soap opera, and I hope that you will be able to do this with no hint of self-criticism. When beginning a self-improvement process of almost any kind, most people make the mistake of siding with the angry voice within them in an attempt to bring about behavioral change. Most of us still believe that we can denounce ourselves into being more responsible. But in fact *remorse does not truly motivate,* and it usually backfires. It can have a temporary effect at best because it comes from the side of our nature that values conflict and attack. From conflict arises pain, and pain will take us only so far. Lasting change must be grounded in happiness. A new course must reward and continue to satisfy unremittingly or it will eventually be turned from. So I am asking you to be very careful about this. Try to look at your chronic mistakes without attempting to motivate yourself through disgust and guilt. Attack is the problem, not the answer.

1. Close your eyes and think in a very general way about your experiences with money. Just let various scenes come to mind. As you do this be conscious of your anxiety level and write down the kinds of things that are the most broadly disturbing. You are not looking for just one or two embarrassing or difficult moments, but for a pattern, a recurring unhappiness in your life. (For example: Needing to offer things of monetary value in an attempt to cement relationships. Being periodically short and having to forage about for money. Always scrimping in an insensitive, unkind way. A history of spending sprees. Recurring feelings of superiority or inferiority based on money.) Briefly describe one or more patterns of this sort.

2. Take only one of these recurring problems, perhaps the one that is the most pervasive and time-consuming, and ask yourself in what context it occurs. In other words, what are the kinds of thoughts and feelings, and especially what are the circumstances, that precede and surround an outbreak of this pattern? (Examples: "When I am physically tired and discouraged." "After I have fantasized how a truly advanced person would live." "While shopping for other things." "When in public and think I am being judged.")

Your goal here is not to engage in deep analysis but merely to look for obvious triggers. For instance, you might notice that you go on a spending spree just after a bad argument with your spouse. That much is all you need to write down, even though there are of course deeper reasons for spending sprees than this. Another example: You notice that you overreact to getting a lot of money at once, for instance at payday. Describe as many of these connections as you honestly see. Be sure to include anything that you can remember feeling just prior to or during the times you have acted out this particular pattern, and please remember to do all of this without self-censure.

3. Using whatever relaxation technique or mental trick you wish, quiet your body and mind and rest for a few seconds. First, look at the set of circumstances that usually attend your special problem with money. Then look at the problem itself. Continue to shuttle your attention back and forth between the problem and the circumstances that commonly surround it. After you have done this for a moment, ask yourself if there are some simple ways to bypass the circumstances that trigger the problem. You are not necessarily interested in discovering how to change the circumstances themselves so much as in seeing how to avoid them. For example, if you frequently overspend when you have to walk through the mall but tend not to overspend when you drive to an isolated store that has what you need, one obvious way to eliminate the triggering situation is not to shop at the mall.

As of now, do not act on the changes you see are possible but merely write them down. Describe more than one way you could avoid or nullify the circumstances that appear to generate your problem. In making this list, once again it might be good to start with ridiculous and fanciful options and then try to add a few that are more reasonable.

4. Do not decide on any action at this time. Instead, concentrate on exactly what is happening around you whenever you are the least bit excited or fearful about money matters. To do this you must become very conscious of anything at all that has to do with money. Look more closely, be more present, as you make a purchase, pay a bill, watch a financial report on TV, balance your checkbook, drive past the bank. Do this for a week, but do not attempt to make changes as yet. As you practice this kind of awareness, record anything you observe that you had not noticed before. (Examples: "No matter what mail I have received, I always open the bills first." "The service seems worse and I leave a skimpy tip when I'm worried about my own predicament.")

5. Once you feel certain that you have a better grasp of what is going on in your life and of how you participate in some of your chronic money difficulties, return your attention to the one pattern you chose in #2. Sitting quietly, taking all the time you need, ask yourself what do you now want to do about this problem. Remember to allow yourself any option and then decide on one simple step—not an infallible step, not a step you even hope will solve everything forever, but merely one you think has a chance of bringing improvement. (Let's say your recurring problem is that you run short of money, and let's say your income is seasonal rather than monthly. A beginning step might be to open a second bank account into which you place all income and out of which you pay yourself a fixed monthly salary.) Let it be a plan that you are confident is within your present readiness to carry out. Record this plan, and then try it.

6. Keep repeating #5 and trying new measures until you have walked past the pattern. Write the date and the step you try first, and below that, the dates and steps you take later. Finally, record the date when you think the problem is behind you. You need not be absolutely certain of this, but do wait until you have a sense of honesty about making this last entry.

CHAPTER IX

Possessions

Money is not worth having unless there are signs of money in our life. So reasons our ego. No good for it to lie there like some overfed cat; to get our money's worth out of money there has to be hard visual evidence that it's a power we personally wield: At least a consoling bank balance printed in a little gilded book that we can take out in private moments and gaze at warmly, like pictures of the grandchildren. If not that, then perhaps an occasional highly conversable vacation and "just marvelous" food. Or the latest tech in wristwatches. Good seats and good service. Respect for one's business opinion. Or even an ornate spouse might do. Otherwise we feel cheated. Money seems to call out to us to be translated into some *thing*. We think it's a tragedy for money to just remain money.

Or if money has become important to us as a symbol that must be avoided, this attitude will also have its display: perhaps a bare-bones and rigidly secondhand furnishing job. The kind of clothes that indicate one is certainly not interested in clothes. Only backyard-grown or bulk-bought foods. Clearly no hair spray. Or a meticulous avoidance of first-name boutiques and little French restaurants. From this point of view, money should be translated into a sacrifice of options. Here again it is unacceptable for money to be merely money.

Inner Simplicity

The desire for more and more (or its corollary, the desire to be deprived) has as its root a belief that what you see is what you get. But of course form is not everything, content is everything, and inner simplicity is the permanent sigh of relief that this has been recognized.

People who have reached an advanced stage of happiness invariably lead simple lives. Their household environment and personal affairs are free of chaos and clutter. They eat simply, dress peacefully, and follow a harmonious routine. If compassion requires that they break with any of this, they can do so easily and quickly, because for the truly happy person simplicity is not just another fetish, it is an enduring internal state.

Whenever we are afraid we are to some degree tense and intractable, and that is why a scattered approach to life is rigid whereas a simple one is not. Yet this is not recognized by most people. They think accumulating is satisfying and buying an endless list of things they don't want and can't use spells real freedom. Or they make the equal mistake of drawing back in fear from all signs of wealth.

Another word for simplicity is clarity. Deep inner clarity about one's purpose and way. Now there is space to see. Simplicity is freedom from mental and emotional litter. The heart has room to love and enjoy. Simplicity is guileless, carefree, and straightforward. It is the uncomplicated way, the easy step, and this soft internal order is expressed outwardly in an instinctive avoidance of excess or its counterpart, deprivation and self-imposed loss. However, because simplicity is a core condition, there can be no exact formula for how it should take form within one's life-style.

Simplicity of heart has a calming effect on one's environment, but the particulars will vary with each individual. There are no rules for determining how many changes of clothes must hang in the closet, whether one should own a yogurt maker, or if mounting Uncle Toby's stuffed moose head in the den is immoral. But it is there to be seen by anyone who cares to look that all possessions are subject to loss and deterioration. Hair and toothbrush bristles develop split ends, cars fall apart, guppies die, jogging shoes go out of style, and the neighbors you acquire along with your new house put pressure on you either to keep your sidewalk edged or tear up the lawn altogether and put in the crushed red lava stone. Even though it would seem too obvious to miss, these flapping distracting streamers tied to every new possession are almost never considered as we go about the supposedly happy work of accumulating ever more. And still we wonder why we can't go through a single day in peace.

That from time to time purchases must be made is obvious, but this does not negate the fact that consequences attend. We can't even bring home a few cut flowers without ramifications: In what will they be placed? Must something be added to the water to keep them fresher longer? In whose room will they go? Should the cat be allowed to nibble? Which family member's role is it to remove the wilted ones? It never seems to be this intrinsic nature of possessions that gets our attention; only the latest symptom of it is noticed. So when the refrigerator suddenly starts making a strange noise we think that all it will take for life again to be worth living is to get someone out quickly to fix it. And of course it should be taken care of. Yet what do we do? At the repairman's recommendation, who demonstrated his reliability by keeping the appointment only after the fourth call and a few threats, we purchase a new refrigerator: the three-door Maxi Deluxe 500-X with Chooz-a-shape ice-maker and chilled-water busboy. Far more can now go wrong than could before, but it stands so shiny and handsome in the corner of our kitchen that we don't think of this until several weeks later when the "busboy" refuses to drop crushed ice in our Dixie cup and the repairman we called before now tells us he isn't certified to work on the 500-X.

We are often so tyrannized by our home that we cannot be comfortable in it. We walk into a room and see only a collection of mistakes. Or we have a nagging little question about the chairs. The decor is atrophying and we're not sure what to do. Our mind is filled with equal parts of fear and decorating hints. In a very real sense we do not have a home because we are uncertain what this place we live in is for. A showcase of our talent and creativity? An example of our energy consciousness? A display case for our wealth? Or merely a place to sleep? You truly want to feel welcomed by your own home. You want it to be a place of relaxation and rest. You want to be able to "come home," but as long as you view it through the eyes of anxiety and condemnation you will not be able to.

One of the many unhappy solutions to this dynamic is to begin neglecting the things we do own because we suddenly decide "I no longer care about worldly things; I'm beyond all of that." It is true that in this way less of our day is devoted to maintenance and repair, but the underlying distress we must feel when we withhold our love from our very surroundings will delay us more than remaining aware of what is occurring within our habitat and caring for the things that need care.

An equally unhappy solution is to begin fearing or, worse, hating possessions and refusing to acquire what would be a comfort and help to ourselves and those around us. Once again there is no list of what these things might be because this would vary with each family or individual. For a long while I resisted buying a word processor. Now that I have one I am turning out my columns and completed manuscripts in about half the time. I owe this to Gayle, who got me to look closely at my reasons for not wanting one. There was a self-image—that of the log-cabin and candlelight kind of guy—which I did not want shattered. When I saw this honestly I recognized how silly it was and bought the equipment that would help. Now if I had to operate the word processor myself (Gayle is a computer genius) this would not have simplified things for me personally because the part of the brain that remembers the difference between a dip switch and an escape key was cruelly left out when my body was assembled. So simplicity is neither a new word processor nor a gadget-free life. Simplicity is the openness that sees what will add to our freedom or what will only complicate our way.

What Have You Put Around You?

A feel for genuine simplicity is fairly easy to develop if you will take it in small steps. This being a section on possessions, I am of course suggesting that you begin with these, but another area of your life—your relationships, your diet, your finances —could just as easily become the starting point.

The following set of exercises is designed to deepen your awareness of the little atmospheres that swirl about you. While it is true that we are affected by our possessions on an unconscious level, it is not true that we must forever remain unaware of what these influences are and where they are coming from. The dreams we have at night are a good example of one way we set up an environment for ourselves and then choose to forget our part in forming it so that the surrounding events can appear to be happening *to* us. Except in certain extreme forms this is all very harmless in the case of dreams, but certainly it is not without pain within our life.

It is possible to have positive associations with what some people would consider messy surroundings. Clutter to one is austerity to another, but what is important to your happiness is not these comparisons but your personal sense of an environment that is in harmony with you. The mind is in a vulnerable state while learning how to focus, and you are probably more affected by the things around you and how closely they match your sense of order and cleanliness than you may realize. Until you learn to see, it is perhaps best to look at fewer things.

Very few people suffer from progressive austerity. The common ailment is overaccumulation, and I will assume you have not escaped this entirely. It is therefore important to consider the number of things around you and also the comfortableness of the memories you have about each item. Both are equally affecting. If you have an overall sense of excess, or the perception that there are spots where things are too crowded together, and if you believe these conditions exist in part because you have been negligent, it would be unlikely that you do not at least occasionally feel oppressed by the glut and mentally muddled by the clutter.

Your possessions also have an impact individually. You are reminded, often on an unconscious level, of a theme in your life every time your eyes glance at an object. I don't wish to be theatrical about this. You never need to be afraid of anything, and it is quite possible to possess at times a serenity that remains untouched by the particular influences of which I am speaking. Your household environment, if it is not simple and free of fear, can be like a mild allergen that affects you only when your immunity has been lowered. And yet you may become susceptible more often than you realize, and this aspect of your life should be adjusted to interfere as little as possible with your mental comfort.

EXERCISE IX-A

1. When embarking on a broad external change it is a good overall rule to begin with the smallest and easiest step. So sit quietly in your least important room. (If you have only one or two rooms, perhaps you could begin inside your car, or before your refrigerator, or at your locker or desk in the building where you work.) Slowly look around. Look at what is behind you, under you, above you. Try hard to take in each thing you see without adding a single judgment or criticism to it. Look at this room as if you were a stranger to it, and see it, really *see* it, for the first time.

Relaxed, and with your eyes now closed, take in the *atmosphere* around you. How does this room *feel* to you? Do certain areas seem congested? Does some part need cleaning? Is there an unhappiness or sadness around a particular object? Is something being neglected? Are there places that seem comfortable or bright with welcome? Describe in writing the various atmospheres you sense above, below, and around you.

2. The above exercise is not meant to make you paranoid about the room you were in or to harden your judgments against certain objects. Nor is it meant to catapult you into a flurry of alterations. It is very difficult to learn that our observations do not require automatic action. We are accustomed to converting every insight into behavior, whereas no change need be made until we are clear within ourselves that the change will add to our mental stability. Until you are certain, it is best to wait calmly. Every ambiguous action causes a disturbed aftermath. Likewise, to withdraw or become slovenly is not a solution because inaction, if motivated by fear, also has its disrupting consequences.

Except for the written part, repeat #1 within a second room. As you do each step pay particular attention to any desire you have to alter the room, e.g., to clean it, throw something out, make repairs, add things to it. When you notice an urge of this sort write a brief description ("My impulse is to pull up this dirty old carpet and burn it").

3. Then close your eyes and imagine undertaking one of the alterations that seems feasible. Project into the future what things will be like as you make, and after you have completed, the change. As best you can, see everyone and everything this will affect. Do not worry whether your fantasy is accurate, for of course it is not. Your aim is not prediction, rather it is to undergo a deliberate mental process that will allow you to see how peaceful you are *now* about making this change.

Write a short list of any disturbing consequences you imagine.

Close your eyes and fantasize *not* making the change, then write down the ramifications you can picture flowing from not acting.

4. Although this step entails seeing more clearly what you want, please notice that it still does not call for any overt action.

In the same general way that you absorbed the atmospheres of the rooms, use a similar general approach in comparing the two lists. Look at them serenely. Do not raise any questions. Do not place importance on their separate lengths or try to rank the individual points. Simply review their contents, then close your eyes and ask yourself what your peaceful preference is, what it is you want to do as of now.

If you would like a more visual way of learning whether you prefer making this particular change to the room, here are two imageries you could try: Think of peace as light and, with eyes closed, observe which list seems "brighter" to you. Another possible image: Picture yourself standing between the two lists and watch your body lean in the direction of your more peaceful inclination. Say to yourself, "If my purpose is to be happy, which way do I lean?" Should there be a sense of something else deciding *for* you, a strong sense of the abnormal, mystical, or psychical occurring when you try either of these visualizations, remember that you do not *have* to continue using them. What you want is to come to know your own heart in all matters, and that is a natural and comfortable process. Fear, in any form, is no part of it. If anxiety heavily surrounds your use of any practice suggested in this book, it is best not to persist, since conflict itself is the principle component of unhappiness.

You may have noticed that this exercise did not concern itself with the question of whether the contemplated change to the room was "right." Issues of right and wrong can almost never be resolved without residual conflict because the grounds on which they are made shift constantly. Is it financially right? conveniently right? aesthetically right? conventionally right? Is it right according to a particular book—but which passage in the book? Is it right for your spouse but not for you? Is it safe? Is it proper? And on and on. There is clearly no clarity in "right." But it is quite simple to recognize your peaceful preference—if you will give yourself time to recognize it—and also not question yourself once you have noticed what it is.

5. Repeat #1 in the remaining rooms of your house, place of work, or any other areas that contain your personal items. If in order to have a clear idea of what you are feeling in each of these locations you need to break the area into smaller units (closets, drawers, the freezer, the glove compartment, etc.), then certainly take the time to do this. A project such as the one suggested in these exercises, if done adequately, could take a long time, and there is nothing lost in giving yourself that time. Do only as much each day as you feel comfortable doing, and do not get caught up in the excitement of some potential change. In itself the change of throwing things out is no more conducive to your mental well-being than the change of acquiring still more.

Once you have mentally wrapped yourself around your array of possessions—clothes, food stock, tools, pictures, pets, books, toilet items, children's toys, accumulated mail—and know what emotions you have about them, not only individually, but also how you feel about the quantity of things you own and how they are arranged and cared for, you are now ready to begin imposing on them your present sense of simplicity. As mentioned before, it is good to begin with the least important area and gradually work up to those rooms or places that seem more complex and evoke greater anxiety. Another helpful procedure might be to work on one area until you feel it is complete before going to the next.

Sit quietly in the place where you have decided to begin. First look at it honestly, then with your eyes closed, drink in the atmosphere around you. Be very aware of areas or items that disturb you. Then open your eyes and consider the first possession, which, if possible, should be one you do not care a great deal about.

Look calmly at this item and ask yourself the following questions (you can write out the answers if you wish, but after the first possession or two you may sense that you can be deliberate enough to do this mentally):

1. Do I still use this? (As a decoration, a tool, a symbol of certain memories, etc.)
2. Am I still taking care of this? (Dusting it, servicing it, polishing it, etc.)

3. If I am neither caring for it nor using it, in what specific ways do I fear letting it go? ("I may use it someday." "I might offend the one who gave it to me." "It's costly and I don't see how I will ever recoup its value.")

If after answering these there is still a question whether to keep this particular possession, close your eyes and project *into the future* both keeping it and not keeping it. Then ask yourself, "Which course of action will add to my *present* peace?" The answer to this question will not guarantee that in days to come your ego will be happy about the decision you make today, but isn't it clear by now that it is our fear of the future that has caused us to hang on to so many things we truly do not want? To become consistently happy you must learn to trust your present sense of peace more than the dictates of your anxieties. Buying sprees, overaccumulation, clutter, chronic disorganization, and such are the result of consistently deciding on the grounds of fear. A peaceful approach to life will not eliminate all mistakes in the terms that your ego judges mistakes; for example, you might throw out something that later you wished you hadn't; but a peaceful approach will allow you to be happier *now*—and there will never be a time when it is not now.

Although it takes a sustained effort to form the habit of listening for and choosing only our peaceful inclinations in all matters, this is indeed a quality of mind fully within reach. The prerequisite is the recognition that it is desirable. Exercises such as these in which the benefits of an imposed harmony can plainly be seen give weight to the alternative to chaos. It is not enough to begin seeing that our ongoing mental patterns are hurting us. An experience is needed to spark our faith in the existence of another way. That is why something so seemingly minor as bringing a degree of peace and order to our physical surroundings can become a rallying point for further extensions into more complex areas such as relationships. If it can just be seen that love is a possibility *anywhere,* even in reorganizing a room in a gentle and self-caring way, then the journey to the deeper realms of love has begun.

CHAPTER X

Your Body

Perhaps more than in any other direction we look to our body, and to our relationships with bodies, for a sense of happiness. It is these major areas of disappointment that we will take up in the next two chapters.

When the performance of our body fails to meet our need to be somebody, as inevitably it must, often our last and best hope appears to be in having children, or lots of friends, or employees, or supporters, or bodies in some other role that we believe can be relied on to finally realize our hopes in the world. Most relationships, even those with our spouse or children, cannot withstand this kind of pressure and fall away beneath the weight of what we expect from them. Whether the focus of our need is on our own body or on bodies in the form of relationships, we are misplacing our trust, and although we do not realize it, a loss of happiness is inescapable. There is indeed a limit to what the body can give us, and yet what we demand of it appears to have no bounds.

Seeing the Body As It Is

The world's present preoccupation with the body approaches hysteria. More poetically, it is reaching a state of "demonic frenzy, moping melancholy, and moon-struck madness," to borrow from Milton. Thin bodies, young bodies, beautiful bodies, bodies with lots of hair, bodies with super energy, bodies with glorious tans, bodies that look presidential, bodies that never show their age, bodies that can run impressive distances . . . This blur of images held up in acclaim before the public eye has created an almost total sense of unreality about a very ordinary and not so endurable piece of machinery, which everyone owns and almost no one can see. Very simply, we have made ourselves too afraid to look.

By cultivating impossible ideals we have been left paralyzed in dismay at our own hopelessly inadequate anatomy or, perhaps even worse, have sent ourselves racing blindly after some voguish physical prize that multiplies and scatters as we approach it. Understandably we do not want to look at how our body matches up. And so we don't look at all. Yet we truly do not need to be engrossed in all this madness, for it is irrelevant to happiness, or being loved, or anything else of enduring value. It is irrelevant even to feeling good. All we need is to recognize that our body *can* become our friend, but in order for it to assume this role, we must first see it as it is.

At present, anxiety is blocking our vision—for what horrors might we see if we did take an honest look? That our mouth size makes our smile insincere? that our inherited metabolism shortens our life span? that our voice is too high for us to be promoted? that the sport we have mastered is not cardiovascularly balanced? that our skin tone clashes with Nature? Or possibly that our body has suddenly gone out of style—for don't we observe that "refined" facial features are admired only to give way a few years later to faces with "more character." One moment the hair is to be wavy and of uniform color, next it must look naturally blond and straight, then overnight it should somehow become genetically curly. At present we must lose not five but twenty-five pounds, and even if we manage that, the bone structure of our legs and pelvis is all wrong and we will still not look svelte enough from a distance, even though up close we are patently anemic.

Perhaps more anxiety-provoking still is the current emphasis on super health, which, when added to the evidence we see daily that it is hard enough just staying alive, results, not too surprisingly, in our thinking of our body as a walking time bomb, or at least as a plain menace and time-consuming reclamation project that stretches drearily into the future.

Obviously the body is currently an unhappy subject. Not only must we keep pace with the world's ever-shifting ideal of attractiveness, desirable personality mannerisms, and meaningful physical attainments, but the stream of new and vital "facts" about the ways our body can torture and attack us has become a torrent that has thrown every breath, bite, and atmospheric vibration into question. We are told that our race subjects us to high blood pressure or skin cancer, our sex to uterine or prostate tumors, our age to whooping cough or stroke, our evenings out to car accident, our job to lung disease, our exercise to back pain, and our play to bad knees. And we are informed that the most reliable remedies for all these consequences are themselves very risky.

At a glance it certainly might seem best just to leave our two-legged tangle of disappointments and dangers completely out of mind. Unfortunately, we cannot separate ourselves from our own perception of our body, and our attempts to do so are merely keeping the dynamics of our pain in the shadows so that any real improvement in this area remains out of the question.

The Body Is Changeable

The body cannot be perfected but it can be changed. Its changeableness is its fundamental nature and the dominant rule of its reality. So if you are overweight and out of shape, your body is changeable. And if you are in the bloom of youthful loveliness, your body is changeable. It will not remain the same whether you are lethargic, droopy, and prepubescent or have great upper-body strength for your age and are presently graying distinguishingly at the temples. You may play a part in its future course or not, but nothing you do or neglect to do will anchor your body in permanence. If the body lacks value this attribute is one obvious reason, and yet it is also its changeableness that allows for hope no matter how much of a plague upon your mind some bodily condition has become.

Changeableness is not desirable, nor need it be fought, but it will most certainly be feared until the ancient human habit of longing sadly for what once was, or of trying to fend off an imagined future, is finally broken. People go through old photos and think that is how their body should still be. But does anyone *really* want to be ninety and look eighteen, the only person whose body never changes, a phenomenon unique in the world to be feared and stared at? Of course the answer is no, yet we persist in believing that because a particular stage was more attractive, more commanding of respect, more employable, etc., it was therefore good and right, which makes our present state wrong. Good and right to have the advantage? How very unhappy is this attitude. *The period in which the body can have all possible benefits is very short indeed, and to try to freeze it in time is disastrous to mental well-being.*

Perhaps the old photos show us obese or seriously ill. Then it will not be the past we regret losing but the future we dread, and to even consider our body at all makes us unhappy because of this fear it brings up that something might return. The body's future is not made more secure by our dwelling on its previous stages. It is cared for best when we know it very well as it now is and remain sensitive to its present needs.

The body we have at this moment is the only body we have. It was not nor will it be again what it is now. Our present body is the one we must finally come to terms with if we are ever to make this part of our world comfortable to live with. We simply do not *have* the body of five years ago, but undoubtably we are still reacting to those old images as if they were flesh and blood, and this is hurting our health, our energy, our appearance, our moods and a hundred other bodily aspects that have a history of influencing our happiness.

EXERCISE X-A

1. I want you to try a rather silly exercise. I want you to take off your clothes and stand in front of a mirror and *see* your body just as it is. Do not judge it. Do not recall how it once was or tell yourself what there will soon be more of that you can't escape. *See your body as one who truly loves you might see it,* with kind and gentle eyes. See it in the present.

2. After having a good and long look, close your eyes and begin taking inventory of your state of comfort. How does the body feel? Are there any places where the body hurts? Is there something that is not easy to live with that could be fixed? Are there recurring problems with certain parts?

You wish to see the overall well-being and comfort of your body and identify the particular areas of trouble that keep cropping up. Make a list of anything (the hips, something about the digestion, a sense of deterioration and neglect, the back) that tends to constantly come to mind as a problem as well as those aspects that seem relatively problem-free. There are of course preoccupations that are always shifting. It's the hair one day, the eyes the next, the stomach, the posture, the wrinkles, and so on. But if you will take a calm overview you should have little trouble recognizing the areas that are a recurring disturbance to your happiness and those that are not.

In this, as well as in #1, you want to continue regarding your body peacefully and sanely. Are you truly overweight or just not thin enough in terms of the prevailing insanity? Do not let your mind fall into its old preoccupations—"Is there a pouch on the hip?" "Is the bone structure good?" "Should my eyes be some other color?" "Am I too thin in places?"—for if you begin this kind of critiquing you will soon be unable to form the clear honest picture you very much need as a starting point.

3. Once you feel that you have written a thorough account of your body, sit quietly for a moment and let this gentle and truthful picture sink in. Remind yourself of the pointlessness of fighting the simple facts. This is merely your body. It is certainly not all there is to you, but for now this is what you have physically and you *can* live with it in peace. Actually you can live quite comfortably and happily with it if you will accept it as it is and let it be.

4. Letting your body be does not mean that you refuse to take steps that would help you feel more at ease in your body, whether this entails an operation, enrolling in a diet center, scheduling a daily walk, or having your hair permed. If you will not judge your body and not be afraid to hear your own counsel without first having to gather a hundred other opinions, you will begin to sense what to do that could help.

There is something in you that knows. So start by practicing acceptance, and follow this by practicing trust. *Practice knowing and you will know.* Only comparisons and judgments can block this thoroughly natural process. It is an indication of our current disorientation that this point would even need emphasizing, for what possibly could be more natural than for one to have a deep sense of how to care for one's own body?

After you have surveyed your body in a mirror and in your mind's eye, and after you have made your written inventory, take up one of the more chronic problems and look at it with your peaceful mind. By this point in the book you should have some sense of what this means, so use whatever ability to see that you have thus far developed. Then proceed in the usual way of opening yourself up to all options and choosing, with this same peaceful aspect of yourself, some first steps to try.

Write out a small program for putting this particular distress behind you, and then, without unnecessary soul-searching and worry, simply begin implementing it. Prove to yourself that it is not necessary to remain mired in *any* form of unhappiness.

The Purpose of the Body

In most people's lives the body functions as a background noise of varying unpleasantness—an anxiety, a burden, a source of regret. At first the body seems pure promise, a bright comet racing across the future. And for a time, in its changeableness, it appears to move toward the fulfillment of many vague anticipations. But what is expected of it is as insatiable as it is ill defined, and the body has not the resources to meet an ever-growing list of conflicting demands. Increasingly it appears to fail just when it is needed most. Thus it settles into its more permanent role, a thing to mistrust, a source of fear.

The body has only one true purpose, to be a servant to our happiness. It can fulfill this function perfectly if we will merely look at it calmly enough to see that it is not a great and magical servant but, once stripped of its adornments, humble and vulnerable and of limited strengths. The current overemphasis has distorted its wonders and its horrors but has not succeeded in transmuting it into anything other than what it has always been.

You need a degree of awareness of your core before you will begin to see your body in perspective, and building this inner sense has been the objective of many of the previous chapters' exercises. However, if you think it will make you happy to get all fixed up and be extraordinary-looking and then go to a party for the purpose of being seen, you are still confusing what we have been calling here the "ego" and the "heart." *Your body can serve your happiness by not interfering with your mind, but it cannot* make *you happy.*

The reserves of peace we carry into an event will determine how enjoyably we spend our time and not our muscle tone, array of jewelry, height of our heels, eminence of our name, or the pitch of our laugh. No matter how cute, severe, or "laid back" a body may be, it simply cannot manufacture an inner state such as happiness. Yet please observe that most of the world operates from the opposite premise.

Possibly you are like me and made some version of this mistake many times before you finally caught on that to present yourself to the world in ordinary terms rather than "daring to be different" creates far fewer distractions. *Dare to be ordinary and you will concentrate better.* There is precious little courage involved in striving to be special since this universal "need" is what makes the world go round, or, more accurately, chase its tail. It obviously is not a need at all but a tired old love affair that has never led home.

It should be no mystery why getting a great deal of attention does not satisfy us. The attention is directed at the body, not the self, and we feel somehow outside all the words and looks that swirl around us. Even though it can be very exciting, we feel somewhat abandoned and forgotten. But, once again, a degree of awareness is needed for this distinction to be seen. It should at least be recognized that part of us remains the same whatever is occurring to the body. Sometimes you will hear an elderly person say "My mind is as it was when I was young, but look at what has happened to my body. It is very hard for me to get used to this old body."

Several years ago I had been working on seeing through the various "charges" and prejudices I had about certain body types and came to realize that it was very difficult for me to look at *anyone* without making at least some small judgment. I decided to try an experiment. I explained what I had in mind to Gayle and asked if she would like to accompany me to Baskin Robbins in our pickup (sufficiently battered and run-down to be inconspicuous).

We parked close to the entrance and, after getting our cones,[1] sat in the truck and just watched the people go in and out. It was summertime, business was good, and every conceivable body type was there, old and young, fat and skinny, buxom and bald, in varying skin shades, and dressed in a surprising variety of attire. As each customer emerged I said to myself, "Is that a good body or a bad body? No, it's just a body."

What I expected to come of this was a degree of neutrality. The peculiarities and features of a body do not reveal what a person is at heart, and to see that fact with a little more honesty was all I hoped for, yet what occurred was entirely unexpected. I was suddenly flooded with love for these people. I began to see how innocent we all are in our little fleshly cos-

[1] Gayle: jamoca almond fudge. Hugh: rocky road.

tumes, that there is no harm in any of this, that in fact there is a certain richness, abundance, almost a blessing to the assortment of physiques that sprinkle the earth.

After awhile we backed out and started heading down Cerrillos Road toward home. In recent years the city of Santa Fe has begun beautifying Cerrillos, but in those days it was a place of cheap motels, little shops with no parking, and fast-food franchises. You could always find grounds for agreement with a new acquaintance at a party by deploring this exception to Santa Fe's historic charm. Possibly you can imagine my surprise when in the midst of our drive home I realized I *loved* Cerrillos Road. I loved the red SALE signs painted permanently on the store windows, the cars that were being forced to back gingerly out into traffic flow, the motels with masonry facades and frame sides. I even loved Long John and Colonel Chicken.

Love, just like judgment, cannot be confined. Whatever we turn our gaze upon is bathed in its gentle light, for love is the recognition that although the uses they are put to may be selfish, even cruel, the *things* of the world are guiltless—and our body is merely a thing. However we have used it in the past, it remains innocent and untainted. Once we put the body back into perspective and start looking at it honestly, our sensitivity to it increases and our concern and care for it becomes more constant.

EXERCISE X-B

This old exercise is one of my favorites. Maybe you are familiar with it also. It never fails to leave me feeling a little more sane. It is not proof of anything, just a means of having an experience. We confuse so many strange and silly things with our identity, our self, that any trick we can use to sort ourselves out becomes a valued aid to our happiness.

1. Sit comfortably and close your eyes. Relax your mind's grip on any concerns you may have, and in a restful and peaceful way, bring your attention into the present moment.

2. Free of any anxious need for specificity, but seeking only a growing *awareness* of an answer, begin asking yourself, "Where am I?" Repeat these words slowly and without fear.

3. Follow by asking yourself, "Am I in my hair?"[2] and pause for a gentle sense of the answer. "Am I in my eyes?" (pause). "Am I in my head?" "Am I in my brain?" "Am I in my shoulders?" In an easy and pleasant way, continue down the body with similar questions and pauses—"Am I in my torso?" "Am I in my heart?" "Am I in my hips?"—and so forth, making the questions as general or detailed as you wish.

4. When you have finished you will probably have an increased awareness of that part of you which is always you, regardless of age, haircuts, amputations, or any other bodily changes, and this awareness may possibly be quite strong. Even if it is slight, carry it with you as you rise and go about your day. And take notice of the little ways you begin departing from it.

How Do the Mind and Body Relate?

In order for us to be happy, what role should our mind take toward our body? It certainly should not be afraid of it, which is its attitude about the body on most occasions. If you found that you were able to do the above exercise enjoyably, in the

---

[2] The balder I get the less trouble I have with this one.

course of it your mind assumed its natural role of leadership. When the body is pushed forward to receive the benefits of life, if it is the body and not the mind which must be in a position to gain from your goals, you have set yourself up for inevitable loss because of the changeableness of the body. You want your enjoyment of life to eventually become steady and reliable and consequently you must not choose as your place of reward that which is inconstant. The body is innocent, it cannot help its nature, change is simply its governing law.

Whatever the body may not be, if taken in the present it is indeed a good servant. A good servant does not have to be anxiously watched over and second-guessed, for that would hurt his confidence and disturb his performance. Certainly instructions are needed and boundaries must be set, and out of simple consideration care should be taken that his tasks do not exceed his capacities and that he is generally pleased with the hours and working conditions. Similarly it is the mind's function toward the body to set the guidelines and then to permit the body to do its job in peace.

It is not only permissible but good to seek the body's overall comfort in very direct ways. A gentle, consistent discipline can add to its happiness as well as to the mind's because boundaries are in fact a symbol of caring. This is why such measures as working out an excellent diet and finding safe and pleasant ways to exercise often have a lifting effect on one's attitude and outlook. What hours do you keep? What kind of bed do you sleep on? Do you now need rubber gloves for dishes? Is there a better shoe? The reason we are reluctant to take the time or spend the money for improvements that would obviously make our body feel better is that we have a very old belief that because we are not consistent we do not deserve good treatment. But observe how much more difficult it is for you to be reliably kind when your body is disturbing you. You will think more highly of yourself as well as be a better friend to your

children and everyone else if you will act *as if* you are worthy
of your own love.

Whenever the mind becomes *anxiously* focused on the body
—does it look just right? does it smell right? is it thanked
adequately? does it get the best seat?—their natural roles are
reversed and the mind ceases to function as a calm overseer.
Have you noticed how often drivers speed up just a little when
you start to pass them on the highway? The four of us recently
took a vacation in a rented twenty foot RV that could do
everything except accelerate. This slight increase in speed on
the part of the car you are trying to pass becomes very noticeable when you are the size of a small house and in the wrong
lane. Why do people suddenly go faster than they want to?
Why do they break line at ticket counters, need more service
than others at restaurants, and (Gayle tells me) rush into the
beauty parlor unannounced for "a quick comb out" while you
are left sitting there with perm solution collecting precariously
on your eyebrows? It is because of the undue self-importance
they assign to their body, which is where self-importance must
be assigned since the mind does not exist on the level of these
petty competitions.

The purpose of the body is not to give the mind reason to be
distracted, and the purpose of the mind regarding the body is
not to constantly worry whether the body is receiving everything that is its due. The usual alliance of fear gives way to one
of harmony when the mind leads in certainty and the body
follows in peace. For this to happen the body must be treated
and thought of gently.

It must be clothed comfortably but not distractingly. It
must be fed in a way that its well-being is enhanced and pro-
tected and yet not so austerely restricted that it is imbued with
feelings of sacrifice and deprivation, which are themselves in-
disposing. It is unhappy to adorn the body, yet to neglect its
appearance so that it becomes unpleasant to look at is equally

unhappy. Letting the body go brings no true relief to the mind, nor is it satisfying to attempt to push it to enviable levels of health and energy. Neither should the body's safety be neglected or left to magic, as is so often done today in the name of a spiritual path. On the other hand to become fanatical about avoiding all conceivable mishaps is simply a miserable way to live.

All these familiar extremes in food, clothing, exercise, appearance, and safety disturb the basic friendliness and compatibility of the body and turn it into a mental annoyance. *A middle road can be walked whereby the body is comfortable in all respects and thus is not a preoccupation.*

To walk such a course in the present climate is difficult because of the excessive stands people are taking on every possible issue touching on the body. When Shrikrishna Kashyap first came to this country to practice medicine, a woman came to him with a mild stomach disorder and he suggested that she drink a little dill-seed tea each day. Two weeks later, when she came back, he asked how she was doing. "There hasn't been much improvement, I'm afraid. My stomach is not feeling very well." He was surprised to hear this. "Have you been taking the dill-seed tea every day?" "Oh yes," she said. "Well then, tell me what else your diet has consisted of." "Oh nothing else!" she assured him. "I have been drinking only the dill-seed tea."

This now being the general approach to life that surrounds you, you wish to stay alert to any tendency you feel to go to extremes. Gently decline to be influenced, and return instead to your own natural intelligence. It is possible, for example, to discover for yourself what combination of foods makes your particular body happy, gives it stamina, and allows it to sleep well, and what saps its energy, lowers its resistance, or stirs it up in some disagreeable way. If you will go about this sensibly and not rush the process, you can come to have a confident sense of what to eat and how to eat it. So, too, is it possible to develop a very pleasant and sure instinct of what to wear, whether to use makeup and other aids to appearance, when and how to exercise, what to do when ill, and which allowances to make for your age.

The happiest body is the one that does not stand out in either a negative or a positive way. It is a body that is comfortable with itself as well as comfortable to look at. Even a very elderly body can be gentle on the mind and on the eye if the mind that inhabits that body is at ease with the body's age and physical state. As we develop a loving sensitivity to our highly individual constitution we will become accepting of its changes, even of its illnesses and injuries, and also of the diminishing capacities that accompany advancing age. It is possible to be sick in peace, have one's period in peace, menopause in peace, grow bald in peace, become less sexually arousable in peace, and be quite old and withered in peace. The time will come when you will look in the mirror and know that the call to be the centerfold will never come, and that very afternoon you may be warmly praised by some member of the younger generation for making it up the post office steps. None of this *has* to cause anguish, but for it not to we first need to be genuinely at home with our body so that its changes in appearance and physical possibilities are not feared and denied.

Giving Form to a Decision

During the last few years of my thirties I set out to get into the best physical shape of my life by my fortieth birthday. I had been jogging since I was twelve, but only five or six miles a day; now I upped the distance to about three times that figure, and instead of running on dirt as before, I shifted to sand. I added daily calisthenics and weight lifting and I also became an authentic "health food nut." For a period of several years, at least a third of every day was taken up with this ill-defined quest.

One afternoon, a few weeks before I turned forty, I was on the final mile of my two-hour run when I suddenly found myself asking, "Why am I doing this?" I was surprised that I couldn't think of a single good reason. On the spot I stopped running, and for the next four years I did no exercise at all, ate whatever I desired, and gained fifty to sixty pounds (I don't know the exact figure because I also stopped weighing).

I probably would have continued in this way for many more years if my health had not started failing. I began getting more colds and flu, and they would hang on for weeks. One day, after having had a virus for over four months, Gayle once again asked if I would consider going to see a doctor she had confidence in who used some alternatives with which many MD's were not familiar. She furthermore suggested that we sit down and meditate about this.

I was born into a family with Christian Scientists on my father's side and generations of MD's on my mother's. Although that marriage did not last long, I nevertheless picked up two separate biases: one against doctors and the other against anyone who was not a "real" doctor. The man Gayle was suggesting was both unreal and a doctor. At this time in my life I was also giving occasional lectures and seminars on the uses of positive visualizations to facilitate physical healing, and so of course I thought I *ought* to be able to handle something so piddling as a flu virus. You can see that what Gayle had on her hands was a clear case of false dignity and prejudice. However, meditation sometimes has a way around ego attitudes, and by the time we got through I realized that I needed help and immediately got up and made an appointment.

Here I had been giving talks on the role our attitudes play in initiating or lessening bodily distress, but I was not prepared for the relief of symptoms I felt within seconds of completing this phone call. By acknowledging my pride and taking a step to discard it I had loosened, to a small degree, my mental grip on the illness. It is important that we give symbolic form to a decision, and the mere act of doing so is sometimes all that is required. More often, as in my case, a number of these steps are needed to put the problem completely behind us. *As long as we are receptive to trying new options our mind remains open to healing.*

If you wish to be happy in the world, you must sooner or later begin the process of translating that wish into worldly terms. It must have application within *all* the circumstances you encounter or else your true decision is to leave part of your life in misery. If you are like most people you probably do not believe you are deserving of even a moderate effort. Do not underestimate your desire to continue punishing yourself and others for the rest of your life. Do not underestimate your fear of happiness and the appeal of the rationale that *your* happiness is of too little consequence to act on.

What Are You Swallowing with Your Food?

Aside perhaps from the amount of rest we get, nothing we commonly do affects the comfort and well-being of our body more than what, and especially how, we eat. When I saw that the weight I had gained would have to come off, I first made a list of every food that I suspected I could eat in peace, those that were questionable, and those that I believed triggered anxiety for whatever reason. This list had nothing to do with calories, but only with my degree of mental ease while drinking or eating a particular substance. Then began a three-year practice of carefully watching my thoughts to determine my

actual fear level about everything I consumed. *The specific outcome we fear does not usually happen, but any fear we entertain will take form in our experience in some way and often in several.*
For example, if you are having dinner with friends and drinking "just one cup of coffee," even though you know that your particular system no longer handles coffee well, a line of thought is set off that very faintly undermines your mood and the ease and focus of your conversation (and thus the comfort of others at the table), as well as tenses certain muscles and triggers other anxiety symptoms, long before the caffeine has had a chance to work. Still to come is this slight but familiar feeling of depression and self-betrayal as once again you find it difficult to get to sleep and begin worrying about the ramifications of not being fully rested for tomorrow. Coffee itself is obviously not the problem, because many people tolerate it quite well, but if you can't take your coffee "straight," if you must always have it with fear, then the effects, even though slight, will be widespread, and when they are added to a hundred other anxiety-arousing ways you may have of treating your body, you can see that there is not a great deal of room left in your mind for simple happiness.
Fear is the core of most physical disturbances, and unless the treatment sought removes it along with the symptoms, it will only remanifest itself in the same or another form. This dynamic can be plainly seen in our eating habits. Consuming meals unconsciously and in a rush has become a Western preoccupation. Even though we may be strictly following some regimen, we are anxious about so much of what we eat that we ram it down quickly just to resolve the conflict. Now we don't have to look at it. It is gone. And then we tell ourselves this way of rushing through a meal is a virtue because there is some more important place that must be hurried to.
But just look at the results. The body does not feel fed. It

has no sense of having really eaten the food. It certainly has not been treated as a priority. It quite naturally feels hungry and deprived and can exhibit this upset in any number of ways. Meanwhile we have gained no clear idea of what foods are causing our trouble, because we have shunned our right to sensitivity, and in place of our capacity to know have at most substituted some shotgun approach by the latest authority.

People just don't understand why they have reached a state or an age when they can no longer eat the way they always have, and it seems an outrage. You know well the typical solution: to continue as usual and simply suffer. No wonder the later years are so universally miserable. A doctor (a real one) told me that his mother visited him a few years ago and that he knew in advance of her coming that she had developed arthritic symptoms in many parts of her body. He got together with his wife and children and they came up with the plan of going on what he believed was a good overall diet for this condition. After she arrived they all acted as if this were their regular way of eating. So for three months, without being especially aware of it, she had no red meat, little salt, very few eggs, lots of vegetables, rice, skim milk, and skim milk yogurt —in other words, a low-fat, high-vegetable diet supplemented with natural calcium.

By the end of her stay she had lost some of the weight that had been exacerbating her condition, but even more surprising to her, all arthritic symptoms had vanished except for one spot in her neck. She asked her son what in his medical opinion was the reason. Of course this was the moment he had been waiting for and he related how the whole family had agreed to change their usual way of eating just for her. He told me that she seemed very deeply moved—and then went back to Florida and resumed her old diet. "Naturally most of her symptoms came back within days," he said. "But you know, she's simply like so many of her generation. She thinks she would rather have two hours of eating pleasure and pay for it with twenty-two hours of pain and pills, and there is nothing I can do."

Indeed there is very little that can be done for most people regardless of age, and to try guilt or pressure only hardens their stand. They are simply not yet willing to face their terror of altering their diet, and it is best to let them come to this recognition in their own time. As with every other area of life, *we can prejudice a person against a good idea by introducing it too soon,* and especially by being righteous and insistent.

It is very difficult to stand by while others hurt themselves, but more than they need changes in diet, relationships, religion, or whatever, the people in our lives need our absolute and unwavering friendship. *Do not join them in it, but support your friends even in their mistakes.* In this way you will be teaching love rather than fear.

Don't be scared to touch your untouchable eating habits. We do not even know what we are afraid of, because the body *is* changeable, including its taste and appetite. I no longer *like* foods that I feel anxious about. I don't like the taste of fear. And after much practice and hard work I have finally grown fond of treating my body as a friend. A thought coats each bite we take, and once we are aware of it, this thought is noticeably appetizing or distasteful. Many reformed alcoholics have had the experience of accidentally tasting alcohol and being so surprised at their dislike of it that they could not understand why they ever thought it enjoyable. Because the body is changeable the stage of liking bad food and disliking good can be surprisingly short if you will gently persist.

Losing Weight

The perception that one is overweight is so universal that perhaps a few thoughts from a former fatty could be useful at this point. As I said earlier, it is first necessary to cut through all the current silliness on this subject and decide for yourself if you are genuinely overweight. You cannot do this by consulting the ever-changing charts, "pinching an inch," or measuring the flab content of your underarms. This will only give you someone else's idea of what the general population should look like. If you take nothing else from this chapter I hope you will have a stronger recognition of the desirability of patiently developing a sense of what is good for *your* body. Above all else you want to arrive at a place of faith and confidence in your own mind's ability to know how to read the body it inhabits—how to care for it and what to do to keep it comfortable and happy.

The question of weight is also a question of comfort. Does your body seem to function comfortably at its present weight?—not does it function perfectly, but does it function reasonably and adequately? Is your mind basically at ease about the long-term effects of your present weight? Perhaps you first need to have your heart, lower back, blood pressure, or gall bladder checked in order to put some question you may have to rest. If so, for the sake of your happiness get the answers and test results you need.

If the issue is more one of periodic self-consciousness and you know that you do not have a real weight problem, you can use dieting, just as you can use anything else, as a way of maintaining your mental equilibrium. If you wake in the morning feeling fat, cut back on breakfast. On the way to work if you pass a fellow who is lapping over the sides and you suddenly feel quite trim, then go back to your normal way of eating for lunch. At dinner you can either moderate or not, depending on what size your self-image is at that time. This way of proceeding is slightly insane to the world, which puts great emphasis on the *appearance* of consistency. But as I have pointed out before, you must choose between inner and outer consistency because there is no possibility of accommodating two such divergent values.

If it is clear that your overall comfort and strength would benefit from a definite weight loss, here are some suggestions I would make based on my personal and counseling experiences:

1. *As in all aspects of life your success hinges on your freedom from conflict about the goal.* In my opinion no one can take it for granted that he is free of conflict about what he perceives as a problem, and especially a chronic problem. I would strongly suggest that you first take at least two to three days to clarify and bolster your reasons for losing weight. It does not matter how convinced you think you already are. If you gained the extra pounds in the first place, and if you have kept them, you can safely assume that you are unconsciously conflicted about losing them. *Never attempt to guess why you are conflicted*—this is a great waste of time—merely strengthen your heart's desire to lose the weight. If you will do this *first,* you will eliminate much of the struggle and perhaps all possibility of failure.

Once a day, for twenty minutes, sit at ease and search your heart for every conceivable reason for losing weight. (During these days of consolidating your positive desires, continue to eat as usual.) Go over and over these ideas, thinking deeply about each one in turn, and deliberately encourage yourself with them. As usual, it is extremely important that there be no shadow of self-recrimination in any of this. See yourself as innocent. See your history as innocent. Be certain that you see your body as innocent. And then *know* that you wish to put this problem behind you.

The reasons you come up with will be very personal to you, and any reason that deepens your recognition that you want to take the weight off is a good reason. One person told me that while working on the conflict she realized that whenever she was thinking about her obesity she was not thinking about God, and so for her, freeing herself of conflict meant deepening her commitment to God. Another person told me that he suddenly saw what his chronic weight problem was doing to his family: how it hindered his play with the children, how it made his wife worry about his health. Since he knew that he was fully capable of doing anything—if it was for his family— his confidence was thus greatly strengthened.

2. Give yourself every option. Nothing needs to be done all at once, and nothing needs to be done in a hurry. Rush is a symptom of hating your body, and hate always hinders. So don't rule out a formal diet. Don't rule out going to a diet center, Weight Watchers, or Overeaters Anonymous. Often it is wise not to try to do it alone but to get help and have reliable support, especially if yours is a long-standing problem, because very often in these cases people lose their hope after the slightest setback or if the weight doesn't come off quickly enough and, in discouragement and defeat, dive back into their old ways of eating. Having a sense of being cared for, which a gentle group can provide, will often keep hope alive.

If you do decide to seek support, get help that is long-term and that will surround your efforts in a consistent atmosphere of goodwill and encouragement. Do not remain in a group in which you are being criticized or in one that is fostering guilt. If you decide to try a diet on your own, pick one that will be easy on you and your body, and also one that can lead to a permanent adjustment and not a diet that promises overnight results yet disregards your health and the stability of your life. *Haste wastes happiness.* I once asked an Indian swami about the advisability of using a microwave. "Tell me about these microwaves," he said. "What do they do?" "Well," I said, "they can cook an entire meal in five minutes!" He looked at me curiously. "But why would anyone *want* to cook a meal in five minutes?" Ah yes, why indeed?

3. Do not attempt to lose all the pounds at once. In fact, if you can form a very general goal rather than deciding on a specific number of pounds in advance, you will remain more sensitive to your body and avoid setting yourself up for dejection. For instance, do not try to lose a hundred pounds. Lose a few pounds, take a look, see how you feel, then perhaps lose a few pounds more, and so forth. If you reach a weight that feels good, do not be afraid to try it out for a few weeks before going on. During the two and a half years I lost my sixty or so pounds, I did this several times, once staying at one size for four or five months before I was *certain* that I wanted to lose some more. These breaks and calm reassessments tend to prevent the conflict from reentering your mind and halting your progress altogether.

4. Form a good plan and stick with it. Do not jump from diet to diet. If a way that is *clearly* better comes to your attention, or if your present approach is found to be inadequate after a fair and thorough trial, then sit down and make an unequivocal decision about what to do. It is the degree of certainty you bring to a plan, and not the particulars of the plan itself, that will determine its effect. Therefore, choose some adequate program and simply begin, and remind yourself frequently to have confidence in it and not to think or speak against it.

5. Do not eat with a sense of fear. Look at the food that is consumed. Look at each thing carefully. Chew and swallow in peace. Perhaps it would be helpful to mentally surround the meal in light before you start, or to take several deep breaths, or to surround the contents of your stomach in light afterward. Do not be afraid to use any trick that lessens anxiety, because the problem, especially if it is chronic, is held in place by fear; it is a pattern of fear that has become established in the mind and has taken on a life of its own. But without more fear to nourish it, it will die.

Whenever the fear comes you need to have something else to turn your mind to, something that will take you physically out of the home perhaps, or some other effective way of redirecting your thoughts, such as calling a person in your support group. One device that helped me was that whenever I had a sort of anxious sense of appetite—and yet I knew I was not really hungry—I would sit down for a minute or two, calm my mind, and slowly drink a glass of water. This kind of "hunger" passes so quickly that almost any break will work if it is preplanned. For some people a specific imagery can help, such as picturing the brain and the agitated parts of the body being drenched and washed out with a thoroughly fear-cleansing liquid or light.

The Body as Pet

There is now a trend, some of it within the spiritual and new age movement, to identify less with the body. Unfortunately this has an effect that is opposite to what is wanted. Instead of increasing communication with our deeper self and bringing into sharper focus the part of us that is not always changing, it tends to confuse our sense of identity and set up little wars within the mind. For the time being at least *the body is part of the mind and the mind cannot remain peaceful while denying what the body genuinely needs.*

The key to a happy body is to treat it like a pet dog. If we project our emotions onto our pets, we respond to them inappropriately, but if we look closely at them and identify with what they are truly feeling and thinking, we can be of comfort to them and consequently they become little gifts of affection and funniness to us.

If you are like most people, you have a far more balanced conception of how to treat your dog than your body. You can love your dog today, but you cannot love your own body because you are waiting for it to be different. By not being afraid of your dog you have given him the gift of seeing him as he is. You know that on summer nights he likes to be in the fenced backyard where he can practice defending you in his highly vocal way, without worry of being challenged. Perhaps in the winter you put him up at night on an old blanket in the corner of the kitchen, or maybe you get him his own doggy cushion printed in blue and green bones. You don't wash his bedding too often because you know that he likes things that are well worn and have a familiar smell. Neither do you insist that he sleep on the king-size bed while you take the couch. This would distress him greatly, and he might end up on top of you, licking your face and asking for forgiveness.

You are acquainted not only with his pleasures but also the diameters of his health and constitution, so you feed him a good but simple diet. You don't scrape just anything into his bowl, nor do you thaw out every cut of meat in the freezer and pile it around him just because he would think this very exciting. You know that these kinds of indulgences could make him feel sick.

You are familiar with his psychology and how to use it. You have noticed that a few consistent "no's" and a degree of discipline make him happier, and so every now and then you order him to shake hands and then pat him enthusiastically and tell him what a good boy he is. You see his limitations well. You keep him off the highway and far from skunks and porcupines. You brush him and exercise him and take him to get his shots, and you do not expect him to understand why. There is no war in this relationship with your dog because there is neither neglect nor a battle for perfection. He is just a dog, and he is your dog, and so you love him and guide him and treat him fairly, and in return he is your innocent friend and harmless companion. And as long as you have it, why must your body be anything less?

It Is Innocent to Be Sick

In this chapter we have already discussed several ways that we often refuse to look at the body, accept it, and treat it gently. Perhaps at no time are these practices more flagrant than when the body is ill. Our definition of what it means to be sick has become increasingly narrow, and this is a reflection of our tendency either to denigrate or romanticize the body, but never to see it clearly. Having a cold or flu is being sick, but to be unhappy or afraid is not. Bone cancer from radiation received at work is considered an illness but damaged legs and hips from skiing or jogging is not. I was once at a party and a man who owned a large motorcycle saw the bandage on my forehead and asked if it was a dirt-bike injury. "No," I said, "I had a small tumor removed." I watched his estimate of my character instantly plummet.

It is unnatural for one to be sick because sickness itself is looked down on as unnatural. Anger, on the other hand, which can resemble an emphysema attack, is treated as a sign of courage and self-respect. Somehow the illness, whatever it is, should not be happening to us. Even though we live in a world of sickness, *we* should not be sick, and if we are, someone is to blame. Maybe a friend was negligent and selfish while contagious; maybe we somehow "chose" the illness; maybe there is someone who is a negative influence; maybe it is the fault of the FDA, the AMA, the dairy lobby—our ego can never settle on where to place blame permanently. It is certain of one thing only: blame must be placed. Small wonder then that we limit so absurdly what we call sickness, and that when we can no longer escape even our own arbitrary definitions we try to run away from our sick body and out from under the time of our sickness: "When will this be over?" "Why did this happen to me?" In the course of thinking these thoughts we once again do not *look* at our body; we mentally avoid it and oppose it and never wholeheartedly give it time to rest and heal.

As I sit writing this, Jordan (sixteen months) is having a typical delayed reaction to his first measles-mumps-rubella shot, and John has a mild case of a flu that is going around Santa Fe. Some would think that Gayle and I were to blame for John's condition because two days ago we took him to a birthday party even though it is the height of flu season, and that it would be appropriate for us to feel guilty. Some would also, and even more stridently perhaps, believe that we were the cause of Jordan's feeling bad. There are authorities and their followers who advocate never giving shots and those who say always give them. More often than not both sides believe that any who do not do as they warn deserve all the consequences they get, and not surprisingly many of them are secretly glad when the child gets sick because this appears to prove the position they have identified with.

These are miserable lines of thought that Gayle and I studiously avoid getting caught up in either by defending our position or by urging it on others. *The fact is that we do not know.* Who really does? So we admit this to ourselves and make the best choice for our children that we can. Although we never *know* what the future will bring, we, like every other

parent, have available to us a peaceful preference about what
to do at the moment. This we can always feel when, together,
we dwell on our love for our children rather than on our many
noisy fears of making a mistake.

Earlier I said, "Practice knowing and you will know." It is
good to distinguish between these two kinds of knowing because much of the world's unhappiness comes from lumping
them together. We can always *know* what we *believe* in the
present, and this form of knowing can be practiced until it
becomes a calm and steady certainty. Gayle and I did not
know what the results of the birthday party and shots would
be in advance, but we sat down together long enough beforehand to discover what we *believed* was the most loving option
for each child. It is always possible to become quietly sure of
one's beliefs, but it must be remembered that this way of making a decision cannot magically place its hand upon the future.

It is our desire to somehow see our way *through* that blocks
our present knowledge of our beliefs. We all very naturally
wish to protect ourselves from making a mistake and so avoid
blame, but mistakes and blame—as the world perceives them
—truly do not matter. Remember that your goal is now happiness and that this state of mind is constituted of kindness never
delayed but exercised always in the present—not what merely
looks kind but what feels kind in your heart. You cannot seek
to be perceived as right by the world and at the same time be
gentle to yourself and others because these goals apply to different times. You can be right in the future, but you can only
be kind now.

Kindness toward children is the same as toward relatives,
friends, and strangers. It is a touching of hearts, an acknowledgment and an embracing of a common bond, a *seeing* of no
differences. It is the gesture of the inner spirit and as such will
not be judged by the future, for it is only felt and received now.
In this case of birthday party and shots, the one factor that we

had in hand and did not have to guess at was our love for our children and our desire to protect and care for them, and it is because we work very hard indeed to make this factor the deciding one that our children are happy today, even though today they are sick. Very simply, putting this consideration first means more to them than our being right.

Being Sick Naturally

Frequently children can be sick with more happiness than adults because they do not get entangled in guilt, panic, blame, worry, and other pointless turmoils. They are simply sick. Jordan and John would no more think of faulting themselves or us for their present symptoms than it would occur to them to assign guilt to being out of breath from running, feeling groggy at night, having weak arms after carrying a heavy load, experiencing chills from certain noises, being blinded by headlights, or any number of other symptoms of the body's limitations accepted by the world as "perfectly healthy." They have not yet taken illness out of context and consequently their minds are relaxed enough to adjust to it when it comes. Being at ease with an illness is also an attainable state for any adult.

Most adults see nothing unnatural about their body being temporarily younger, stronger, more smooth-complexioned, or more eye-catching than other bodies, and do not feel compelled to conceal these disparities. Yet they are reluctant to call in sick. In contrast, most little children think nothing of stopping abruptly in the middle of play and telling their playmates, "I have to sit down now, I have a tummy ache today." As yet they have no silly healthier-than-thou self-image to uphold at all costs.

Children are also happier because they seek no special meaning in illness. We who are supposedly wiser believe we must find great significance in the way we get sick. Before they run off, his playmates do not counsel the little child with the tummy ache to work on his unwillingness to digest new situations. Yet let the average new-age adult get sick and he feels he must torture himself with books, articles, and snatches of conversation that relate every known character trait to some infirmity. No longer does a person have simple constipation; the individual is now tagged as emotionally repressed. Gallstones point to latent hostility, sore throats to being uncommunicative, and lower back pain to fear of money.

It is not that there could never be such connections in individual cases, but it should be obvious that these formulas are so generalized as to be meaningless. And what real purpose do they serve? I heard another one just today. A friend went to a seminar and told me the speaker said that cancer was an inability to love. In my work I have known many cancer patients and this statement is completely untrue to my experience. I don't even know if that is what the speaker said, but I do know it is what is being repeated, and understandably so because of the general interest in these new ways of classifying people. Is it realistic to think that the promulgation of this concept will result in cancer patients becoming gentler and more loving people? Will it deepen the bond between them and their nurses, therapists, and doctors? Will it add to their peace and lessen their misery?

When you get sick it is good to become like a little child, to not mark time but concentrate on the moment at hand, to be completely and unresentfully responsive to your body's needs, and not to confuse your mind and agitate your body with unanswerable questions about what this "really" means. It means that you are like every other person who occasionally gets sick, and that in a world of sickness this is natural. An illness is simply our body's way of calling for a halt, of calling for rest, and in addition it is the egos' age-old way of withdrawing. To stir up our body with reasons for shame and to further increase our sense of alienation by filling our mind with still more questions as to why we are separate, different, and alone in the world will merely deepen and prolong the illness. So instead, be quietly and comfortably sick.

Never ask yourself why you got sick. It is an interminable question. Simply look at the illness carefully and then do the things and take the remedies that will make this one day a little easier. If this means bed and a good book, let it be this without guilt. Have no fixed belief or even interest in when it should all be over. Set no goals, think no thoughts that put you at odds with your condition as it is this very instant. Be a child again and remain sick in the present.

The unhappy part of your mind is always trying to get you to do what you need not be doing in the present. If you are ill it is always best to cut back on everything you can and to arrange the situation so that you can be as comfortable and peaceful as possible. Many are reluctant to spend the money that would get them the assistance they could use, and so they end up feeling burdened and resentful. It is better to spend money than to retreat deeper into fear and separation, or if one does not have the funds, to ask a relative or friend to help out for a time. So often there is indeed someone who would be glad to help, in fact would feel loved by being asked. Trading away your longer-term peace of mind to save yourself the temporary embarrassment of asking for help is a poor bargain.

Do not carry on as if you were not sick; this is arrogant, not noble. There is no logic in punishing or pushing your body just because it is ill. Once again, illness is *not* evidence of some character deficiency that you need be harsh with yourself about or run from like a secret sin. So do not become alarmed and begin chasing about for an all-encompassing remedy or rush around trying to shake the illness as if it somehow could be ducked out from under. Be honest with yourself quickly.

You are sick. Then resolve to be thoughtful and generous to your body. Many people are now afraid to take medicine, thinking it is a sign of weakness, and when they do succumb they tend to overdose themselves, trying to eradicate every last telltale symptom of the shameful state. Use medicine as a kindness to your body, to comfort it in the present but not to force it. Make these periodic illnesses—whatever they may be or however you may fit into the national average for having them—a time like all other times—just another opportunity to practice gentleness of thought and action, and you will prove to yourself that it is possible to be happy even while sick.

Life-threatening Illness

Very often when people learn that they have a life-threatening illness they become profoundly confused, and sometimes even physically disoriented, because they unconsciously believe that they have been singled out for special punishment and, quite naturally, they do not understand. The disease appears to have picked them from thousands, and there seems to be no sound reason why they were selected. And indeed there *is* no reason, and no authority or book has ever succeeded in making it completely and finally understandable to anyone. If it were genuinely understandable it would also be reasonable, and in what conceivable way is it reasonable to find yourself in pain and dying of a rare disease?

Although people with a life-threatening illness cannot be expected to recognize this at first, they hopefully will see very early on that to continue pursuing this question of "Why me?" is to enter a dark and hopeless pit from which it can sometimes take a very long time to pull themselves out. Any line of thought that leads inevitably to guilt is of no use to you, for it will merely increase your sense of misery and so distract and disorient you that you will not be as sensitive to needed steps as you might otherwise be. *It is never helpful to "assume responsibility" in the sense of taking on blame.* Attack in any form is neither responsible nor truthful, and yet criticism and guilt are frequently more prevalent in cases of life-threatening illness because of the bewilderment those involved are often thrown into. It is not more honest to blame or more humble to feel guilty. These attitudes are unworthy of you. They will not relieve your mind and they will never truly succeed in rallying your friends to draw close. So do all you *can* do to direct your mind into more helpful channels.

Because confusion over the true cause of the illness is so common during its early stages, the individual, above all else, needs to get into a very calm and peaceful state—as calm and peaceful as is possible—and try to begin seeing what steps he wishes to take. As in all other matters, every option should be considered. If done without panic this will bring a small measure of relief into the mind as it becomes increasingly clear that indeed there are a number of courses available.

Do not be afraid to try or not to try anything. This is your body and you are free to proceed as you choose. So look at your disease with your peaceful instincts. Freeze the situation in calmness and examine it carefully. Then open yourself to all possible alternatives and begin with whatever first steps you find are the most comfortable ones to think of taking.

It is never a good idea, and this is especially true during the period just after learning that you have a life-threatening illness, to begin indiscriminately mentioning your situation to others. Very few people can resist the urge to warn and advise. One or two people in whom you have deep confidence could possibly be confided in, but you wish to avoid the inevitable confusion that comes from just *hearing* contradictory opinions. Do not assume that you are beyond being influenced by very well-meaning people in just this way because conflict can enter your mind almost unnoticed and suddenly you find your-self doubting your own peaceful knowing and do not under-stand where your uncertainty came from. *Confusion comes from worrying about making a mistake rather than being open to taking a step,* and very often the advice one gets from rela-tives and friends is tainted by their quite natural anxiety and will agitate and fragment your mind rather than calm it and focus it.

Follow a course that is your course. If you wish to die in peace, that is your right. If you want to try many approaches, to do everything medically that you can, this also is your right. To first inform yourself is fine and can be a definite part of coming to your own way, but you do wish to monitor carefully your tolerance for new articles and pronouncements. Remem-ber that these will never stop. There will never be a final an-nouncement made on which all minds suddenly agree, and so you wish to chart your own course through all of this, taking what information illumines your way and not fearing to de-cline to read more once you are settled on an approach.

If you have great confidence in a particular doctor or some-one else in a position to guide you, then it is best to begin with this person and to listen deeply to what is said. After you have received the counsel, take it into your heart and gently arrive at your own decision. Frequently an individual will reach a peaceful decision but then it is thrown and tossed about in his mind, he talks about it to others, he receives a new article, and very shortly he is again dismally uncertain and confused. Please observe that these bulletins, articles, and so forth con-flict dramatically. It is essential that you plot a course within all these opinions that is your own course, your own way. Do not be afraid to trust yourself, to think your own thoughts, and to walk gently and easily toward your goal, whether this is to go all out to heal the condition, to learn to live with it in peace, or to die in an atmosphere of your choosing. Honor your heart in all ways, and your choices will be good and kind to all.

We Are Not Alone

Fear is the great companion of all illness. There is always a tendency to withdraw into that fearful part of oneself, to shrink inwardly into a frightened little object and to be one who is alone. Plotting one's own course does not mean diving into martyrdom, loneliness, and isolation. As I mentioned before, the ego involvement we all have in illness, any illness, is always a form of withdrawal, or, more precisely, a withdrawing into our unhappiness and a withdrawal of our love from others, regardless of whether our outward contact with them remains the same or is increased.

In learning to develop and trust your own instinctive knowledge of your body and what it needs, and thereby becoming less dependent on the inconsistent opinions of the world, you will actually develop a stronger rather than a diminished bond with other people, because your bond with everyone is found rather than lost within your own basic nature and knowing. Even in being less open to relatives' and friends' surface anxieties and advice, you should have a sense of joining them on this deeper level, of overlooking their fears and siding with the real love behind their gestures.

If your illness requires that you rest and be physically alone, as most illnesses do, then hold your loved ones closely to your heart. Do not let guilt over your condition, or false pride, create within you vague feelings of distance and estrangement between you and *anyone,* for this is *never* a necessary part of being sick. You will find that it is often easier to see beyond other people's weaknesses when they are not around, so take advantage of the perspective that your physical isolation affords you by resting easy with any relationship that may come to mind.

In any discussion of the body it must be remembered that if we become engrossed with how we differ from everyone else we automatically lose sight of the deeper connections that bind us all, and we can even come to believe that they do not exist. The desire for happiness, for simple peace, is a continuous stream running through the core of every person and joins us all in one unseen family. Again and again our heart calls us to come back to our love for each other, to remember our oneness, and to treat as we would be treated. By recalling our debt of gratitude to all who touch our life we do more to promote our health and to lend a sense of well-being to our body than any procedure, exercise, or regimen that could be performed without love. So many of the things we do for our body are carried on as if we existed in a vacuum. This is true even within teams, exercise groups, jogging clubs, and the like, where so often there is the form of joining but not its heart content. This is needless and sad waste.

EXERCISE X-C

You will live to see everyone you now know die, or they will live to see you die, and this simple fact puts the body's value into perspective. If we have nothing more than this to hold out to each other, our reasons for despair are boundless. So let us once again turn our gaze on the human heart, our core of commonness, for it is there that something else can be recognized. Is there indeed any part of us that does not live and die alone, that does not wear out its welcome, that is capable of peace and knowing, that can feel loved and give love in freedom? No exercise can establish it as a reality, but a persistent openness to seeing beyond the surface of things will always increase vision. So the key, as ever, is in the trying. Let us then try once again to experience the level on which all living things join.

You must realize that you will be attempting to pass beyond the very foundation of the world's unhappiness, and so it is not realistic for you to expect easy and dramatic results, but a little gain now will remain with you for a very long time.

The unrelenting image that the world holds up for all to gaze upon is the image of separation—everything standing apart and no realistic hope of all hearts beating as one. Whenever you get caught up in even the most trivial of worldly problems you will instantly take its picture of reality to heart and suffer loneliness in some form. The problem will cry out, "Are you separate? Are you separate?" Learn *not* to answer this question, for only one small obsession with the world will be sufficient to "prove" that indeed you are.

A person can feel separate in a crowd, with a group of friends, even in the midst of a large family. *Loneliness is not a friendless state; it is the major symptom of the world.* It is the unavoidable price of taking the terrain one presently travels too seriously. The world does not work and this still seems to surprise us. The feelings of not ever being completely understood, of having to be wary of using up other people's goodwill, of being saddled with certain relationships, of having too much to do and having to do it by oneself—these emotions are a constant and almost universal undercurrent to thought, and stem from placing great stock in how things go for us instead of how deeply rooted we are in our core. Yet if there is no real awareness of the core itself and what it implies, no other outcome can realistically be expected.

We will not first believe in a place of quiet within us and *then* experience it. We must have an experience first, and then another, and another, until our faith in its reliability and its locality begins to flower. A distant light is dimly seen, but not quite believed. Nevertheless it is walked toward. And with each step it grows brighter. There is no mystery to this process. The following exercise could be such a step.

Once in the morning and evening, for five to ten minutes (longer only if you can do so without tension), silently and slowly repeat these words: "I am gentle. I am peace. I am one."

As you say this try to become gradually aware of a place in you that the words point to, a place of utter stillness and peace, the one part of you where there is no loneliness.

While continuing to repeat the words, let this little spot of stillness grow. Let it expand. Watch it bloom. But do not *want* it to grow, and do not expect it to. You are simply focusing on a reality, and as you do so it naturally becomes more obvious. Merely experience whatever you are aware of without measuring or judging a thing. Remember that you do not know this part of you well, so you are not in a good position to calculate what it should be doing for you now.

What you do not yet believe is that this part of you is you. You are you, and because of that simple fact, you are not alone. Isn't it obvious that an experience is badly needed? So do this little exercise faithfully for two weeks.

CHAPTER XI

Relationships

What We Have a Right to Expect

I have spoken often in this book of the little part of us that is always looking in the wrong places for happiness, or possibly it would be better to say, is always looking in the wrong *way* for happiness, because, potentially, happiness can be had any place, with any person, under any circumstance, provided it is carried and gently laid there by the seeker and not grasped for as if to fill an emptiness. In no place is happiness sought more hopefully and dashed more consistently than within relationships, and still we continue to see in them our ultimate delivery from a wilderness of pain. This is doubly tragic because our insight into the potential of relationships is actually well grounded, but it is as if over and over in life we walk into a room of extraordinary beauty and peace, our room, set aside for us, overflowing with the riches we long for, and each time come away with nothing, perplexed and angry and resolved not to try again.

And yet there is this feeling of not knowing where else to turn. With a new relationship at least one has hope. It seems that an aging man can be renewed by a young woman, an aging woman renewed by a young man. That a husband and wife who are not happy together can be renewed by a baby. That a child can be renewed by a pet. The expectation placed on the new body—the new friend, the new doctor, the new spouse—is so great that very soon, perhaps only in little ways at first, it fails to live up to what we wanted. The pet is not cooperative; the doctor makes a mistake; the newfound friend is discovered to hold the wrong political views; the baby will not sleep through the night. Disillusionment gradually sets in and soon the person or animal must be turned from in some way in order for us "to keep our sanity."

It seems impossible to expect that this pattern could ever be reversed. And yet it is possible. As with all dynamics, we must first see very clearly how we participate. Until our part in these little dances of doom is recognized, we will continue blaming the new body, whatever its description, for the failure *this time,* and be tempted to run after still one more relationship to save us.

What we expect of a relationship before it begins sets up an initial disappointment and ultimate failure. Many children come to have a very narrow range of toys they expect adults to give them, and when someone does not know what the acceptable gifts are, a child can show sharp disappointment upon opening a present, even though later, after giving it a try, that toy might become the child's favorite plaything. Here it can be seen that expectations are based on the past and are blind to the present. The child has had fun with robots and so now his first board game looks like no fun and downright ugly.

It is a mistake of course to turn against a present because it is not what one expected, but it is a tragic mistake to reject a person for this reason. Although children learn to prejudge toys fairly soon in life, it is usually only much later that they start this with other children, and consequently they are often able to play happily with an unknown group at a park or playground with very little time needed to "warm up" to them. Children play well with strangers because they have no thoughts about what it all means. They don't worry about where the relationships are going. Many adults are as afraid of getting along too quickly as they are of immediate dislike, because they believe these emotions imply something about the future—a burden that must be avoided or an opportunity that must not be lost.

Adults have long since learned the unhappy lesson that they should size up a new person before opening their hearts completely.[1] Unfortunately the sizing-up period never ends because the ego is incapable of deciding when the point of total trust has been reached. There may still be some undetected weakness there that could rise up and injure one, so it is forever best not to love too much. The ego rationalizes judging as necessary to avoid the potentially dangerous entanglement, but most people are not genuinely dangerous, and the ability to see clearly another's capacity to do us harm is actually lessened by our attempts to judge that person.

Forming an enthusiastic first impression is always an equal possibility, and this can be as blinding as the many negative first impressions we are always having to reform. Judgments do not look, they compare, and *all expectations are a judgment.* There is no relationship, whether between a parent and child, between two couples, or between an animal and a person, that expectations will not undermine.

[1] Naturally, opening one's heart does not imply opening one's home, one's purse, one's front door, or any other action. Being a component of happiness, acceptance is purely mental.

The parent has expectations of the child, but the child also has expectations of the parent. The parent is to provide the perfect childhood, and of course the child does not even know what this is or should be. As children grow older their ideas of what is needed constantly change, and later as adults they are uncertain whether to denounce or be thankful for the conditions under which they grew up.

The expectations that the parents have of their child are perhaps more conspicuous. It should look a certain way; definitely it should be intelligent and try hard in school; it should have many friends and be pleasing to adults as well, and so forth—whatever the values of the parents are. Even with a new baby there are these same souring expectations: It should not hiccup too much in the womb, it should come out easily, it should be the right sex, it should sleep through the night, it should nurse or drink its little bottle well, it must not have colic or unsightly rashes.

Much is also expected of a new relationship between an individual and an animal, and even of a fish taken into the home. A pet must fulfill the needs of the entire family, and this is obviously very difficult for it to do. It must behave, especially when there are guests, and of course it should cooperate in being quickly housebroken. A new fish must not give signs of dying, even though that is what some fish seem to do best. It should live happily in the water, eat the food it is given, and be attractive. If it hides away too much there is obviously something wrong with it.

Certainly great expectations are placed on a new friendship, and even more so if it is a romantic one. The long-term relationship is highly valued by the world, although at present it is very chic to be fearful and overly cautious of forming even short-term ones. Friends discuss these liaisons incessantly and tell each other they must not remain in a relationship that demands too much. Thus for one to have many superficial relationships that have the appearance of both depth and "freedom" is in vogue now, and this sets up the curious expectation that the new friend should not try to be too much of a friend. In romantic relationships just where to draw this line causes constant strife, especially since in the back of the participants' minds is the counter ideal of wanting to experience the one invulnerable love, the great love of one's life.

There is this myth that somehow a special few can have a lifelong union in which they stare meaningfully into each other's eyes, hang upon each other's words, and are thrilled by each other's touch year after year. There is much pretense at this and articles are written about how to maintain this type of relationship, how to add new mystery and spice, and giving rules for ways to draw back the other person and hold him or her spellbound and in love with you forever. The expectations thus created are very sad because they are so far off the mark that they tend to drive wedges between people who had a perfectly fine relationship before one of them got carried away with an impossible ideal.

EXERCISE XI-A

An expectation is looking for something rather than looking at something. We anticipate one thing and do not clearly see the other thing that is at hand, and because what we anticipate is not there, we place a veil of mourning and loss over all that lies beneath our gaze. If you could but look at it and want nothing, this day could comfort you and make you glad far beyond what you expect. You expect too little when you want only another version of the past. Discard fantasies and open your heart to reality. This is indeed feasible, but first you should assume that, unless you have already done the specific work involved, every relationship you presently have is to some degree obscured by what you expect of it. And, secondly, it is crucial to your happiness that you understand that expectations, like cataracts, must be removed; there is no way to see around them.

1. Set aside fifteen or twenty minutes and during this time take up only one relationship, perhaps the one that is presently receiving most of your attention from day to day. Mentally stand this person before you and look very carefully at everything that comes to mind. Search each thought for expectations, for how you *want* this person to be, and write these down as you uncover them. Consider his or her body, occupation, personal mannerisms, past and present behavior, selection of friends, dress habits, state-of-the-world opinions—anything at all that you associate with this individual.

Whenever you feel a tinge of irritation or disapproval, you can be sure that you have an underlying expectation. If, for example, you are considering one of your parents and are recalling, say, a recent phone call, if during or after the conversation you now remember being upset about something that was said, you must realize that you expected your mother or father to somehow be different. Naturally this could be a very long-standing expectation. The fact that people prove over and over that they are not a certain way does not lessen our wish that they were. Very few individuals stop clinging to their tired old expectations of what role their child or parent should have played in their lives. One can also have quite enduring expectations of a past employee, of one's therapist, or of how one's wife or husband should behave. A divorce, followed by years of absolute estrangement from the ex-spouse, will often have very little effect on the anger felt over how he or she should have been.

2. If you find it difficult to become aware of the expectations you have of the person you have selected for this exercise, you might try the old Gestalt therapy technique of pulling up a chair and then vividly picturing this individual sitting in it. With your eyes either open or closed, tell this man, woman, child, or even animal, exactly what you want of it. Speak straight from your heart and hold back nothing. You can do this silently, but if that does not make the person seem real enough in your imagination, try saying it all out loud.

When you feel finished it is very important that you physically get up, sit in the other individual's chair, mentally become that person in every way you can, and answer yourself back.[2] This will show you that to have expectations of others generates in them opposing expectations of you. An even more important effect will be the possibility that you will sense more deeply the common core, the gentle bond, which exists between the two of you. If you feel an unreasonable reluctance to switching chairs it will be because of this possibility.

3. The easiest way to have no expectations is to identify and discard them before the relationship begins. This is often feasible. A baby is due, the family decides to switch dentists, one sees the need for a watchdog—and so a list can be made and added to of what is *already* expected of this upcoming relationship. Then the mind must be carefully watched for any signs of disappointment or judgment once contact begins.

4. Once your expectations are identified you must lift them from your mind so that the relationship can be experienced in the present. This discarding process cannot be compromised. For example, no matter what erasing technique you used, if

[2] Some people find it helpful to shuttle back and forth between chairs until everything has been said on both sides. You might think of this as your acting out a dialogue between you and the individual. Notice that as you proceed a gradually increasing level of understanding and sympathy develops and your initial stands and judgments begin to weaken. The resistance that I mention above, which you may experience quite strongly, comes of course from not *wanting* to understand and feel at one with the other person.

you were to continue describing to others what you had to endure as a child, there is no conceivable way you could see your parents as they actually are today. So the first and most obvious means of freeing your mind of expectations is to stop complaining or telling witty stories about your ex-spouse, your new housekeeper, your teenager, or the people down the street. *Your mind will not accept a new truth while your conversations continue to deny it.*

5. One very simple and direct method for relinquishing expectations is to bring the person to mind and then go down the list you have made, saying with each item:

"__(name)__, I no longer want __(specific expectation)__.
I want *nothing* from you. You are free."

Say the words until you can sense that you mean them. Do not expect your first efforts to have permanent results. Expect nothing. Merely do the work, every day if necessary, until no vestige of these expectations remains.

With children, and especially with a new baby, it will be a little easier to complete the work if the parents do it together. Frequently *both* parents have an unconscious expectation that a mother should be able to do everything an infant requires, and as a consequence of this attitude and of the physical setback caused by the birth itself, very often the mother is deeply exhausted for the first year and therefore can very much use this form of mental support from her husband. *There is great power in agreement.* The specific expectations do not have to be agreed upon, only the need that both parents look at their child with freshness and softness. Children of all ages are extremely sensitive to their parents' unfulfilled anticipations and are utterly helpless to satisfy these. They usually do not know where the unhappiness they are experiencing is coming from, but they feel it acutely, and often act it out. Until the approximate time of adolescence the child identifies more with its parent's mind than with its own. Thus the importance of the parent being unconflicted in his or her attitude toward the child.

6. For many people, using mental imagery is another effective way of discarding expectations.

• One that I find helpful is to picture each expectation as a string I have tied to the other person. With a pair of golden scissors (why "golden," I don't know; feel free to use the material of your choice), I cut each attachment until the individual stands free. Since the strings we tie to a relationship always connect at both ends, we are released along with the other. Remember always that the freedom to love and to be at peace is the only freedom there is. There is no genuine liberty in being insensitive.

• Another visualization is to imagine your list of expectations going up in smoke. I suppose one could literally burn it; I have never tried this.

• If you could detect just a little of the ugliness that your expectations have spread across your image of the other person, perhaps you could use an imagery that begins to strip this away. Maybe a mask or a costume could be removed to reveal the basic blamelessness, if not the loveliness, of the person as he or she is. As I write this I am thinking of a friend who, even though he has consistently been this way for the ten years I have known him, I have always expected not to be competitive.[3] I notice that in my mind's eye his features seem hard whenever I want him to be different. I say to him now, "[Name], you are free to be competitive. You do not have to

---

[3] It is important to see not only our own but also our friends' egos clearly and without judgment. It is equally important to remember that our friends are not guilty merely because their egos differ from ours. For example, we can (and definitely should) see that someone is dishonest, but without thinking that our way of being dishonest is somehow superior.

change for me to be your friend," and I picture my expectations lifted from him like a suit of unattractive armor.

I know from experience that this person will look slightly different to me the next time I see him because of this moment or two I devoted to our relationship.

7. (SUMMARY) As just implied, this work will gradually take you to something more than just release from self-induced pain. You will come to see the face of innocence. This is not the culmination of years of ascetic strivings; it is a present possibility. It is the one reward you have a right to from any relationship you now have.

Let us take one step further the example of the parents and their newborn. After they have identified and released their expectations, perhaps they sit together for a moment and just look at their child as if they were saints, as if they were holy guardians sent to watch over it, to love it and comfort it and to meet its every need. Can you see that if this were sincerely done—for in their hearts there *is* the desire that they be able to look in just this way—how much more they would now be able to receive from this little baby? They would see before them not a crying demanding burden, but the opportunity to turn their minds to something better. They would see a chance to love unselfishly, to love without wanting, to love without sin. They would look a little past a needful body, and there they would view hope and happiness and gentleness of spirit. Above all, they would gaze upon absolute, pure innocence. The fact that they could see this would be their gift, the gift that just one relationship free of expectations had given them.

We will never have our expectations of any relationship met. Fantasies cannot be lived out. But held in each one is a far greater reward—the opportunity to see innocence.

A Relationship Can Give Its Gift Only in the Present

We have all witnessed this great wasting of good relationships now going on. It seems that no one knows any longer how to have a relationship. Even people with very strong and enduring bonds will impulsively separate. As if struck by a disease, a person will one day wander off into the arms of another and give up everything—children and the friendship of half a lifetime—all for the possibility of some great romantic play. Thus beneath the layers of expectations that each person carries into a relationship there is still another, growing in strength. It is the very understandable anticipation of abandonment. The one who has been loved for so long may leave, and indeed this is the way of the world. The spouse may die or find another. The best friend may become enchanted with individuals who move in another sphere. The pet may be killed. The parent may become old and mentally withdraw into some unreachable world.

Somehow a way must be found to set aside all these sad images if we are ever to be free enough and present enough to have a real relationship with anyone. Yet it seems so unlikely that such a task could be completed because the possible distressing turns that each relationship could take are too numerous and real—many teenagers do in fact turn sullen, babies are often surprisingly demanding, animals frequently become uncomfortable when they get old and are no longer companionable—and how can one be expected to just ignore these realities?

Of course one cannot ignore them if they are occurring now, but at least one does not have to anticipate them if they are not. With all that *could* happen to our loved ones being shouted at us from every corner of the world, the only hope we have of partaking of the rich potential of our relationships is to want them and to have them in the present only. So often it seems that someone has to die before we realize all the opportunities we missed to be happy with this person. If only we had settled down and gazed at what was within our very hands rather than looking fitfully around in a blinding attempt to worry away all possibilities.

Ignoring what is presently disturbing one's enjoyment of a relationship is never called for. Even though this approach is extremely common, all it really accomplishes is to allow issues to remain in place and fester. The problem does not go away and neither does the habit of not addressing problems. New ones are continually added to the old until one day there is an unexplainable and permanent pall over the relationship, and it is no longer worth the effort. The ego's solution to this dynamic is to bring up any hint of difficulty forcefully and at once and to "attack" the problem on the spot, which in practice means attack the relationship. In today's rush for self-fulfillment it has not been widely recognized that *most relationships can withstand very little pressure,* and consequently these frequent confrontations so valued now as signs of "being yourself" and "owning your own power" produce the same long-term effect as ignoring problems—the relationship is eventually turned from in some way.

Resolving Issues

If the other person has just done something that sets you off, this is usually not the time to bring it up because you will probably not be able to do so without some element of attack, and this will precipitate, not a deeper understanding between the two of you, but merely a counterattack. I realize that if you are like most of us your urge to be the fastest gun in town is deep-rooted and that relinquishing the quick-draw habit, whether it takes the form of quiet martyrdom, raucous carping, or "a little sanity," does not come without hard work and concentration. Our weary old desire to be right does at times feel like a need. And yet I also know it is worth the effort to question the value of seizing our first reaction and waving it like a red flag.

Relationship problems should be recognized as they occur, but dealt with when the possibilities of cooperation are greatest. If you feel even a slight sense of urgency and rush, your ego is involved in some way. What harm can come from your waiting for this to lessen? The other person will also tend to react less defensively about what he did as time passes because it will not be as immediate and dominant in his mind. Your chances of a resolution are further improved if the individual senses that you are bringing the subject up because your motive is friendship and not anger. Therefore, first take a moment to think through why you are mentioning this at all. Naturally you may still have some residual anxiety, but at least become clear that you are seeking to strengthen the bond between the two of you and not trying to correct an equal.

If the no-fault concept can be applied to insurance, surely there is room for it in relationships. Friends, and especially couples, frequently spend all their goodwill and most of their time together in vain attempts to assess blame, when this is far more hopeless a task than determining right-of-way in a car accident. And what a bloody and awful achievement it would be even if it were possible. Why not set the easier and happier goal of being a genuine friend to the other and looking for ways to link hands and walk past the issue?

In order for an issue to be solvable you must quietly and guiltlessly admit to yourself that you have taken part in whatever has occurred. This procedure shows your mind the necessity of *joining* with the other person to solve a mutual problem.

Do not confuse acknowledging your part with taking on blame. To feel guilty is to draw back, not to join. Simply recognize in a general way that each person always plays a roll in any disturbance within a relationship. If this were not so you would not *feel* disturbed. Acknowledge this theoretically and silently, but do not be specific. It is not required. In fact, it will be a hindrance for you to tell yourself what your part was, for you will not be able to indulge in this form of self-analysis without guilt. Guilt, being painful, is always shifted and is therefore a very separating emotion.

Participation is not always overt. Very often one person is merely acting out what both individuals are feeling. Among the most common and disrupting relationship problems is some undermining doubt that circulates in one of the party's minds. Within a marriage, for instance, as long as one spouse dwells on the question "Should I get a divorce?" there is no hope of commitment, and you can be certain that the lack of it is always felt by the other. A simple device such as completely committing oneself to the marriage for one week, one month, or one year at a time can give the relationship a chance to breathe and show its potential. Anyone is capable of answering the question "Do I want to take the first step toward a divorce *today?*" And if it is seen that at present there is no such wish, then to try hard to have the best marriage possible for that entire day.

How to Argue in Peace

If a relationship is not to be slowly crushed by the weight of its unanswered issues, a way must be found to eliminate them as they arise. We have already reviewed some prerequisites to attempting a resolution—releasing the mind of fundamental doubts about the relationship itself, recognizing our own participation in the problem at hand, waiting for a good time to bring the matter up—but once these conditions have been met, how can two people put a disagreement peacefully and permanently behind them? An issue can appear solved, but because one person intimidated, cajoled, nagged, or reasoned the other into compliance, and because the one who complied was not sincere, a residue of resentment remains, and although there may now be surface agreement, the relationship certainly has not been helped.

A way is needed to reach wholehearted agreement and leave goodwill in its wake. Due to the high risk of setback, naturally it is best not to allow the mind to lay the grounds for disagreement in the first place, but prevention of this sort is not a practical goal at first, and even to attempt it often leads to the more severe problem of denial and unconscious hostility. It is healthier for the relationship when any sense of estrangement and distance is quickly and honestly seen, even though the decision may be to defer mentioning it. Once brought into the open and correctly resolved, a conflict can literally add to the peace between two people.

The means for correct resolution of an issue is always the same: The individuals must bypass their separate ego positions and gently unite. What form this takes does not matter, but in most cases, without some outward form, the process is never quite completed and, once more, evidence of incompatibility is accepted and believed by both. By breaking a disagreement into its separate parts and arguing it out in a more formalized way the mind can concentrate better and the heart has time to be heard. In a sense the following steps are the stages of an ideal argument. Even in the worst altercations there are good moments, but they come at the wrong time. Our habit is to express our second thoughts and goodwill when they are most likely to be batted down. When the ten steps are applied they tend to sort out the jumble of pieces that make up an unsuccessful argument and put them into a workable whole.

1. Deal only with the present. The relationship may have already grown past the problems you keep recalling, so wait until an issue has genuinely entered the present before concerning each other with it. Simply because you are unhappy or excited, do not dredge up old injuries. Remember that the relationship is always an easy target, so be clear in your heart before you speak. Meanwhile, take the relationship as it is today and give it your full attention. See the *relationship* and not its history. Do not endlessly discuss its problems and cherish them as part of its identity. Do not even analyze the relationship; live it. If there are no problems, don't think of any. *Enjoy each other now, for this is the reason you are together.*

2. If something comes between you—and it has if even one person thinks it has—**sit down together as soon as practical.** What your bodies do symbolizes your priorities. Thus to discuss a subject on which there is a difference of opinion while doing something else (fixing dinner, driving, eating, etc.) tends to deepen the conflict. If either of you is angry, both of you should first calm your minds before talking. Sit down together and quietly remember your purpose. Of course for one of you to pressure the other into doing any of this will defeat your very aim.

3. One at a time, state your ego position in as much detail as you wish, but do not justify it or argue its rightness. Describe your stance in complete honesty and openness, but do not attack the other person's stance.

4. Do not interrupt, and do not call each other on breaking these guidelines. Your aim is to join in peace and so you do not want to needlessly stir up the other person's resistance by listing faults or calling attention to mistakes.

5. Deal only with the specific issue at hand. Avoid the inclination to lump together so many problems at once that resolution becomes impossible. Do not try to think of causes or connections. Do not bring up the past at all unless you are absolutely sure this will add to the chances of resolution.

6. Rather than saying what you want, say what you are afraid of. You will always be willing to let go of a fear, once you see it as fear, but you will be tempted to feel resentful and deprived when you consider compromising on what you think you *want*.

7. While the other person is talking, truly listen. Say to yourself, " __[name]__ really means this." There is a tendency to think that the other's stance is pretense or that the person is merely being perverse—because he or she is so obviously wrong. Respect is not earned, it is given. *Unless you take this person seriously you have no hope of uniting with an equal.*

8. Once each of you has given your ego position and described your underlying fears as best you can, **close your eyes and remember your debt of gratitude to the other.** Be willing to use any mental trick that allows you to see what the other means to you. Perhaps list to yourself any recent signs of the other's thoughtfulness or gentleness.[4] Perhaps recall when you first met. Keep up these efforts until you are certain you have once again recognized the value of this relationship.

9. With your eyes still closed, decide on the gifts you would like to give the relationship. Earlier you would have thought

[4] Although #8 is usually done silently, Gayle and I sometimes put this in the form of a game. Taking turns, we have to cite ten instances of the other's goodness (some specific act that was unselfish, generous, kind, etc.). When you are angry you can't think of a single redeeming quality, especially one you are going to have to say out loud. So if you play this, remember that the first few may be hard to think of, but if you persist you will loosen up a little and the others will come more easily.

of these as compromises or concessions, but if you did step #8 such an interpretation is now impossible. Make sure that your gifts relate directly to the issue being resolved and truly serve to narrow the distance. *Do not make grand off-the-subject gestures.* [5] Simply think of a few specifics that are within your present ability to carry out happily. And make them genuine gifts that you *know* the other person will appreciate.

10. Open your eyes and, in turn, verbally share your gifts. There will now be more than enough flexibility to resolve the argument. Maybe it will be seen as a non-issue by both. Maybe one of you will recognize that you do not feel strongly, and the fact that the other *does* is all the reason you need to want the same. Maybe new options will have been thought of. Maybe the accommodations you both make will split the difference between you. If not, repeat the steps or perhaps just live happily with the effort made for a while until you both feel ready to try again.

Here is an example of how these steps were used. An estranged couple that Gayle and I began counseling loved each other very much but could not spend time together, even on the phone, without constant battle. The argument they had most often was whether the wife should move back into the house. The husband thought that her unwillingness to do so was proof that she did not love him, and never had, and the

---

[5] We were once counseling a couple whose long-standing issue was the husband's desire to control the family's finances versus the wife's desire to purchase whatever she thought best. Specifically, the husband wanted her to buy only what was on the list she left the house with, and the wife said this was not always practical. They went through these ten steps, and when they opened their eyes to share their gifts, the wife was so filled with love for her husband that she said she would get a job and buy a house so that their family would no longer have to rent. As you can see, this was a lovely idea but did nothing to remove the issue at hand. On the second try they agreed on an exact percentage of spending latitude for both of them.

wife took the husband's ultimatums on the subject as further evidence of his desire to dominate and control her.

We met with them on Wednesday evenings for several months, and during the first few weeks we had them take up one issue each session and apply the ten steps. Although this is not always necessary, we started them out on minor problems before attempting the major one. In this couple's case several weeks were needed before they could even listen to each other calmly.[6] As is true in so many marriages, they had grown very afraid of each other over the years and read their own anger and judgments into every word the other person uttered.

"Jumping to conclusions," whether done overtly or silently, is always a symptom of genuine fear, and is not lessened by being challenged. You do not *want* your friend to be afraid of you because to the degree one is anxious one cannot love. If you wish to be more loved, as of course you do, you must be very careful not to say or do anything that increases the other's fear of you, whether or not you judge his or her concerns to be unfounded. A person can be hushed up but cannot be made less anxious by being shown to be irrational.

By the time the question of their living together was taken up, they had learned to make their gifts concrete, in other words to be very specific in their accommodations of the other's position as well as intelligent about not "giving up" so much of their own position—if it was deeply held—that they later regretted what they had done and became resentful. After the first application of the steps the wife offered to stay overnight three times each week, and the husband agreed not to

---

[6] There is always one who seems better at listening than the other, but often this is an appearance only, because although the individual may be able to repeat back what the other said, it has not been truly *understood.* That is, the words have been heard, but the ideas have not been taken seriously and respected.

question, even in the most indirect way, what she had done with her time when she was away.

Over the weeks that followed, many problems arose (What time in the afternoon should she arrive?; Should she call if she was going to be late?; Should he question her if she didn't?; Should they have sex if she was very late?, etc.). Each step was handled as it arose, and although this couple worked hard, they unquestionably needed support and guidance during the early stages of their reconciliation, which quite naturally involved far more than learning to argue in peace. Because of their extraordinarily persistent efforts these two eventually developed great sensitivity to each other's needs as well as the kind of mutual affection that could grow over the years.

Never Fight the Ego

Many of the questions that keep a relationship stirred up are unanswerable at the time the mind is reviewing them: "Will my husband die before I do?" "Is my wife capable of having an affair?" "Will adolescence mark the end of this closeness my child and I now feel?" "If I become incapacitated should I go to a nursing home or live with my children?" There is simply no way for a relationship to attain its lovely potential while questions of this sort are in the background. *Unhappy questions are not put to rest by being answered.* No final answers exist. Therefore the questions themselves must be seen for what they are—the fear of being happy in the present—and discarded. This is not an easy feat, but it is one that in each person's lifetime has already been accomplished many times.

When you were still young you may have walked into a store, seen something you thought you really wanted, and asked yourself, "If I take this will I get caught?" Of course there is no real answer to the question. If you did in fact take it and were not detected, or even if you were caught and reprimanded, you probably recall that the question did not go away.[7] Perhaps you tried to answer it in many different stores before you realized what an unhappy question it was and stopped considering it. Just as you may have decided never again to take this question seriously, you are also free to choose not to consider any other question from your ego. *Because they are felt by the other, private lines of thought always affect the course of a relationship.* The ego is a garbage bag that has collected every contradictory experience you have ever had, but not one thing it contains can possibly harm your relationships—unless you begin chewing it over in your mind.

It must be remembered that the ego part of us does not want a relationship—any relationship—to endure because union of any sort threatens its sense of autonomy. To our ego all value lies in being different, so for one to strive to have no differences with another is self-destructive. When we first started counseling couples several years ago, we met with a man and woman who had maintained a three-year argument over whether to get married. The woman said that the man's refusal to consider this was the root of all their troubles. The man appeared to love the woman, but since he was obviously having difficulty explaining his position to her, we asked if he would please close his eyes and quietly search his heart for his true feelings. To Gayle's and my surprise, when he finished he said that he had just realized that he *did* want to marry her. Turning to the woman with this piece of magic, we waited for her profuse thanks. She said, "Well, I don't think I want to marry him," and thus began six more months of the same dynamic, until finally, they broke up.

This was only the first of hundreds of examples we were to

[7] With me it was Grapettes. Do you remember Grapettes? They were the pocket-size (I thought) grape drink, whereas Nehi Grape tended to live up to its name.

see in the coming years of people switching sides just to keep a fight going. "You are never upset for the reason you think," says *A Course in Miracles*. Our ego is upset because upset prevents joining, and it guesses correctly that joining will be the death of it. You may have noticed that you are not exempt from the tendency to bring things up too quickly and in the wrong way, and that when you do so you are often surprised at the other person's overreaction. However, if you will look a little closer you will see that you are not *truly* surprised—you simply took up your desire to be right rather than worked to increase the strength of the relationship.

Being right is our primary way of being different, and it always yields a feeling of distance and estrangement between us and the one we cast as wrong. The remedy is to recognize our far deeper desire for closeness and oneness, and to use our considerable understanding of the other person, first, to avoid unnecessary rifts and, second, to do only what will be *received* as love.

Our Knowledge of Other Egos

If the particular gesture you have been making is not being interpreted as a friendly act, perhaps you should reconsider its form. Most children love water; most cats do not. To take a cat into the bath, as our then two-year-old once tried with Tuba, will not be greeted with good humor. Tuba was appropriately named and there are times you can hear her through a three-foot adobe wall, but unless you give a human your full attention, you may not accurately sense that individual's lack of readiness for what you are about to do. *Our habit is to say what we would like said and to consider this reasonable,* even though we often have sense enough not to follow this procedure with children. Since likes and dislikes are formed by past experiences, and no two people's histories are the same, if we truly wish to treat others as we ourselves would be treated, we must learn to take an honest reading of the other person before we act.

Except possibly when dealing with strangers, it is not accurate to claim that we do not know other people's egos well enough to predict what will be received happily, for in an argument we clearly know them well enough to say exactly what will hurt most. Gayle once gave a memorable display of her knowledge of my ego when we were living in a small converted schoolhouse in Pojoaque, New Mexico. We were having our argument in the kitchen, and I must have said something quite unfair because she stopped talking and pulled a leftover broccoli casserole out of the refrigerator. Piece by piece she sprinkled it over the entire kitchen floor and left the room.

What she knew about my ego was that the mess would get to me before it got to her, and although I was determined not to relent and would loudly announce her childishness and immaturity whenever I had to walk on-toe through the kitchen, in the end I was the one who cleaned it up.

Those long warfares—which are funny to look back on but were highly separating at the time—have been put behind us for several years now, and we are working very hard to progress beyond the smaller flare-ups that still occasionally occur. As we have discovered, this is a reasonable goal, and the love between us grows with each little gain made. However, I want you to know how surprisingly deep the resistance can be to changing from misusing to using one's knowledge of the other person. There were many times during a period of several years when I thought the task was proving impossible. Now I realize that it was not the task but my conflict over the ultimate goal that was holding me back.

Gayle and I have seen this same resistance to "giving in" with almost every couple we have counseled. We have also observed that in relationships between parents and children, and in all other relationships in which a very deep union is being attempted, the resistance surfaces as the individuals draw closer.

Giving In

In order to understand this phenomenon a little better let us consider again the part played by the ego. As I have been using the term throughout, the ego is our shallow or surface personality. Being impressions of our past, it was formed mostly in childhood, but has been added to ever since. It is merely a collection of conflicting lessons and beliefs that constitutes a self-image that does not match what we feel on the deeper levels of our mind or "heart." In every possible sense we are not our ego, even though we each definitely have one, carry it around with us at all times, and are influenced by it continually. As we increasingly turn to our peaceful core, we gradually come to realize that we do not even believe all of this superficial nonsense we have been thinking for all these years, and when this point is reached the mind begins shedding its ego identity at a very rapid rate. As it starts to melt away we become increasingly capable of uniting with other people on their heart level.

We have in effect two identities, one that can join and one that cannot. As long as we *defend* our ego, our imaginary and totally separate identity, we will feel a strong resistance to giving in to a union of two hearts because we accurately recognize that our sense of separateness will be weakened in the process. And yet we have never really examined this thing that we get so defensive and stubborn about. Indeed we are protecting something, but do we even want the something we throw so many relationships aside to guard?

No one who begins the practice of watching his mind can long fail to notice all the garbage it contains, and yet it is this garbage that we all cling to and insist be respected and deferred to by our parents, friends, employees, children, and even the hapless salesperson in the store. This is the self-importance we so vigilantly watch over and preserve. Whenever you feel a strong need to be right you are merely failing to take out the garbage.

Nothing you truly want can be lost by loving too much. This fear, this resistance to giving in, only protects your unhappiness. If for just an instant you could see how utterly unimportant are these stands you are always taking, these opinions that must be respected, these personality traits that must be justified, then you would know that sacrifice is never what is being asked of you. *You do not want what you fight for; you want what you betray in order to fight.*

What could you possibly lose by seeking the peace of another person—by literally making another's peace your single-minded goal? You can certainly lose by destroying another's peace; in fact, loss will be the one reliable outcome each time you must be right. You can certainly lose by loving too little. But to love too much is to dare merely to be your self, to be your own heart, which is all you have ever wanted to be.

In the West, especially, many have assumed that the way to have a more reliable life and a more consistent state of mind is to get tough. To be hard on it makes it hard, rocklike, and predictable, whatever the "it" may be. To attack and scare it makes it behave. One must not for a minute let up on one's body, one's behavior, or even on one's children and friends. And so throughout America teenagers are pursued through the house by irate parents yelling "Once again you didn't take out the garbage." In another version of this mistake, young people see the painful lives of their elders and believe they can avoid their aching loneliness by learning to keep their distance:

"If it's inevitable I will suffer little desertions all my life, I must avoid getting close enough to anyone for it to hurt."

The unexamined assumption is that all this pain and chaos we have so much of comes from closeness and gentleness. Thus parents assume that incessant scolding and other forms of "parental distance" result in better control of their two-year-old or that pushing their own body past its limits will eventually hush its little ways of whining. The thought of showing their body constant compassion seems as unreasonable to most people as being a true friend to their child or viewing strangers as their brothers and sisters.

The actual pain of betrayal, faithlessness, and mockery enters through the ego and not the heart. Hardness, bitterness, withdrawal, anger, and other compassionless qualities that are turned to as means to steel oneself against the falling away of friends and loved ones make the mind more vulnerable to suffering rather than less. It is not by withholding thoughtfulness and caring that we protect ourselves and live more happily. You will never suffer by being too faithful to another, provided this does not entail taking sides. If you do suffer it will not be from love. The notion that the risk we must take if we want to draw closer to another person is the pain of rejection is as impractical a piece of advice as it is false in its supposition that love can convey us to loneliness or that light can increase the dark. There are definite causes of suffering, but gentleness, kindness, and acceptance are not among them.

The Ego Alliance

There is no way to get egos together since they differ at every point, as they naturally would, being outgrowths of personal experience. Yet the hearts of all people are highly compatible. Therefore the key to making a relationship real is for the individuals involved to step past their separate self-images, and yet it is in the course of this attempt that resistance is experienced so acutely. A shift from an ego-based relationship to a heart-based one is indeed difficult to achieve, but I can assure you that because of its absolute gentleness, no other source of happiness in this world compares with it.

Although egos cannot unite, they can form alliances, and most relationships are no more than this. The nature of this foundation makes them eminently vulnerable to fallings-out and breakups. They are also increasingly unhappy because there is always a basic dynamic present that should be understood and bypassed. This is found within relationships of all forms, between lovers, children and parents, acquaintances, and of course within marriages, and essentially it is the feeling of "you and me against the world."

Within such an alliance there may be a strong appearance of accord between the parties, especially on what is wrong with everyone else. A community of like interests is discovered or formed that generates on both sides an impression of agreement and closeness, yet when it is examined more carefully it can be seen that these links are not so much mutual loves as similar dislikes. The ego is never wholly certain of what it likes. Nothing ceases to be scrutinized. Yet it can feel somewhat more definite about its dislikes. The basis of the average relationship is a mutuality of targets: the reprehensible conduct of the government and which candidate is "loved" for saying it like it is; the destructive policy of schools and which authorities are recommended because they agree; the movies that are poorly done and which are the temporary favorites; and especially the behavior on the part of certain individuals that is laughable or reprehensible, and what contrasting behavior on the part of other individuals that is just wonderful.

There is no true love and acceptance in any of this. What makes this foundation of a family's bond, of two couples' enthusiasm for each other, of a crew's spirit, of a friendship's fidelity so tenuous is that fear and anger are self-immolating. *Disapproval cannot be felt for anything outside of a relationship without also being felt within it,* and so all such relationships are ultimately destructive of the participants' happiness.

This last summer the four of us took a trip to the San Juan Islands. We rented a small American-built station wagon at the airport and transported it to Orcas on one of the large ferryboats that shuttles there. In Santa Fe we live on a long rough dirt road, and we have had to switch to foreign-built cars because the various domestic ones we have tried have been demolished, usually within a few months. Without being particularly aware of it we had developed a prejudice against all American vehicles.

It was about three days into our vacation before we realized why the tone between us was not good. It seemed that every few hours something new would fall off the station wagon, and so all the time we had been driving it we had kept up a running commentary. On one particular day Gayle was outside a grocery store when a man came up and asked how she liked her new wagon. "It is a terrible, terrible car," she said, and delivered our by now well-practiced list of horrors. "Oh," he said sadly, "I just bought one." Gayle is a very kind person and she backtracked as fast as she could, blaming the rental agency, retrograde planets, and everything else she could think of, and told the man she was certain he had not made a mistake, that it was actually a fine car. And of course he didn't believe a word of it.

Once we realized that a critical frame of mind will not stay put—even if the target is inanimate—we surrounded the station wagon in light, resolved to think of it gently, and as an inevitable result the happiness we felt being together increased. Quite naturally this also spilled over onto John and Jordan.

Gayle and I had long since recognized that it utterly destroyed our gentleness toward each other for us to indulge, even momentarily, in judging other people, whether done together or in private fantasies, but we had not seen that to merely deplore the car one is driving, the house one is renting, the food one is eating puts the relationship temporarily back on an alliance-of-hate basis and wipes out the quite fragile flow of loving feelings. Of course some couples have not yet had a sustained enough experience of peace for its absence to be particularly noticeable but, as we have found, once a real relationship begins to form, the amount of work required to keep it growing is eagerly and happily given.

What Is a Real Relationship?

What then is a love-based or heart-based relationship? The feeling tone is "You and me *for* the world"—the precise opposite of the ego-based one. Upon first consideration this may seem not only an unattainable but silly position. Yet far more effort is required to misunderstand others than mentally to let them be. The tension a relationship comes under when trying to sustain an attack against outsiders is enormous. The betrayal is felt within the relationship, and a wedge of guilt is driven between the two who are attempting to band together. It is never feasible to unite *against* because the uniting force is love.

It is very possible of course to take the ideas of acceptance and gentleness and turn them into rules for behavior, even though they are a mind-set rather than the overt acts of a body. Being gentle does not mean becoming a doormat and saying yes to everyone's whim. And acceptance of others does not mean joining them in their selfish or hurtful acts. In reality such an approach identifies individuals with their shallow rather than their deeper feelings and only pushes them further in the wrong direction.

Love says no as effortlessly as it says yes because it seeks far more than to be inoffensive. Love is kind even to another's ego, but it is never afraid of it. Instinctively the love in you will side with the basic goodness of the other person. Perhaps you have noticed that to gently and unequivocally say no to someone's ego request often has a noticeably strengthening effect on both of you.

How can you be certain that a request comes from another's ego? Your happiness never entails judging anyone, and so you do not have to concern yourself with where a request comes from but merely with its effect on your mind. Any request that calls to your fear should be looked at carefully. You will often have a sinking feeling or a tinge of guilt just before you start to acquiesce to a demand that will hurt you. Just as with any question that comes from your own mind, *practice looking at the fears it generates and never at the question itself and you will know what to do*—provided that you are absolutely clear that your single goal is peace and genuine happiness.

Although there is no general understanding of this, *gentleness is firmness*. To the world only some form of anger is firmness. Far too many parents discipline out of their mood, and because of their unpredictability merely end up making their children afraid of them. One moment the child is ignored or thought funny for kicking the parent while being dressed for bed; on another night the child is snapped at or worse for the same thing. This approach increases resentment, even in very young children, and can end up making them as erratic as their parents. Parents who are deeply gentle refuse to react out of their passing moods and are therefore consistently in a position to steer the child away from the unhappy approaches to life that any youngster will be sure to try out from time to time.

Acceptance is frequently seen as a dangerous concept, and it obviously runs counter to the prevailing values of our times. Unfortunately these are particularly hostile to the formation of real relationships. I know a young couple who have a twelve-year-old who loves the outer-space type cartoons now on TV. They regularly tape those they feel are not too disturbing and let her watch them after school, but they allow no TV during meals and certain other times of day. About two years ago the couple took in the husband's elderly father, who is mentally sound and relatively healthy but no longer has the stamina to support himself financially. For over a year feelings between the father and the son were stirred up daily by the son's insistence that his father's long-standing habit of watching TV during dinner could not be permitted in their household.

In the course of receiving counseling the son discovered that he was the victim of an almost universal attitude within relationships: He could not give in because he had already lost too much ground. In this case to his wife, daughter, and, in years past, to his father. Once he recognized the meaninglessness of this "fact" he was also able to open his eyes to the many options he had to resolve the issue. The one he chose was to buy another TV and invite his father to watch his programs and take whatever meals he wished in his bedroom. His daughter did not object to unequal treatment as he had feared; in fact, she was relieved at the improvement in atmosphere.

The feeling of always losing ground, of always having to be the one who compromises, is of course the core of the resistance I spoke of earlier to forming a true relationship, and yet it is a much encouraged attitude of our time. Many articles, talk shows, interviews with celebrities, and new-generation books feed the current wisdom that one's personal "growth" comes before all else. One needs one's space, one's energy, one's time. Every individual has a right to sex at a certain level of excitement, to a job that fulfills, to a partner and children who know just when to leave you alone. This is what you have coming and you must not back down on any of it. The many pronouncements on this subject can sound very virtuous, practical, and even mystically or spiritually grounded, and perhaps every person you know has been unconsciously influenced by them to some degree.

If your approach to your relationships is not to be infected by these popular arguments, you must see with honesty that any idea you have that calls to your autonomy comes straight from your ego. *The need is never for you to stand more strongly, more self-sufficiently alone.* The great and fatal wound of humanity is this ancient fiction that selfishness works. What we have before us now is just a new version of a very old sadness. The true need—as it has always been—is merely to love, to accept, to be quick to help, to be slow to judge. And the reason is very simple. You *are* forgiving and kind at heart. *The one trait you will never be able to change is your gentleness,* and on the level where it exists you are united with and not at odds with the true interests of every living thing. This basic truth gives you enormous potential for forming real relationships.

What then must we do to join rather than merely ally ourself with another? First we must look deep inside and see there someone who knows peace, someone who knows genuine love. We must feel the existence of such a self somewhere within, no matter how layered over. And then we must be willing to step out of ourself, out of our little scared defensive identity, and into that person we wish to be: one who does not look for faults, one who is not temperamental, one who is not jealous, one who does not judge. And we must be willing to do this a thousand times a day if necessary.

This may seem so terribly, impossibly beyond your abilities. But I am writing this book to assure you otherwise. Indeed I am a very ordinary person, and my past personal problems were, I can tell you, as severe as you may think yours are now. I had no fancy mystical experience, I just finally got down to work. And after several years of a very simple approach, the one I have been describing in various ways throughout this book, I am more the kind of person I want to be than I am my ego. The balance has shifted. Still I have miles to go, but they can be good and happy miles. Anyone can take this journey, and that person will come to know what a real relationship is —and it need not be a "love" relationship that provides the first opportunity.

The makings of your first real relationships are before you now. They are already within the bounds of your present daily routine. Two friends, an individual and an animal, a child and an elderly parent—there is no end to the many potentially tender and lovely relationships. If only a start is made and the effort continued as best one can. Simply remember that the effort is to see innocence and is not a flurry of smothering gestures; it is to think gently and *not* to get a response. Then you will discover that the distance to the heart is very short indeed.

EXERCISE XI-B

The aim is to begin recognizing that as you put yourself in a mental position to have real relationships, they occur naturally. It is not wise to target a specific person and place your hopes on this one individual's reaction. If you will in a sense make yourself one half of a real relationship, the other halves will blossom around you. But, again, avoid anticipating changes in particular people because you will be unable to do so without building up your expectations and becoming increasingly selfish.

It is important that you rule out no one with whom you

have contact. Just practice being an absolute friend to the person before you now and you will gradually discover the many who feel the oneness you feel. Even though the world puts great value in numbers, you do not wish to count your friends like a miser counts money. Merely be rich in your ability to stay at peace. Be the kind of person you want to be, and because of the nature of the human heart you will see the like-minded.

Since it is the repeated small beginnings and not the grand breakthroughs that carry us forward, I want to suggest a limited but very effective way of practicing being one who is capable of a real relationship.

1. Select, as they come up, three events in which you will be encountering one or more people over a sustained period, such as a party, a visit with your parents, an outing with a friend. As close to the beginning of each occasion as feasible, schedule a period of at least fifteen minutes for mental preparation.

2. During this time first decide how you wish to be. Look in your heart and feel the simple answer. Do you want to be strong? kind? peaceful? centered?—whatever qualities epitomize your heart's desire.

Once you recognize the attributes you want, take the upcoming occasion into your mind and visualize your being this kind of person within it. Start at the beginning, perhaps your arrival at the place, and picture your every response to be as you would wish. Remember that you alone are the focus of this exercise. Therefore imagine people and events as they will probably be and not as you would like them. Go through the occasion in great detail. Fantasize any range of expected or unexpected occurrences, but see your calm, steady self remaining the same. Be very disciplined about this, picturing each happening carefully until you have seen yourself through the entire event.

3. During the event itself, let yourself be. If at some point you realize that you have forgotten your purpose, take a break (go to the car, into the rest room, or use some other excuse) and gently remind yourself of it, and then return to the occasion as free of tension as possible. Do not anxiously monitor yourself. Your preparation before the event was like giving yourself a shove—so now let yourself glide.

Select Your Encounters with Care

It would be possible to have a real relationship with anyone if we could somehow refrain from seeking certain signs of reciprocity. If we would not place our hope in another's ego, we could sense quite strongly the person's true feelings and would experience a lovely and enduring kinship with this individual, whatever form that might take. Even though this is always true, often it is not helpful to have frequent contact with everyone available. Egos never love but they do fight more disturbingly with some than with others. This is merely a dynamic of the world and there is no blame to be apportioned.

How much another's personality clashes with yours needs to be considered. If you see that you simply cannot be around some individual without it upsetting you, there may be other ways of practicing love that will carry you forward more quickly, for if the situation is not happy for you, you can be sure it is not truly happy for the other. Perhaps a complete break is not necessary, and of course no action need be rushed into or, once taken, defined as irrevocable.

Never abandon anyone in your heart, and if your actions symbolize rejection, refuse absolutely to give them this interpretation yourself. *Whenever you step back with your body, step forward with your mind.* Maintain within you a place of constant gentleness and warmth for the person, and do not confuse yourself by thinking that you must discard your peace because of appearances. Your ego *will* argue this, but continuing to love is your right.

As we have discussed before, you must to some degree shelter your inner happiness in order for it to grow. This you will not be doing if you insist on relating in only one way to someone who is difficult for you. Whenever feasible do not put yourself in circumstances where you are likely to make more mistakes than usual. You subject yourself to discouragement when your mistakes come too closely together. If situations that are hard for you personally go on too long, your reserves of peace become depleted and you begin losing ground. Stop and see that this is not necessary.

Naturally there are relationships such as with family members that must be maintained in some way because to turn completely from one's child or parent is more disturbing to one's mental health than occasional contact. However, these encounters, if difficult, can very often be modified. A mother may discover that she is lectured less by her son through the mail than on the phone, and so finds ways to shift their communication to letters. A father may use formula to feed the baby on periodic nights in order to give his wife a needed break from the child. A sister may find that her brother is less argumentative if the visits take place at his house. I have a friend who phones his mother only during the day because the cocktail she has after dinner always makes her maudlin and manipulative. The ego has great reluctance to take the simple step that will make a difference. The battle must be fought out on the same grounds until won, yet *in relationships there are no triumphs.*

The Gentle Option

The relationships one has should rest gently in the mind, cradled there like little flowers. They should refresh and brighten one's life. Truly there is no need for any association to torture us and to go on as a plague upon our life year after year. And yet so many commonplace encounters can no longer be thought about sanely—the grown child and elderly parent, the couple of many years, the parent and adolescent, the "terrible two's," the in-law's dreaded visit. . . . It is believed that these and various other interrelations *must* be endured with some degree of unhappiness. There is even a certain pride taken in the sacrifice everyone "knows" is inherent. Jokes are made and sympathy given as if no option to misery could possibly exist within these situations too numerous to count.

The couple, the parent and child, and all the rest must not allow their minds to fall into these traps of dark categorization, for when they do they will find themselves playing out a needless tragedy with no insight as to any way out. It is not that there are no inherent difficulties in these situations, for of course there are, but no implacable law of unhappiness is at work within a relationship, no matter what stage it has entered. Those involved must not only free themselves of preconceptions but should be wholly open to aids of any sort. They should actively bring themselves every option that would facilitate moving beyond an impasse.

The Parent with Teenager

The relationship of the parent and teenager is an excellent example of a situation set up in the mind to be miserable, whereas in actuality it is often the first straight opportunity the parent has to give back to the child a little of what the parent has been receiving for the past twelve or so years, because until adolescence most children, despite many obvious problems, are remarkably pure givers. Now, as a teenager, the child is ready to make mistakes. And it *can* be the parent's pleasure to stand aside and allow these explorations to occur in an atmosphere of understanding and support. For don't we all remember what it was like?

This is essentially the time of learning, of the bird leaving the nest, and of course the child makes mistakes. Parents can become very frightened if they unthinkingly assume that the mistaken behavior is permanent. So many of the actions that parents feel compelled to stamp out will not be carried on for more than a few years. The chances are that your son will not be wearing a two-tone Mohawk and Day-Glo muscle shirt when he is forty. Our son Scott seemed to have no financial sense as a teenager and cost us a great deal with his neglect of cars and other family equipment. Today, in his twenties, he has his own financial management company and is knowledgeable and imaginative and surprisingly conservative with his clients' money, and he gives *us* financial advice.

Occasionally teenagers make mistakes that have lasting effects. But would judging them have helped? Of course not. Would judgment have saved anyone? Of course not. Naturally the parents wish to prevent any serious error they can, but so frequently their degree of upset is not warranted and merely eliminates them as the child's friend just when a friend is most needed. Thus the parents must *decide* to stand by and allow their teenager to make mistakes—not catastrophic ones if they can help it—but still not to try to control with the desperate angry control that one sees in so many families.

The teenager will of course do things that the parents would not do, and the parents can be strongly tempted to feel hopeless. They must find dependable ways to hold on to their perspective. They must work hard and consistently to look at their child with innocence, still being firm when this is necessary, but a firmness wholly free of disapproval or anger. At this age the child is not yet ready to make every last decision, and this fact cannot be ignored and the teenager wishfully imagined to possess a maturity not yet gained.

Nevertheless, parents who want to bridge these transitions with love must give their children the opportunity to keep choosing, to continue experimenting in complete confidence that they are still deeply appreciated, and especially to grow happily and to develop without fear of ridicule and retaliation. If communication has been kept open with the child all through his growing years, the teenage years will be easier. If the child can confess without being attacked, if he is not constantly nagged, if he is surrounded by a great deal of affection and the certainty that he is as he should be and not this secret longing that he be something else, then he will not become quite as fearful and withdrawn during this difficult time.

In this way the teenager will learn to choose from the heart rather than from anxiety—for this will be the dominant lesson that the parents are teaching—and adolescence will become a time of true flowering. Yet because of their tense concern about this stage, instead of parents gently liberating their child, they usually close down at just the time they should soften and open up and not be confused by any of the silly fads or the pleasures that their son or daughter seems to derive from appearances or from language or secretiveness or whatever it may be at the moment.

Parents simply cannot become caught up in any of this. They must choose to have the strength, not only to keep their own peace, but enough strength for their child as well. During this period adolescents may become scattered, confused, and conflicted and incapable of the degree of selflessness and concentration they had perhaps even a year or so earlier. A wise parent will not add duties during this stage but may even cut back on them if their child's mental distraction warrants this. What to do can be accurately sensed from the standpoint of strong friendship for the child but will be consistently misjudged when the child is thought of disapprovingly.

Take this still very young one into the soft understanding of your heart and patiently bathe it in love. Have confidence in your child, even though your child may have little in himself, and resolve to remain a constant friend throughout this time, one who can be turned to, one who will support and never judge, and one who emanates hope by a quiet knowing of how it will all turn out.

The Long-term Relationship

In a long-term relationship the other person will change, and this is the great fact of life for which we are ill prepared. It always seems to take us by surprise and we respond to it badly. Of course the relationship is quite promising at first. It is an alliance based on mutual likes and interests.[8] Although it may not be this dramatic, it can even seem as though we have known the other person before. Pleasing coincidences abound. There are veiled signs and coded indicators pointing to the rightness and wonder of it all. And we may discover an almost psychic ability to read the other person's thoughts, to antici-

---

[8] The attraction of war can be very great and occasionally two people come together because their egos *clash* and they find this exciting at the time. These relationships seldom last because it is more difficult for the individuals involved to see each other as innocent. Even though there will be some initial "attraction of opposites" in all relationships, those that are founded principally on this dynamic are quite rare and most couples need not worry that they have made this mistake.

pate his or her every action. Or at least so it can seem at the start.

Then as if by some sinister magic the person is different. There comes a morning that starts just like every other morning. You are the same. The house is the same. Your toast is medium brown the way you like it. But suddenly you look across the table and see a complete stranger. Do not panic. This is a problem in perception.

Perhaps as you stare at the interloper you begin listing to yourself the little ways this person has been changing recently. The temptation—and many there are who fall for it—is to believe that the spot of corruption was always there and you are only now discovering it. You were deceived, the individual is not as represented, and so you have no choice but to turn against your former friend. Please acknowledge, though, that although you do not like the direction this person has turned, these very changes are probably being viewed as an improvement by someone else. In other words, your interpretation is not compulsory, and it is a good first step to question it and to loosen and shake it a little.

Have you ever known anyone who kept a pet monkey? With a few exceptions, monkeys tend to be loud, destructive, and impossible to house-train. If not constantly caged, they hang on the drapes, swing from the light fixtures, and do embarrassing things with their bodies when the boss comes to dinner. And yet their owners continue to be loyal and understanding in the face of every known definition of bad manners.

My friend, if there are people who love a pet monkey, *you* can love your spouse.

How do they succeed? They sacrifice their house, their possessions, and their sleep and get not one word of apology from the monkey. They succeed by making a decision to accept the monkey as it is. They demand nothing, they expect nothing extra, and consequently they can see the monkey's many good and entertaining qualities. "Look at its little dimple," they will say. "Look at the cute way it eats its banana." They want nothing more than the monkey can give.

A monkey can give a lot, but I assure you that your spouse, no matter what change he or she is going through, is giving far more to you. Once again, the problem is in the perceiving. Naturally there can be deep deviations that you will not continue living with. If the person has become insane and violent, you will leave, and so you should, because lost causes can end up losing you, and martyrdom never serves your purpose. But if you genuinely desire a long-term relationship you must be very honest with yourself about this. Is this truly an evil direction your spouse has taken? Of course you do not like it, and you may even have guessed correctly that it is not a particularly happy one for your spouse. But does the change really extend to this person's core? Because if you do not face this issue sincerely, all the relationships you try are doomed to this same fate, since you simply will not succeed in finding a person who will remain forever the same.

You can be sure your ego will not greet enthusiastically some, at least, of the new directions your partner will eventually try. This comes in the course of all long-term relationships no matter how auspicious their beginnings. Gayle and I would not have remained together for over twenty years if she had not allowed me to undergo so many changes the first ten or twelve years of our marriage. Many of the things I did were not happy for anyone, and her friends were almost unanimous in thinking her a weakling for not leaving me. The world has an upside-down view of strength; it sees flexibility as weakness and attack as power. Gayle was carrying the marriage by herself because I was too weakened by selfishness to uphold my part. This is a function, and not a sacrifice, that each partner must assume from time to time in any long-term relationship. You must not be afraid of these changes and become rigid.

As was often true in my case, the direction the person takes may even be somewhat self-destructive, and yet you still want to be supportive and understanding. You must continue to be a friend, and you must see that you want to.

Do not let grievances accumulate in your mind during the periods in which you alone must carry the candle of the relationship and hold it steady. Do not keep some vague balance sheet of how much you have coming. Do not even remember. To be selfless is an act that is little understood—not to be some sort of drudge, not to be one who suffers for the rest of the family, one who feels unfairly treated and saddled with a hopeless situation, but one who is *truly* selfless, one who does not see the past at all, who simply sees what must be done for the relationship at the present, one who can look gently at one's children, who can see that the spouse tried, that the spouse's parents did the best they could, who knows that in the world things occur that are not particularly happy, things that do not make sense and are not especially just, and yet one who still decides to be peaceful, to look with innocence, to be happy within oneself.

Remember that change is always a very real possibility. Suddenly your life can open to the spirit of peace. If you will merely persist in being the kind of person you want to be, this must eventually occur. It is a matter of working with your own heart, your own desires, until at last you are living them straightforwardly and are not set spinning within every worldly current.

Why wait for the world to change when it is a present possibility for you to be like some gentle water lily that rests in the corner of a bog unsullied by the mud and scum that washes over it? The lily provides a resting place for fauna because it does *not* sink. Many people, in an honest desire to be compassionate, miss seeing that they can't be of help by shouldering the same discouragement and sadness that is weighing heavily on another, for they will not lessen his burden but merely spread it to themselves.

Instead of jumping into the quicksand of another's emotions along with him, offer a strong and steady hand. Offer, but do not insist. And let us also keep sacred the unalterable fact that we are not in a position to judge what is best for another, to judge what will come of this thing he has just done, even if it *was* a mistake. Haven't some of our own mistakes resulted in our greatest gains?

Let us expect more of ourselves *now,* for in the present we still have a choice. But once it is done, it is done, and there is truly nothing more of ourselves we can look back and expect. This is equally true of a one-year-old, a twelve-year-old, a ninety-year-old. There simply *are* no grounds for judging another person or ourselves.

In counseling couples who have gone through a great deal or who have been together a long while, Gayle and I have repeatedly seen that the sheer volume of grievances accumulated over a period of time often becomes the one inaccessible issue behind all other problems, and until it is erased no amount of resolution of current differences will make the couple happy for very long. Even a divorce will not eliminate the knot of resentment and anger that has built up over the years.

As I have discussed in several chapters, this accumulating process is never a necessity. Yet very few couples are motivated to do the work required to prevent it and often end up trying to separate bodies to relieve minds. There may be good reasons for stepping back from a relationship, but this will not in itself heal the mind whether it takes the form of a "trial separation," remarrying, or sheer sustained hatred. The only way two people come to live in peace with the thought of each other is the same as is required to disencumber a relationship while it is still intact: They must finally see each other's absolute innocence.

So many ideas and exercises have already been given for accomplishing this that I will not present any new ones in this section. I will merely remind you that it is the willingness that does the work and not the particular practice chosen to give it form. This bitter residue did not collect overnight and will not be let go of with a few halfhearted efforts. Work must be instituted, and you must persist until your mind can at last see guiltlessly, can see the other *now,* can look upon this one you have known so long the way a truly good and loving person would view this individual upon their first meeting.

Why should you be open to laboring so hard? Because you will carry this unhappiness to your grave if you do not complete the work, and any other love relationship you may form will be limited in its depth by the great shallowness you still cherish. Therefore, whether you remain with this person or physically leave the relationship, let go of the *history* between the two of you completely and absolutely. To this end use any approach we have discussed. Perhaps begin by writing in a notebook that you always keep with you every thought that you have of this person as you go through the day. Nothing you do, no place you enter, is the same as it would have been before the two of you met. As you continue with your work you may be surprised to discover that in a very real sense this one you have been with (or were with) for so long is *constantly* on your mind. Perhaps the notebook could be used for one or two weeks, or until you have a substantive sense of what there is to let go of, and then you could use one of the many relinquishing imageries already presented each time you become aware of some disturbing remembrance or anticipation involving this individual.

I am being intentionally general about this because by now you should have some sense of your own about how to proceed. Your goal is innocence. It is to come at last to peace with the person in your mind. If you still occasionally find yourself attacking this individual in little ways in your casual conversations or in momentary fantasies, the work is not complete. And as long as any trace of hatred remains, it can start growing again. So see the work through. Be kind to your mind. Clean it out and make it your friend, your resting place, your home. You deserve to be happy, for you, too, are innocent.

The Grown Child with Elderly Parent

Another example of a very natural relationship that has within our times been turned into an arena where hopes are stamped out and all questions are morbid and impossible is this coming together of parent and child late in the parent's life. Perhaps the parent is not only old or dependent but is dying as well. Why must this situation strike guilt in the heart of the parent or terror in the child? Why must even one's mother or father moving into one's own home, if this is the form the contact takes, descend like a shattering blow to all one's dreams? This situation is *not* a tragedy no matter how the world is now choosing to view it.

Every relationship has its work because of what is being attempted—the bypassing of egos so that hearts can unite. In this sense only, the relationship of child to elderly parent can be very difficult. Of course the parent often feels ashamed, but the child, too, may feel quite bad about the unhappy alternatives that must be considered. There often is a considerable backlog of anger and resentment to be set aside. The child may feel inadequate to make the right decisions and frustrated that all this had to happen now.

As we have discussed so often in this book, there is no right and wrong in these matters. It is not more virtuous to take one's parents into one's house than to set them up in a publically financed institution, or with another relative, or with a roommate in a separate location, or in a mobile home behind the house, or any of a thousand other options. So perhaps the first rule that the child should observe is to *seek clarity, not rightness.* Seek to *know* your heart. Seek to make each decision out of the trust you have for your own instincts. To this end, do not rush into things and do not open yourself up to too much advice. *Advice is often another voice that does not echo the voice of the heart.* If you will first let go a little of your fear of mistakes, you will be able to make each choice in its time, and you will remain clear and at peace as you proceed.

Do not hesitate to act once you have a gentle sense of something to try, and do not be reluctant to change your mind if you see it is not working out. No decision need be eternal; therefore refuse to be timid. *You will always make some advance toward happiness whenever you are confident and organized.* So if a little research must be done first, give this time willingly because of how it will smooth your way later. This is a form of remaining in the present just as surely as acting out of uncertainty is a form of leaving it.

One who has not forgiven his parents cannot expect to have a settled state of mind. This holds true whether he is unable to remember his parents and has only an impression of them to deal with, or whether they can no longer be confronted because of incapacity, or whether they are both healthy and constantly under foot. Often the increased contact with a parent that sometimes comes as a result of his or her advanced years provides us with a shortcut to completing the forgiving process. The more frequent encounters "forced" on us bring the various resentments we still have into conscious thought where they can be dealt with. It is very revealing how many people think they have risen above their pasts *until* they are thrown into close ongoing contact with their mother or father.

If this opportunity is given you, do not throw it away by denying your emotional reactions. Look carefully at each feeling, and at the close of the day relinquish thoroughly all that have surfaced. If you can succeed in seeing your elderly parent as innocent *now,* the weight of your entire childhood will begin slipping from your shoulders. This is your chance to do what your mother or father may not have been able to do for you during your adolescence—to become strong enough for both.

The elderly can be very distracted and confused. Even though it is not called for, or even a possibility, it may seem to them that now they must somehow assess the course of their entire life, and even perhaps that the puzzle of death must be solved. These answerless questions can be a shattering weight upon the minds of the very old. As you can see, this is not necessarily the time to try to manipulate a parent into giving professions of love and loyalty. It is *your* time to love. If you sense that confessions or dramatic displays of your emotions will not make your parent comfortable, choose some simpler, gentler, and more easily understood way of being kind. *Your helpfulness does not have to be direct.* Do not get caught up in some sense of ego urgency, some impossible striving to have at last the moment of truth and oneness that you have always longed for. Very often love is not given or received through the histrionics so currently popular.

Choose peace for yourself and your parent will feel it. Only this is necessary. All is known within the heart. You have nothing to prove simply because someone's death is nearer than your own. Merely be a comfort. Out of your debt of genuine gratitude, be a strong and consistent friend in whatever ways are happiest and most peaceful for you to do this.

Feeling at Home

The list of precondemned encounters does not end with these few examples. If all our individual prejudices were gathered together probably no aspect of any relationship would escape some degree of self-fulfilling dread. In this chapter we have gone from observing how, on one side, the world looks to relationships for solutions to all its problems, to seeing, on the other side, how it sets up various ordinary interactions to be little inescapable hells. Another illustration of this dichotomy is a wedding. The day of one's marriage is supposedly the happiest of all days, and yet as a minister I always scheduled a quiet meeting with the couple I was to marry just prior to the beginning of the ceremony because I had found that by that time the two would usually have gotten themselves into a state over what had gone or could go wrong—what someone had said, who didn't come, what had been or could be forgotten, and from all the earlier planning and compromising of plans. I was so addled on the "happiest day of my life" that after the service I actually forgot Gayle's name while standing in the reception line and had to introduce her by saying things like "And of course you know my wife."

During these meetings we would hold hands and I would simply remind the couple of what they knew in their hearts this day was for: merely to unite with each other in happiness and love. Therefore nothing *could* go wrong because this one thing they could do perfectly. All the other busy activities, which seemed so important at the time, would quickly be forgotten. What they would remember and carry with them was the affection they held each other in, the friendship that they had blessed and deepened.

Once they remembered their purpose, the day indeed became happy—not happier than other people's days, for a true purpose is not an attempt to be favored. And this is the key to enjoying any relationship, that the relationship itself not be marked for particular service, not be used as a mere foothold. If we see each relationship in a different light, we have no splendor. It is in approaching all relationships, and all stages of relationships, in the same way that they yield up their common gold. Naturally this does not imply that we talk to the produce clerk the same way we talk to our mother, but merely that we carry the same gentleness of mind into all contacts.

Another time of relating that should be very happy, according to the lip service accorded it, is the evening of the day. One is now off work, household chores are finished, and there is nothing to do but enjoy one's spouse and children in perfect bliss. People actually commit suicide because they believe so completely in this fiction, which their own life has never offered them. This is as insane as throwing away one's family in order to be single, because the facts in either case do not warrant the motivating fantasy.

Because of sitting in schoolrooms much of the day, or in front of TV, younger children often have a store of energy that they have not released, and come evening they are ready to play. Their idea of fun usually involves acting out their imaginations in some energetic and, to the adult, repetitious way. Adults on the other hand are usually tired and slightly discouraged by the end of the day and their idea of fun is often some quiet activity like reading, talking with friends, eating leisurely, or watching TV. And so the prevailing evening state in most families is a continuous, though perhaps covert, battle of wills. The adults feel constantly interrupted and the children feel neglected, and of course both are correct. Once again, there are always many ways around any unhappy dynamic, but they require openness to options and some initial effort.

The happiness of the family rests in its attempts to join rather than to separate and withdraw into private pleasures. This does not mean that everyone must stay in the same room doing the same thing or that adults must give up their TV or evening newspaper. It means only that the mind itself does not exclude or long for some show of togetherness to be over with so that one can again be self-devoted. The ego does not understand that minds can continue touching even while bodies are separately engaged. Thus the principle is the same: Do not indulge in idle feelings of judgment and fear. Keep thought gentle. Keep the mind soft. Think kindly and easily rather than rigidly and unhappily. And put your mental arms around those who are not beside you. Much less work is required to spend the evening this way than in defensive withdrawal. Just watch and try, watch and try, and your gain will be gradual . . . and immense.

As to what specifically a family can do to begin eliminating the customary evening strain, perhaps a small amount of time could be set aside simply to try different activities. If the children of the family are young, maybe just before sleep everyone could join in letting go of the day.[9] Jordan is still a baby, and his bedtime is much earlier, but Gayle, John, and I do this together every night just before John goes to bed. As children get older there are an increasing number of games that can be played, and often just a few minutes spent this way can brighten the atmosphere remarkably, and the effect can last for a very long time indeed. As an example, a game might be played in which the entire family sits in a circle and takes each individual in turn and surrounds that member in light and sees the person as wonderful and just perfect as is. Of course children frequently have to be helped with these things and gently shown, and you must remember that they may act silly, because acting silly is part of their idea of fun.

In a variation of this, a clock or timer might be used, the alarm set, and when it rings everyone switches to the next person. And so you begin with the individual on your right, surround that member in light, and at the sound of the alarm you go to the second person on your right, and so on around

[9] See Chapter VI.

the circle. In this way everyone is being surrounded in light by someone at all times. A little game like this can be very nice.

In another version, perhaps something is done verbally. Mother begins and says, "Daddy is friendly. Daddy is silly. Daddy is nice." And each one in turn adds some kind points about Daddy, and then this is done with the next family member, and the next, always keeping the remarks gentle, and very soon a sense of joining and oneness has been created.

A family might also do very playful activities such as a time in which the child can speak openly, perhaps even an evening of silly talk. Children love this—just silly, crazy talk. Or songs that each one adds to the lyrics. Or funny sounds or funny faces that everyone tries to guess. Parents frequently think they cannot be silly and still maintain discipline, but this is silly. Of course silliness may not feel natural to some parents and to force a person into this role would defeat the purpose of joining.

Parents must learn not to make decisions out of fear of the future but to make them in the present interests of their family. The games that are played should be ones that strengthen love, strengthen the bond, and that increase the family's real treasure, which is the affection they have for each other.

Because music bypasses words, it can also bring people together. Particularly simple music with gentle lyrics. I have seen the unhappy atmosphere of a car ride quickly change when a Raffi tape was played. And one does not have to be proficient to play musical instruments oneself. If your purpose is love and not a conflicted sense of first having to meet some unclear standard, you can have great fun with a kazoo, harmonica, drum, or just blowing into bottles. And also with drawing, painting, sculpting. And with a thousand other arts and disciplines.

The aim of all these activities is simplicity and happiness, not artistic invention. So many of us are afraid of trying our own ideas because we do not believe they are "creative enough." We carry with us a hampering mental image of how the activity should look, and so we either do nothing or do it in conflict. It is always better to try than to remain stymied because of fear.

If all our relationships—the chance encounters, the short-term, the lifelong—could somehow be stripped of both dread and anticipation, and if we could *look upon other people as merely opportunities to be at peace,* as chances to relax and see innocently, then this anciently agitated aspect of the world could recede into the ordinary and once again be a normal and happy part of life. There is no real reason why this cannot occur. All it requires on our part is awareness, awareness of how we make the mistakes in the first place, of how we set ourselves up for pain through our expectations and see it through with our need to be right. Once we begin recognizing the attitudes and approaches that undermine any chance we have of being at peace while in the presence of another body, we will naturally and effortlessly discard them. Thus it is so very important that we remain hopeful and encouraged. Relationships do not have to be a whirlwind that constantly lifts us up and casts us down, and yet we have indeed gotten ourselves into some unfortunate mental habits that are preventing remedy. Therefore, my friend, work hard, for it is happy work. Do not lie down before the world's insanity on this subject. Do not be trampled by your passing moods and tiny emotions. A deep serenity is still attainable. Immerse yourself in gentleness. The world cannot withstand your love.

CHAPTER XII

May I Wrap That for You?

Happiness is not noisy. It is not a special time set aside, a party, a "happy hour," an event that stands out in the mind above other events. Happiness is not even a thing to do. It may be possible to schedule excitement, but it is not possible to schedule genuine happiness, and as we have seen, these pre-planned forays into fun often end up making real happiness more difficult to come by.

Nor is happiness some fantasy that comes from a song or a movie. Because of its harmlessness, happiness is incapable of giving you more than others. It is not a comparable state, and you will never feel good merely knowing there are those who suffer more than you. Happiness is not a jungle but the clear, quiet stream that runs through. You need neither wits, nor cleverness, nor insensitivity, nor anger to get "your share" of it. In fact, you need very little.

If the handful of principles discussed in this book are ad-hered to, you will unquestionably come to know a reliable and growing happiness. There is not a great deal to learn. As I have said here often, your attainment rests far more in your readiness to make an effort than in the elegance of your approach. Although the ego believes that mistakes have great importance and should frequently be recalled and mulled over for significance and guilt, and must definitely be used for hammering oneself into a better person, the truth is that mistakes are not important. Starting over is important. A faulty approach must first be recognized, and then discarded. While you continue dwelling on weakness you are not practicing strength. It is that simple.

And the components of true strength or happiness are also quite simple. Happiness is gentleness, peace, concentration, simplicity, forgiveness, humor, fearlessness, trust, and now. Of course these qualities have their ego counterfeits, and as concepts they *can* be misused. However, any misuse of one will leave out one or more of the others. In its true form each quality includes all the rest, for happiness is a whole, and one feels whole when genuinely happy.

Simplicity

Simplicity, like the other qualities of happiness, is a characteristic of mind and cannot be judged by appearances. It is an integration, a stability, a settledness, a straightforwardness, a purity of the mind that is often expressed in a simpler life-style —a simpler diet, a more orderly routine, a more intelligent use of time, less clutter, less financial chaos, fewer involvements— in other words, less world, more peace. These are merely common effects, but there are no rules or strictures and certainly no external measurements of one's mastery of simplicity.

It is possible to be quite wealthy and still be simple. One's house may be larger than ordinary, one's business activities more widespread. Likewise, one can own nothing and do little and be thoroughly mixed up and disjointed within. Therefore, allow your simplicity to begin with your thoughts and feelings and radiate outward naturally. Have as few needs as possible. Yet once you have reduced your needs to a minimum, do not be afraid to meet them—in a new way if necessary, but always adequately. Nothing is truly gained by avoiding your desires and waging war with your ego.

Although simplicity is never a form, unless it pervades every area of your life it is not genuine. Genuine simplicity can find pleasure in unexpected and overlooked places, such as one's family and job. And to practice it during all unhappy moments is powerfully effective. The ego's typical reaction to distress is some degree of panic and disorientation. Notice this tendency the next time you are feeling stressed. A part of you will begin casting about, wanting to do more, thinking of irrelevancies. Unless this is checked, although you will become more active you will not do well the few things crucial to your happiness.

Let's say you are a man and that consciously or unconsciously you have the ordinary male-ego position of believing that somehow you should not be saddled with child care. Your wife, say, is sick, and suddenly you find yourself alone with the baby. Observe that your ego quickly engages you in a number of chores not strictly necessary *at that moment,* or at least gets you embroiled in worrying about them, whereas your heart will counsel you to drop everything and concentrate on the essential—caring for the actual, not the imagined, needs of your child. Seeing this, perhaps you plop down in a chair and just hold the baby. And if that makes you happy, and the baby happy, it is enough.

For most people preparing for bed and getting ready in the morning are difficult times, and yet they will entertain almost any idea that could add further complications. Whether it is one of those times or some other recurring distress, remember if you can that happiness is always a possibility. Every life does not have to hold a thousand dark pits. During your moments of difficulty help yourself by doing less, by thinking less, by relating gently, by being one thing. Since you live in it, leave the world undisturbed. Simply be simple. There is nothing more to happiness than this.

Now

It is as if a cult has formed around the concept of "being centered in the now" or "going with the flow," and those who do not speak in present-tense terms and eschew gathering nuts for the winter are judged to be spiritually backward. Allowing one's mind to be at ease now instead of later never entails self-conscious mannerisms or a practiced vocabulary. It certainly does not imply that one should not provide for the future needs of oneself or one's family.

The universe simply does not reward people who have the right beliefs with money. So please do not quit your job, cancel your insurance, or let your bills slip in the name of trusting the present, because all this will do is make you needlessly anxious, and can even result, as it has with others, in your abandoning in disgust a gentle approach to life. It is never necessary to be special in any way.

We expect too much of a memory or an anticipation. What do they possess to give us? We can bring to ourselves little more than tension when we pursue a time that is absent. The present is not somehow more virtuous, it is just that this instant is the only one in which we have the opportunity to be happy, so why waste it? Why seek *anything*, even a chance to be right, in fantasies?

Notice that you cannot have fun thinking outside of the present without your reveries quickly deteriorating. These thoughts have meaning only as comparisons and must always continue into their opposites. The mind cannot be controlled when off in unreal realms. No way exists to be happy this afternoon, this evening, after the divorce, after finals, after the loan goes through. The mind can never fool itself completely that the uncertain is certain. It constantly revises its versions of later in a sad attempt to arrive at one that will come to rest and satisfy. All we are doing is paying for a few mental upturns by falling an equal amount, and we end up with feelings of waste and meaninglessness. And indeed we have wasted our thoughts and our mind.

The future stretches before us like an endless fear, or at best excites the heart with uncertain hopes that make us turn from the present to gaze down a road we are not on. There *is* no better time than now, and the hope that there might be has cost most people their happiness. Therefore, do not send your mind away in pursuit of vain imaginings. Let it stay with you and spread out its calm blanket of acceptance at your feet.

The past drags behind us like an endless string of junk tied to a wedding car. It may sound unusual and attract attention, but in not cutting it loose we are drowning out the gentle music we long to hear. Do not pull the past into the present. In the present you are free. Merely leave behind all that is behind, and know the lightness, the happiness, this little practice can bring.

Never make the mistake of fighting to stay in the present. *There is no code of thoughts to think.* If your mind feels restricted and rigid it is not practicing happiness. So allow the day to come to you. Let each event arrive in its own time. Do not try to override the moment, to judge the moment, and somehow get beyond it. Now is no more than an absence of fear, a presence of ease.

The *literal* content of the ideas we think must always involve some aspect of the future or past. Remaining in the present means staying within a circle of peace. We simply think *from* peace and from ease. We do not make silly rules about good and bad subjects. Tension is the clue that our heart has shifted, that we are no longer interested in thinking in a happy way but have gotten caught up in questions. When this happens remind yourself that truly there is no moment with more potential for peace than the one at hand.

What other time but now can touch the heart and bring rest to the mind? When else is there the chance to forgive and join another in love? Be where you are. Love the ones you are with. Enjoy the moment you are given. Bless the life you have. There is nothing more to happiness than this.

Gentleness

Gentleness is not a physical protector. It is a way of thinking. What must be understood about happiness is that the mind poisons the day, the day cannot by itself damage the mind. A truly gentle mind will remain happy under even difficult circumstances. But if gentleness is interpreted as meaning that we have created an atmosphere in which we are immune to being hurt, then naturally this is not gentleness but self-delusion. What logic is there in going into a rough neighborhood in order to demonstrate that you are gentle? We must not confuse ourselves unnecessarily. Being gentle does not imply that you should continue in a situation in which you are being cheated or finish going through your shopping list in a store whose employees are obviously angry and unhappy.

If we value our state of mind we will easily take the necessary steps to protect it, and obviously this will not include saying things that are likely to be misunderstood or doing what will be taken the wrong way. The reason we frequently do more harm than good is that we have not stopped to see what is actually wanted. A gentle person is thoughtful of himself and others and does not make offers that are unnecessary.

Gentleness can take up any subject without harming it, without *wishing* it harm. It sees no harm in a face, a word, a mannerism, a stance, an opinion. It does not condemn weakness or fear anger. It neither hides from the world nor kicks against it. It is adaptable, it makes allowances, it understands, it has nothing to prove. Thus it has enormous power to remain itself.

To think in a way that allows you to be comfortable with what you are thinking is true gentleness. In this state of freedom the inner self is relaxed and soft rather than defensive and wary. You will always treat your body, other people, and all living things gently when your mind is gentle. So take it easy. There is nothing more to happiness than this.

Peace

Peace, or freedom from conflict, is the absolute core of happiness. It is in learning to watch our sense of peace that we avoid unhappiness. All forms of misery are heralded by a frame of mind that must become immediately recognizable if we are ever to gain mastery in happiness. If you are not clear about what you are starting to do, no matter how small the task, you are on the verge of scattering your thoughts and throwing away your peace. That is why so much of this book has been a description of the symptoms of mental conflict. Not that it is all that hard to recognize, we are just grossly out of practice.

If you have a question, you *are* conflicted, and what you are doing, or are about to do, may not hurt you, but the inevitable state accompanying it will. Peace is the willingness not to rush. You can always tell an ego impulse by the little sense of urgency you feel: "Do it quickly before it's too late." Too late for what? In your rush to be unhappy, notice how vague and confused you will always be about the reasons for not pausing and becoming clear. "Hurry or there will be dire consequences." But what consequences? Do not be afraid to stop and examine this argument. What exactly is it implying? And what do *you* believe? Our little scared ego places tremendous value on not wasting time, on being fast, on the quick opinion, the quick retort. So remind yourself that a moment's stopping is not a waste, and that it uses so little time that this rationale is meaningless. Practice being slow to react, slow to anger, slow to judge, slow to have an opinion.

I have already stressed the following point, but if I were to add a thousand pages and devote them to nothing else, it would be insufficient. *Appearances are not as important as your mind.* We wouldn't think of leaving the house with our bodies in a state of disarray, and yet we are very consistent in disregarding our mental condition. Our ego believes that only what can be seen has importance and since our thoughts are out of sight they signify very little. Provided our life is well ordered they may ramble in any direction and, so long as they remain hidden from others, they can do us no harm. This is the core belief around which all unhappiness spins, and it is the complete reverse of the truth. Unless you translate it into some form of neglectful behavior, you can never repeat the following idea too often: "Appearances don't matter, only my mind matters." For if your mind is in a state of real peace you will deal with appearances quite well.

Take the time to look in your heart and be clear. Walk through life being clear. Practice doing each thing in peace. Make your mind your well-ordered and peaceful home. Do not be afraid to admit to yourself how important your mind is to you, and do not be afraid to act this out by pausing as often as needed. The time has come to be very direct with yourself.

Do you want to be happy? Then you want to have peace. There is nothing more to happiness than this.

Forgiveness

Earlier I said that only your mind can poison the day. When this happens you can be certain that whatever other mistakes it may have made, your mind still holds a grievance. Anger and judgment can sometimes poison circumstances instantly, sometimes slowly, but whether their first effects are "controlled" or "unrepressed," they are never wholly eliminated from the system through some alchemy of time, as is generally supposed. In fact, people tend to become more narrow and bitter the older they get. The buildup occurs because the validity of the judging "faculty" is never questioned, and grievances are swept into corners of the mind, and gradually there is no room to breathe, no room for light and love, which can come to be looked down on as no more than childish fictions. Now the judgments themselves become part of the identity, a point of pride, and one does not like having them questioned. One feels righteous about one's beliefs and can't understand why the world refuses to see.

Forgiveness is the alternative, but forgiveness does not mean releasing all criminals from prison, spending more time with someone who pushes your buttons, or other such nonsense. Forgiveness is a thought not a behavior. It is an inner expression of self-respect and integrity. The grounds for forgiving are simple: Grievances are unworthy of you.

As we go through the day it is as if at some point we are shot with a poisoned arrow, and although not necessarily recognized at the time, the deterioration begins. Something happens, we interpret it, and this little picture, carried in the mind, begins releasing its toxins. Soon we are reacting badly to almost everything and we do not know why. It just seems that "things are not going well," even though on other occasions we have been able to glide through far more than this.

Form the habit of scanning your mind—not second-guessing your motives but staying aware of what your ego, your fear of happiness, is up to and just how seriously you are taking it. The particular thoughts that arrest the mind must be recognized before the mind can be set free. Your own ego can become like the neighbor's dog you have agreed to take for a walk. Your function is to keep it moving along and not let it stop and sniff. When it gets too interested it gets in trouble. And it is when your ego stops to dwell on some wrong that *you* will feel injured. How many remarks were inoffensive until we thought about them? How many mistakes failed to delay us until we turned them into sins?

To forgive means no more than to continue walking toward your goal. If you see that some picture of an earlier event is poisoning you, do not try to dishonestly change the picture, for you will think you are trying to alter reality. Merely look closely at it and then let it go; see what could spell trouble for the dog and then move the dog along. Use any means that allows you to do this at the time, for once you have let go, you *have* forgiven, even if in the future you find that you must repeat the process.

Forgive, but do not wonder how you must act on it. Forgive, but do not try to convince another to forgive. Forgive, but do not hold yourself superior because you have done so. Simply forgive. Wrap your forgiveness around you like a cloak of light, an armor that protects your happiness but closes no one out. Forgiveness is not the-devil-can-take-you attitude. It is a clear shield of love and peace that lets the person in but does not let in judgments that betray the person.

The armor you wear is your goodwill. Put it on every day and the arrow of some daily circumstance will not penetrate.

This will be so because you will not send the arrow back, nor will you take it with you. You will think nothing of it. And there is nothing more to happiness than this.

Humor

A laugh is the most beautiful sound on earth. As it rings in one heart it resonates in others and always has the effect of helping people feel closer, feel understood and liked. It is like a little shower of love, a bubble of happiness that can't help popping. It rises out of peace, passes through an ease of manner, and bursts forth naturally. A gentle nature offers no resistance to humor, because it sees innocence in the world and feels no need to hold back.

True humor is a continual welling up of happiness that very often children have. You can frequently see it just behind their eyes waiting for the flimsiest of excuses to overflow. John makes up jokes. He evidently believes that any sentence beginning with "Knock knock" or "Why did _____ cross the road?" is bound to be funny. Although his jokes come out making no sense whatsoever, everyone laughs because he is so delighted and happy telling them.

Obviously humor is not merely stories, retorts, and being witty. And it is seldom found in kidding and questions. It can be pure and abundant without ever taking the conventional forms. The ego's version of humor requires that you understand what is *meant,* and agree by laughing. And those who don't laugh are "humorless." Clearly that is just another way of comparing and judging, for of course true humor is not a mere sound in the throat. And it never shocks or jolts or makes people feel singled out and tense. Where is the fun in that?

Very often we lose our humor as the years pass and the

problems mount. Our little jokes are increasingly based on separateness and are sophisticated and bitter. Where did the child go? It got lost in fear and seriousness. What the ego cannot grasp is that happiness is not frivolous—only happiness is serious.

Once we somehow knew not to let things become so real. The world danced before us because we looked at it through dancing eyes. This is still possible, you know. You are not going to change the world. And do you really want to be that arrogant? Isn't it enough to help those you *can* help?

Why do so many adults secretly smile when a child—any child—merely walks into a room? Of course there are many who do not, but perhaps the ones who do have not completely forgotten a child's mind, the good healthy way a child often feels and reacts. A child can indeed help the world, but not through twisting it and attacking it, which always gets mixed results at best. Gayle once got so ill with food poisoning that she collapsed on the bathroom floor. John, then three, got out a tube of Cortaid and began rubbing it on her cheek and saying, "Poor Mommy." And it helped! It was not serious medicine, but she felt bathed in the sweetness of a child's spirit.

So be a little funny, a little relaxed, a little bit off guard. Sink back into your inherent pleasantness and gaze kindly at the world. The world is indeed a very funny place. It is a Marx Brothers movie in which nothing can go right. So kick off your shoes, tip back your chair, and thoroughly enjoy the absurdity of it all. Become a little child. There is nothing more to happiness than this.

Fearlessness

Fear is one of the great depressors of happiness, and perhaps fear of happiness itself is first in the heart of the ego. This part of our mind deeply believes that happiness is a sign of weakness, and it is strongly drawn to every witness of this view. This is what, as an example, creates the addictive quality of the news. The ego lusts to know the worst of everyone, of every day. It feeds on fear.

Certainly there is nothing bad or sinister about articles on the famous, news briefs on crimes and disasters, or local stories about the winning streak of the neighborhood basketball team. Most reports, reviews, and even gossip columns are well meant, and many of these attempts to inform do no more harm than waste time. The point is that you cannot realistically expect your mind to function on a level higher than the level of ideas you continuously feed it. If you pepper your conversations with stories of fear and loss, if you memorize every negative statistic that comes your way, if you join every bandwagon against the newest bad guys, naturally you will be a basically anxious and depressed person, no matter how spicy a personality you contrive. Of course the world is a mess. Why does this fact require your constant vigilance?

In your heart you yearn to be at least a small answer to the world's great sadness, and you know that to do little more than dwell on other people's weaknesses is not fulfilling that yearning. A fearless mind heals because it gives hope. Without a word spoken or withheld, it encourages and calms. Certainly you lock up and buckle up and take your insurance umbrella —if those gestures help your mind to be less anxious. Unquestionably you take steps to protect your children, your pets, and the well-being of your own body. Fearlessness is not some silly pretense of being mystically immune to all worldly dangers. It is uninterested in *appearing* fearless because it values so deeply the true state.

What I refer to in this book as our heart could also be called our deeper self, for that is how it feels—more fundamental, more collected, more rooted, more sure. Yet it slips into our chaotic mental courtroom without respectable credentials, for it refuses to promise results in worldly terms in order to substantiate its claim for a hearing. It merely whispers, "Don't always try to decide in advance. Wait, and when the time comes to decide, pause and see what you truly want to do. Do that thing you can do most peacefully. And do it easily and happily."

Notice how the mind has been trained to reject such unencumbered advice. Where are the endless questions of duty and responsibility? Where are the thousand clashing lessons from the past? Perhaps, for just a moment, we know the thing we could do most peacefully, but what can we recall that shows this particular course of action rewarding? And what can we anticipate that makes it safe? Very possibly, nothing at all. And so the only question unanswered is on what will we place our trust.

It is a good thing for one to begin noticing the gentle intrusion of "I want to" into the usual merry-go-round of "I really wonder if I should, because this could happen if I do, yet if I don't there just might be this other consequence which would be worse." Rather than try for the impossible answer to the question of "What will result?" and ending up choosing a course that merely avoids our greatest fear of the moment, we always have the alternative of doing what we want to do. As we look calmly at our mind, taking whatever time is necessary to do this, if we see that its overall state is gentle and kind, then we trust the preferences it contains, but if not, we withhold judgment and devote our efforts to clearing the mind rather than stirring it up with still more points to consider. There is no anxiety in "I want to," provided the desire is seen in peace and acted on in the present.

Because your heart has only one voice, you are free. As you work to know yourself you will stop fearing your own will because you will stop doubting your own goodness, and then you will see why goodness is not confined to you. Therefore, walk gently and walk well. Step into yourself and walk without fear. There is really nothing more to happiness than this.

Concentration

What we look at is what we feel, and in the world we always gaze upon our quality of mind projected out. With each thought we are either judgmental or happy. Every thought is a focus, and it sees a world bathed in darkness or light. Of course for most, concentration is already so shattered that much of the day is a blur of gray which holds little meaning.

In our household there are two adults and two children and therefore at least two divergent sets of reactions to electrical failures (a frequent occurrence where we live), stopped-up toilets (not frequent), locking ourselves out (only once; John cried, "Call the police!"), questionable insects roaming the house (just try teaching the concept of good and bad bugs to a child), or even to what constitutes an interesting rock (there are many rocks in the stream down from the house and the adults and children in question have yet to exclaim over the same ones—except out of politeness). I took John and his friend Luke (also five) into a cave last week and neither of them thought the mice scurrying on the walls of particular interest. I found them rather cute, with their big ears and fuzzy winter coats, but was hurried along to other things. When I passed up a sort of smelly sticky mineral goo that was oozing from the wall, the kids stopped and poked and sniffed and animatedly discussed its meaning, but did not consult me.

Whose judgment is right? Which is better, little and cute or smelly and sticky? We look at thoughts not at things, and the most we can say is that we are true to our personal past. Yet is that all there is to be true to? The way the world argues over what is a big or minor event, you would think the answer was yes.

There is a level of perception beyond our individual histories. It is a choice, of course, but the potential is always present. It is found in our ability to look peacefully and gently. Happiness is always a possibility, because the part of the mind that sees is capable of becoming generous and accepting. And happiness that endures is possible because it can decide to see this way permanently. Narrow and hard or calm and free— those are the two choices set before the mind's eye.

"Seeing no evil" is not concentration, because the decision as to what *is* evil goes unquestioned. I know a man who used to turn his eyes to the other side of the street, or cross over, when he saw an attractive woman approaching on his side. Maybe such a practice could simplify life for someone else, but in this case it was done purely out of fear and conflict. Who can help noticing what the world marks as beautiful, or ugly, or horrible, or any other quality it teaches is worthy of attention? Concentration is not the practicing of blindness. Rather, we notice everything in a new way. This entails gathering together every part of us. Now we will see with *all* our heart and strength and mind. We will notice from our wholeness. Perhaps this man has come to see that the body is guiltless. If so he is now as happy as he is harmless.

You can behold gentleness and peace and innocence in the world provided you understand that they come from you. A way must be found to release the heart of its beauty. When your gaze is on the present and your eyes laugh, you shine on the world you see and the light of your heart goes before you. This is possible because you are something more than a body, and this something more must become interesting in your eyes, more interesting than the list of worries that scatters your thoughts into a thousand contending purposes.

Be single-minded, be purposeful, be focused. Know who you

are and what you want. Be conscious, be aware. Formulate your purpose into words, etch it on your heart, repeat it in your mind, and above all, live it and see it. The truth is true. Happiness is better than misery. Therefore concentrate on happiness. Merely decide "Today I will be happy," and it will be so. There is nothing more to happiness than this.

Trust

We take our bodies to nutritionists, our minds to therapists, our children to schools, and our marriages to magazines. We are so used to thinking that any possible good must come from an outside source that we do not consider the alternative: There is something within us that knows.

The ego takes self-trust and, as would be expected, turns it into ego-trust. To honor this "self" one is called upon to respect one's irritation and selfishness, as if they were the essence of the individual. We *do* know the wisdom of our heart. We *have* felt it. It is just that you and I get confused so often. We are told to doubt, and we doubt.

This is why our inner sense appears to need developing—an absurd concept when you consider it, that we must somehow become more ourselves. But it does feel that way. So let us proceed slowly, but very directly. Simplicity can be quite confusing at first. Let us try ourselves out a little at a time until we are finally found worthy in our own eyes. In other words, do not merely assume the posture of trust—trust also your feeling of when you need help.

Today, begin trusting your own sense of happiness, of what makes you happy and what does not. Let it spread to your diet, your clothes, your relationships, your spiritual yearnings. Let it infuse your spending and saving, your health and your habitat. Sit down often and know your own heart. There is clearly a lot of weeding out to do, so many silly assumptions about what is exciting and desirable that you and I have falsely believed. So if a little experimenting and culling are required, that is a small sacrifice indeed. All it implies is that we will make some mistakes. We will try something we thought we wanted only to uncover a more profound want.

Let the roots of your knowing deepen and expand. Water them with your patience and your clear purpose. Where is the shame in admitting that we have not yet arrived? Let the world rant about its absolute rightness, and then let us respectfully return to our heart for the quiet answer.

Let peace become your friend. Take its hand often. Yield to its soft nudges, its broad and gentle preferences. So it isn't exciting. Where has excitement gotten the world? You are ready now for something kinder than excitement, something that does not take you on its wings only to plummet from under you in chase of someone else; something real, something feathered with compassion that will lay you to rest at the end of the journey, and will watch over you in love. Only the peace of your own heart can be relied on as completely as this.

Simply practice knowing and you will know. Practice trusting and you will have the grounds for trust. Practice your self and you will know a self that touches all living things in true helpfulness. Practice your heart and you will be happy. There is nothing more to happiness than this.

And so, with this little wrapping-up chapter, our conversation ends, but not our joint effort and our mutual goal. We walk together, as do all those who have laid strife aside and set their eyes on love. This is the other way to pass through the world. It requires no special concepts, no excluding vocabulary, no particular beliefs, only enough hope in the possibility of love and peace to pursue them in one's family, one's job, on the streets, in the stores. Just a little willingness to try to be the kind of person we want to be—one who takes others as they are, who helps when a way to help is clear, who sees innocence in mistakes.

Let us then journey together. The distance to the heart of love is short indeed. Where else could it be but where you are? It is your right to be happy. This is what you were made for. And if you will not resist, happiness will find a way to pour from your heart and fill your days. Simply keep a place within you where it is welcomed, and peace will come and abide with you forever.